HUMAN RIGHTS AND F
BRITAIN AND IRELAND

Human Rights and Responsibilities in Britain and Ireland

A Christian Perspective

Edited by

Sydney D. Bailey

for the Project of the Churches on Human Rights and Responsibilities
in the United Kingdom and the Republic of Ireland

Foreword by
The Archbishop of York

MACMILLAN
PRESS

First published 1988

Published by
THE MACMILLAN PRESS LTD
Houndmills, Basingstoke, Hampshire RG21 2XS
and London
Companies and representatives
throughout the world

Typeset by Footnote Graphics, Frome

Printed and bound in Great Britain by
Biddles Ltd, Guildford and King's Lynn

British Library Cataloguing in Publication Data
Human rights and responsibilities in Britain and
Ireland: a Christian perspective.
1. Human rights—Religious aspects—
Christianity   2. Human rights—British Isles.
I. Bailey, Sydney D.   II. Project of the Churches
on Human Rights and Responsibilities in the United
Kingdom and the Republic of Ireland
261.7   BT738.15
ISBN 0–333–46073–1 (hardcover)
ISBN 0–333–46074–X (paperback)

Contents

Foreword

Issues concerning majority and minority rights and responsibilities underlie much of the political conflict in today's world. Where social and political differences are correlated with differences in religious allegiance, the conflicts become peculiarly intractable. It is a sad fact that many of the most violent conflicts and outrages have a strongly religious dimension.

The theme of this book, therefore, has a wider relevance than its title might imply. The special problems of Britain and Ireland may owe much to particular historical events, some of which lie buried – though certainly not dead – in the distant past. They may also reflect some of the national characteristics of the British and Irish people. The religious dimension may have features which are peculiar to Ireland. But the problems also conform to more general patterns of conflict and can serve to illustrate more general principles. Indeed, a simple recognition that such patterns of conflict are not all that uncommon may in itself be a help in reducing some of the animus. And the converse also follows. Any serious attempt to understand the problems in one place, and to search for meeting points, may have unexpected spin-offs elsewhere.

It was the hope of those who first conceived the Project that the effort of standing back and looking in general terms at human rights and responsibilities might help to provide a common starting point and a common language in which old issues might be tackled afresh. Inevitably, though, the Project grew, the authors found themselves forced to deal with particularities as well as with generalities, and also to provide more background information than was originally intended. The result is a wide-ranging study which I believe could do much to increase understanding between separated communities, as well as inform and stimulate many who may not at the moment feel that the problems belong to all of us who live in these islands.

The fact that this is 'a Christian perspective' is central to the book. I have already made the point that religion can exacerbate conflict. It also holds the key to finding constructive ways of reconciliation. At the very least, the Churches have a responsibility to work side by side in exposing misunderstandings, in removing the causes of gratuitous offence, and in learning to speak and hear the truth in love.

The Advisory Board, who sponsored and monitored the work, consists of concerned Christians from both islands anxious to initiate and maintain a constructive dialogue about our common problems based on our shared Christian perspective, but the Report in no way commits the Churches to which the members of the Advisory Board belong. I thank the members of the Advisory Board for the careful and patient way they discharged their mandate.

The calibre of those who served on the Working Party should itself inspire confidence, and I pay tribute to the way they carried out a daunting and complex task. I warmly commend the result.

The Working Party operated entirely independently. The text was edited under the auspices of the Working Party, and the Advisory Board was not asked to endorse the precise way the issues and conclusions were formulated. The Report is lengthy and complex, and deals with a wide range of important issues. Members of the Advisory Board naturally have their own ideas about many of these issues, some of which may diverge from what is contained in the Report as regards presentation or substance. The Advisory Board has now decided to authorize the publication of the Report, not because it provides definitive answers to the issues raised, but rather because it represents a useful contribution to the Christian dialogue to which we attach such importance.

I hope that the Report will be received and read by people of goodwill in this spirit.

Bishopthorpe, York   JOHN EBOR
July 1987

Acknowledgements

We owe a special debt of gratitude to our four consultants: Kevin Boyle, Anthony Lester, Mary Robinson, and Ben Whitaker.

Many other people and organisations have been generous with their help, either by giving us factual information, discussing ideas with us, or in other ways. We thank, in particular, the Rev. Harold Allen, the Rev. Basil Amey, Amnesty International, the Rev. Robert Beresford, the Rt. Hon. David Bleakley, Kenneth Bloomfield, Paul Buxton, James Casey, Arthur Chapman, the Committee on the Administration of Justice, Jerome Connolly, John Coolahan, Robert Cooper, the Rev. Gabriel Daly, Donald Davidson, Noel Dorr, the Rev. Eric Elliott, Frances Elliott, the Friends Committee on National Legislation, John Fisher, David Goodall, Tom Hadden, Dr Jeremy Harbison, Kurt Herndl, Sara Huey, Carol Jackson, Sister Mary Kilpatrick, Jim Knox, Mgr George Leonard, B. G. McClelland, Alf McCreary, Alister McCullough, the Rev. Dr William McDowell, J. T. N. McGaffin, Russell Mishcon, the Rev. Dr Philip Morgan, the Rev. John Morrow, Peter Moss, David Poole, Sir Michael Quinlan, the Rev. John Reardon, Dr John Robb, Stephen Shaw, the Rev. Willy Slavin, David Stevens, Bishop Owen Swindlehurst, Peter Tennant, the UN Information Centre, Lord Wade, M. Whyte, Derick Wilson, Stanley Worrall, Hugo Young.

Project of the Churches on Human Rights and Responsibilities in the United Kingdom and the Republic of Ireland

Honorary Officers
President: the Most Rev. and Rt Hon. John Habgood, Archbishop of York
Hon. Treasurer: Lord Hylton
Chair: Sydney D. Bailey
Hon. Secretary: Lionel Jacobs

Advisory Board
The Rt Rev. John Austin Baker, Bishop of Salisbury
The Rev. Professor John M. Barkley
The Rev. Eric Gallagher
Miss Nicole Hodgson*
The Very Rev. William B. Johnston
Paul McDade*
Senator Catherine McGuinness
Joyce Pickard
Peter Sutherland*
The Rev. Bernard Thorogood
The Rev. George Wadding, C.Ss.R.*
Kenneth Whitaker*

*Co-opted

Working Party

Professor Colin Campbell
The Rev. Alan Falconer
Sean Farren
Sir James Fawcett, QC
Brian Garrett
The Rev. Richard Harries
The Rev. Canon Anthony Harvey
The Rev. Enda McDonagh
Senator Stephen McGonagle (resigned 6 May 1986)
Paul Sieghart
David Trimble
Brian Walker
The Rev. Professor James A. Whyte
Professor John Whyte

Consultants

Professor Kevin Boyle
Anthony Lester, QC
Senator Mary Robinson
Ben Whitaker

Notes on Members of the Working Party and Consultants

WORKING PARTY

Sydney D. Bailey, DCL, (Chair) is a member of the board of International Affairs of the British Council of Churches and Vice President of the Council on Christian Approaches to Defence and Disarmament. He received the Rufus Jones award for contributions to world peace from the World Academy of Art and Science in 1984. Publications include *British Parliamentary Democracy* (1958, latest edn, 1978), *How wars end*, 2 vols (1982), *War and Conscience in the Nuclear Age* (1987) and six books on the political functions of the United Nations. Member of the Society of Friends (Quakers).

Colin Campbell has been Professor of Jurisprudence in the Queen's University, Belfast, since 1974. He was formerly a member of the Standing Advisory Commission on Human Rights, and edited *Do We Need a Bill of Rights?* (1980).

Alan Falconer, a Church of Scotland minister, is Director of Studies and Lecturer in Systematic Theology at the Irish School of Ecumenics in Dublin, Editor of *Understanding Human Rights: An Interdisciplinary and Interfaith Approach* (1980), he has written extensively on the theology of human rights and on ecumenical themes. He is a member of the Churches Advisory Forum on Human Rights and of the Irish Council of Churches Human Rights Forum.

Sean Farren is a lecturer in education at the University of Ulster. He was chairman of the Social Democratic and Labour Party from 1980 to 1984, and was elected a member of the Northern Ireland Assembly for North Antrim in 1982. He was a member of the New Ireland Forum and currently speaks for the SDLP on employment.

Sir James Fawcett, QC, DSC, was a member of the European Commission of Human Rights from 1962 to 1984, and President from

1972 to 1981. He served in the Foreign Office from 1946 to 1950, was director of Studies at the Royal Institute of International Affairs from 1969 to 1973, and was Professor of International Law at King's College, London, from 1976 to 1980, where he is now Emeritus Professor. He is Chairman of the British Institute of Human Rights.

Brian Garrett, LLB., FRI Arb., is a solicitor in private practice in Belfast. He is President of the Irish Association for Cultural, Economic and Social Relations, Chairman of the Law Labour Committee of the International Bar Association, and a member of a number of committees of the Law Society of Northern Ireland. He was formerly Chairman of the Northern Ireland Labour Party, a member of the Standing Advisory Commission on Human Rights (1974–8), and Visiting Associate Fellow in International Affairs at Harvard University (1977–8).

Richard Harries is Bishop of Oxford, and was formerly Dean of King's College, London. He is a governor of the British Institute of Human Rights.

Anthony Harvey is a New Testament scholar, formerly Lecturer in Theology and Fellow of Wolfson College, Oxford, now Canon of Westminster. He was a member of the Church of England Doctrine Commission and of the Archbishop of Canterbury's Commission on Urban Priority Areas.

Lionel Jacobs (Honorary Secretary) was secretary of the Northern Ireland Standing Advisory Commission on Human Rights from 1974 to 1983.

Enda McDonagh is a Roman Catholic priest of the Archdiocese of Tuam in the Republic of Ireland and Professor of Moral Theology at the Pontifical University of Maynooth. He is a member of the Higher Education Authority in Dublin, and a member of the Senate of the National University of Ireland. His most recent book is *Between Chaos and New Creation* (1986).

Paul Sieghart is a retired English barrister with a special interest in international human rights law, on which he has written several books. He is a member of the Council and the Issues Committee of the Catholic Union of Great Britain, and Honorary Visiting Professor of Law at King's College, London.

W. David Trimble is a Lecturer in law at the Queen's University, Belfast. He is an active member of the Ulster Unionist Party and an Orangeman. He was elected to the Northern Ireland Constitutional Convention in 1975.

Brian W. Walker is President of the International Institute for Environment and Development. He lived in Northern Ireland for eighteen years, was a founder member and chairman of the New Ulster Movement from 1969 to 1974, and a member of the Standing Advisory Commission on Human Rights from 1975 to 1977. From 1983 to 1985 he was director of the Independent Commission on International Humanitarian Issues. He is a member of the Society of Friends (Quakers).

James Whyte is a minister of the Church of Scotland. He was formerly Convenor of his Church's Inter-Church Relations Committee. From 1958 until his retirement in 1987, he was Professor of Practical Theology and Christian Ethics in the University of St Andrews.

John Whyte has been Professor of Government and Political Science at University College, Dublin, since 1984. From 1966 to 1984 he taught in the Political Science Department at the Queen's University, Belfast. He is the author of *Church and State in Modern Ireland, 1923–1979*, and of many papers on twentieth century Irish history and politics. He is a Roman Catholic.

CONSULTANTS

Kevin Boyle is Professor of Law, University College, Galway. He is currently on leave to act as founding Director of ARTICLE 19, a new London-based international human rights body working for freedom of information and expression. He has written extensively on human rights and emergency laws in Northern Ireland and the Republic, and is co-author (with Tom Hadden) of *Ireland, a Positive Proposal* (1985). He was legal adviser to the New Ireland Forum. He is a Barrister-at-law and has taken a number of cases to the European Commission of Human Rights.

Anthony Lester, QC, specialises in constitutional, administrative, and international law, and has argued many leading cases before the

European Commission and Court of Human Rights. He was Special Adviser to the Standing Advisory Commission of Human Rights in Northern Ireland from 1975 to 1977. He is a Queen's Counsel of the Northern Ireland and English Bars, and a junior member of the Irish Bar.

Mary Robinson, SC, has been a member of the Senate of the Republic of Ireland since 1969. She practises at the Irish Bar and lectures in European Community Law at Trinity College, Dublin, where she was formerly Reid Professor of Criminal and Constitutional Law. She holds an LLM from Harvard University, and is a member of the International Commission of Jurists. She has presented a number of cases in the European Court of Human Rights and the European Court of Justice.

Ben Whitaker was Member of Parliament (Labour) for Hampstead from 1966 to 1970, and Parliamentary Secretary, Ministry of Overseas Development from 1969 to 1970. He has been executive director of the Minority Rights Group since 1971, and a member of the UN Sub-commission on the Prevention of Discrimination and the Protection of Minorities since 1975. He edited *Minorities: a question of human rights* (1984), and is the author of several books on humanitarian questions.

Introduction

BACKGROUND TO THE REPORT

Our aim in this Report is to consider how human rights may be secured and human responsibilities exercised in the United Kingdom and the Republic of Ireland, but in view of what has been happening since our project was launched three years ago, it is not surprising that we repeatedly found our attention directed to Northern Ireland. Hardly a day went by while we were at work without the media in Great Britain and the Irish Republic reporting some new political development or act of terrorism in Northern Ireland. It is there that the special interests of our two states meet, that human rights and civil liberties are under particular threat, and that the problems arising from different traditions are especially difficult to resolve. It is here, too, that the rhetoric of human rights is used by those who violate human rights by using violence for political ends.

We are not, of course, asserting that all human rights are always fully secured for everyone throughout the rest of the United Kingdom and the Irish Republic, for there are some infringements of human rights and civil liberties in both states that cause us concern. We refer to some of these in the pages that follow, but we must make it clear that we have not been able to deal adequately with the many issues of majority–minority relations outside Northern Ireland. We fully realise that there are minorities in the Republic of Ireland and in Great Britain who may suffer varying degrees of disadvantage or deprivation: travelling people (gypsies), for example, and other ethnic or religious communities, who are as entitled to preserve their own cultures and traditions as are the two communities in Northern Ireland. The fact that our gaze has been so frequently directed to Northern Ireland does not mean that we are blind to or unconcerned about peaceful community relations elsewhere in these islands.

Nor have we sought a 'solution' to the basic political problems of Northern Ireland – or, indeed, of any other part of the two states. That was not within our mandate. As we make clear in Chapter 3, our primary concern has not been the status of territory but the rights and responsibilities of people. We have started from the situation that exists, and have then asked whether better protection of human rights and civil liberties, and better exercise of human responsibility,

1

could ameliorate the situation while remedies for basic political problems are being sought.

It had been our original intention to focus on the role of the individual rather than that of government. It was our wish to draw attention to what individuals, Churches, and voluntary agencies can do to increase tolerance and promote mutual understanding. But this emphasis created some difficulties. Our central concern has been with human rights, but the international law of human rights imposes direct obligations on sovereign states and only indirect obligations on individuals. For every human right which international law seeks to protect, the obligation to ensure that the right is respected is imposed on the state which has that individual within its jurisdiction.

In order to protect human rights within its territory, a state must itself enact such laws and exercise its powers in such a way as to try to ensure that its inhabitants individually respect each others' human rights. So, for example, international human rights law requires that states should protect the right to life. One way in which states perform this obligation is to have laws which make murder and manslaughter criminal offences, to have police and security forces able to respond effectively to murderous assaults on individuals or on the social fabric of society, to have courts which can try individuals charged with offences, and to have prisons which can contain those convicted of them. Were a state to fall demonstrably short of any of those requirements, it might be in breach of its international obligation to protect the right to life. But the mere fact that, despite all its efforts, some murders continue to be committed, does not constitute of itself such a breach: the state is expected to do only what it reasonably can to assure the right to life. Today, in matters of this kind, governments which have ratified the relevant treaties can be called to account before tribunals, both by other governments and by individuals.

Thus in dealing with matters of international human rights *law*, we have had to consider the obligations and actions of states, despite our original intention to focus on the role of individuals. But we fulfilled our original intention when we considered the moral responsibility of individuals, Churches, and groups to respect the rights of others, to refrain from acts of discrimination, and to promote tolerance and mutual understanding. So the moral responsibility of the individual to respect the human rights of others is nearly always buttressed by the legal responsibility of the state to ensure that the international code is being respected.

Our Project was initiated by the Churches and our Report is addressed to them in the first instance, but we hope it will interest all men and women of goodwill in the Republic of Ireland and the United Kingdom.

Parts of our Report deal with past failures by and future opportunities for Christians in both states. We consider that Christians should be ready to admit past mistakes and to receive new light from whatever quarter it may come. Many distinct communities are learning to co-exist peacefully in these islands, discovering positive features in human diversity. We hope that our readers will discover new truths from differences as well as from similarities, as we did while engaged in our task.

When we came to look at human rights and responsibilities in detail, we found that the boundaries were always receding. We would explore a right or responsibility, only to find a new issue exposed. Partly as a result of this, our Report deals with issues which we had initially thought were outside our mandate. We have found that the twin concept of rights and responsibilities covers almost all aspects of moral and social life.

We have repeatedly asked ourselves what is distinctive about this Report. Three features of the Project are, we believe, unique. First, the members of the Working Party, the Consultants, the Advisory Board, and the honorary officers come from both parts of Ireland and most parts of Great Britain. That has made us aware of the wider aspects of the problems in Northern Ireland and the international context in which progress can take place. Secondly, our composition and approach have been interdisciplinary. For convenience we have put labels on parts of our Report – ethics, law, politics, and so on; but the process of drafting and revising has involved us in mutual learning, and we have sought to present our Report in a form which integrates the separate disciplines and approaches. Thirdly, we come from different Churches and traditions which together represent the mainstream of contemporary Christian thought in our two states. We regard it as significant that, despite our different backgrounds and traditions, and despite an initial scepticism among some of us about the validity of the concept underlying the Report, we have come to complete agreement on the theological and philosophical basis of human rights and responsibilities. This is spelled out in Chapter 1 and, indeed, sustains our whole Report.

While we have tried to avoid duplicating what has been written in other reports and books, we found that we had to give some basic information about the background to the troubles in Northern Ireland, especially in Chapter 4. All of us – and especially those from Great Britain – have been struck by the widespread ignorance and perplexity about Northern Ireland on the part of people in Great Britain, often leading to exasperation, apathy, and even hostility. But there is no escaping the fact that Great Britain has a continuing responsibility towards all the people of Northern Ireland which is, after all, part of the United Kingdom.

Rights and responsibilities belong together. Minority rights imply majority responsibilities, and majority rights imply minority responsibilities. Our Report's stress on both rights and responsibilities seeks to correct a widespread tendency today to stress rights rather than responsibilities.

SOME DEFINITIONS

All occupations – whether it be accounting, plumbing, or farming – have their own jargon. We have tried to avoid jargon in our Report, or to explain it when its use is unavoidable. The reader is likely to encounter difficulty only where words in everyday use have slightly different meanings in technical jargon.

Some of the terms used in Chapters 2 and 5, for example, are to be found in international legal documents such as the Charter of the United Nations and the European Convention on Human Rights. In ordinary everyday language, we may speak of minority rights or self-determination without the precision of legal draftsmen. That is perfectly understandable. But when we come to interpret or rely on legal texts, we have to understand words in their legal senses. We have tried to avoid language which might cause offence, but it may be helpful for us to define a number of key terms we have used, especially for the benefit of non-Irish readers.

We give in Chapter 1 our understanding of human rights and responsibilities in the perspective of Christian ethics, but we would stress that the international code which has also guided our work expresses ethical principles many of which are to be found in other religious faiths and ideologies. The international code of human rights is not a product of one ethical tradition alone. Throughout our work, we have tested what is happening in the two states against the international code to be found in two regional and four global instruments on human rights. The regional instruments are the

European Convention on Human Rights (1950, 1953)* and its Protocols, and the European Social Charter (1961, 1965); the global instruments are the UN Charter (1945), the Universal Declaration of Human Rights (1948), the UN Covenant on Civil and Political Rights and the Optional Protocol thereto (1966, 1976), and the UN Covenant on Economic, Social, and Cultural Rights (1966, 1976). The Universal Declaration of Human Rights sets out a catalogue of rights and freedoms to be protected; the UN Charter, the European Convention, the European Social Charter, and the two UN Covenants are formal treaties which bind the states which have, of their own volition, become parties to them.

The Two States

The project is concerned with two states, the United Kingdom and the Republic of Ireland. Most Irish people would regard 'the Republic of' as unnecessary: the state is simply Ireland, and that is the name by which it is known in the United Nations and other international organisations. When we speak of Ireland, however, we mean the geographical entity which contains the 26 counties of the Irish Republic and the six counties of Northern Ireland. We apologise to readers in the 26 counties who find it strange that we refer to their state as the Republic of Ireland or the Irish Republic; but to call the state Ireland, as most of them do when talking to each other, can cause confusion in the United Kingdom. We note that the Anglo-Irish Agreement exists in two different versions because of different national usages (see Appendix 4).

England, Wales, and Scotland together form Great Britain, and Great Britain and Northern Ireland together form the United Kingdom. Wales is a Principality, Scotland a Kingdom, and Northern Ireland a Province. Many people in Northern Ireland object to the term 'the Province', so we have tried to avoid using it. Many of the majority community in Northern Ireland call the region 'Ulster', though the traditional Ulster included three counties which now form part of the Irish Republic (Donegal, Cavan, Monaghan).

We refer to the United Kingdom and the Republic of Ireland together, what used to be called the British Isles, as 'the two states' or 'these islands', occasionally as 'the archipelago'.

*When we refer to international treaties, we give in parenthesis the year in which the text was adopted, followed by the year the treaty entered into force.

The Churches

In the Irish context, Protestants comprise both Anglicans (Episcopalians) in the Church of Ireland and the Dissenting Churches (which in Great Britain might be called Free Churches or Non-Conformists). All the main Churches (Protestant as well as Catholic) are organised on an all-Ireland basis. Most of the larger Protestant Churches belong to the Irish Council of Churches, and three Irish Churches (The Church of Ireland, the Methodist Church in Ireland, the Presbyterian Church in Ireland) are also members of the British Council of Churches.

Majorities and Minorities

In both Ireland and Great Britain there are a number of ethnic and religious communities comprising, for example, Jews, Hindus, Muslims, Buddhists, Sikhs, and gypsies (sometimes called travelling people).

It is well known that there are two communities in Northern Ireland, a Protestant majority (about 60 per cent of the population) and a Catholic minority (about 40 per cent). In political terms, most Protestants are unionist (in favour of the continued union of Northern Ireland with Great Britain) or loyalist (an ultra unionist whose first commitment is to British elements in the character of Ulster). The two main political parties which speak for the majority of Protestants are the Ulster Unionist Party or Official Unionists whose leader is the Rt Hon James Molyneaux, and the Democratic Unionists (DUP) whose leader is the Rev. Dr Ian Paisley. Some Protestants have also formed themselves into more extreme groupings such as the Ulster Defence Association, while others have engaged in the use of physical force through para-military bodies such as the Ulster Volunteer Force.

Most Catholics aim for a union of the two parts of Ireland. Those members of the Catholic community who favour the use of legal and non-violent methods we have called nationalists or constitutional nationalists. The largest political party of the Catholic community representing this point of view in Northern Ireland is the Social Democratic and Labour Party (SDLP) whose leader is John Hume.

Some members of the minority community in Northern Ireland are committed to the use of physical force to achieve political ends. These support the Irish Republican Army (IRA) or its political wing, Sinn Fein, whose leader is Gerry Adams, or the much smaller Irish

National Liberation Army (INLA) or its political wing, the Irish Republican Socialist Party.

The Alliance Party in Northern Ireland (not to be confused with the Liberal-SDP Alliance in Great Britain) accepts that Northern Ireland should continue as part of the United Kingdom in present circumstances. It tries to appeal to moderate members of both communities.

Human and Civil Rights

We draw attention in Chapters 1 and 2 to the prevalent confusion about the meaning of certain key expressions, and especially the phrase 'human rights'. At one end of the spectrum, there are those who question whether the term has any meaning at all; at the other, there is a marked tendency nowadays for anyone who suffers some perceived injustice to complain at once that his or her 'human rights' have been violated.

In order to limit this area of confusion, we shall therefore in this Report impose on ourselves the following rules about the use of these terms in the *legal* context – without, of course, seeking to impose such rules on anyone who prefers to use them differently.

1. We shall use the terms 'human rights and fundamental freedoms' only in the sense in which they are used in *international* law – that is to say, those rights and freedoms which the Universal Declaration of Human Rights and the increasing number of international human rights treaties require the states of the international community to respect and ensure for all their inhabitants.
2. We shall use the terms 'civil rights' and 'civil liberties' when we are discussing legal rights and freedoms under the *national* law of the particular country we are considering – which, in the context of this Report, will usually be the United Kingdom or the Republic of Ireland.
3. Where we use the word 'right', 'freedom', or 'liberty' without any prefix like 'human' or 'civil', we shall try to make clear from the context or by specific reference whether we are speaking of one that is 'legal' – that is, one that can be vindicated before some national or international court or tribunal – or 'moral' – that is to say, one that is supported by moral claims, but not (or not yet) by national or international law.

We can perhaps best illustrate this terminology by some examples. There are strong moral arguments for saying that no one should be forced to kill others, even in time of war, if that goes fundamentally against conscience. Those who take this position will therefore speak of a right to object to military service on moral grounds (conscientious objection). When military conscription was in force in Great Britain, national law made provision for this right, within certain limits and subject to certain conditions. In Great Britain, therefore, there has in the past been a *civil* right to conscientious objection. But the code of international human rights law makes no such provision; conscientious objection is therefore not an internationally recognised *human* right. Some would argue powerfully that it ought to be, but it is not a 'human right' according to our self-imposed definition. It may soon become one, as both the UN Human Rights Commission and the Council of Ministers of the Council of Europe have recently recommended that conscientious objection to military service be recognised as a human right (resolutions of 10 March and 9 April 1987 respectively).

In making a distinction between 'human' and 'civil' rights, and between legal and moral rights, we realise that we may disappoint some who would insist that they have an unquestioned right to something which is recognised neither by their national legal system nor by international law. This would apply, for example, in the case of those Quakers who are unwilling for their taxes to be used for national defence. We should make it clear that we are not in any way challenging the moral character of such a claim, but simply drawing attention to the fact that neither national nor international *law* has yet recognised it.

ORGANISATION OF THE PROJECT

The project was formally inaugurated at a meeting of the Advisory Board at Cumberland Lodge, Windsor Great Park, on 17 and 18 October 1984. The Board is composed of nine men and three women, belonging to Protestant or Catholic Churches from different parts of Great Britain and Ireland.

The members of the Working Pary were appointed by the Board at its first meeting. The Board also appointed four honorary officers, two of whom are Anglicans, one a Roman Catholic, and one a Quaker. Present at this first meeting were observers from the British and Irish councils of churches and the justice and peace bodies of the Catholic bishops of England and Wales, Scotland, and Ireland.

The Working Party includes Roman Catholics and Protestants from England, Wales, Scotland, and both parts of Ireland. It includes various kinds of expertise (theology, ethics, law, history, political science, public administration) as well as a number of persons active in party politics. We greatly regret that there were no women among our number; when considering minority issues in Great Britain, we reminded ourselves that we were all white.

All of us served in our personal capacities. One of the original members of the Working Party, Stephen McGonagle, resigned on 6 May 1986. We are grateful for his contributions to our deliberations and were sorry to lose his help.

We held twelve residential meetings, usually in or near London, Belfast, or Dublin, but once in Glasgow. There were also a considerable number of meetings of sub-groups.

The procedure we followed in drafting this Report was to hold a preliminary discussion of an issue (or cluster of issues), and then ask one of our number to prepare a first written draft. These drafts were considered in detail at several meetings (rarely fewer than four), and revised until we were satisfied that we had reached as near consensus as was possible in the time available. The final editing was undertaken by our Chairman.

In dealing with controversial issues, we have done our best to express alternative views as fairly as possible. On some crucial matters, there remain differences of judgement as to the precise words to be used; and, in some places, one or more members would have preferred to formulate the issues or conclusions differently. But we have worked as a team throughout, disregarding labels as much as possible and trying to be sensitive to other views. We have now reached a point where we have decided to transmit our Report to the Advisory Board, and we hope that the Board will authorise publication, with or without its own comments or reservations.

One member of the Working Party has asked for the inclusion of two footnotes of dissent (pp. 82 and 83). In two other places there are anonymous footnotes recording disagreement (pp. 147 and 194), and in two other places we state majority and minority views (pp. 170 and 178–9).

The preparation of this Report was possible only because of the untiring efforts of our Honorary Secretary, Lionel Jacobs. Honorary Secretaries tend to be anonymous figures who lurk in the background, but Lionel Jacobs was crucial at every stage of our work. His previous service with the Standing Advisory Commission on Human Rights in Northern Ireland gave him exceptional experience and authority. Besides preparing agendas and minutes, he did his share of drafting. We take this opportunity of expressing our thanks to him.

At our request, the Minority Rights Group, which is well known for its reports on divided societies around the world, sponsored a series of case studies of successful co-existence in some plural societies in Europe: South Tyrol, the Swedish community in Finland, Belgium, Switzerland, and the Netherlands. These papers have been published by the Minority Rights Group as their Report 72,[1] and form the basis of part of Chapter 3. We had a meeting with Ben Whitaker, director of the Minority Rights Group, and some of the authors of the papers: Professor Alcock, Dr Palley, and Dr Steinberg. This proved an extraordinarily stimulating and valuable session, and we are most grateful for this contribution to our work.

Needless to say, the Minority Rights Group and its collaborators bear no responsibility for any deductions we may have drawn from their writings or from our discussions with them. Lord Hylton, the Honorary Treasurer of the Project, initiated a debate on the Minority Rights Group report in the House of Lords on 11 February 1987.

The two governments were informed about the launching of the Project, and ministers and government officials in the two states responded promptly and willingly to our requests for factual information. The Project has from the start been entirely non-official, and we sought no official blessing for our work.

All persons concerned with the Project served on an honorary basis. There was no office, and no permanent organisation was created. It was always intended that the organisation would be terminated when the Report had been finalised.

Between March and June 1987, we had the assistance of Paul Hunt, seconded to the project from Quaker Peace and Service. Paul Hunt is a young lawyer who had previously worked for the Quaker agency in the Middle East, dealing with human rights issues. He received a very modest maintenance allowance while he was working for us, the cost being shared between our project and Quaker Peace and Service.

The project was financed by contributions from Churches, charitable trusts, and individuals. Almost all the major Churches in

Great Britain and Ireland made at least one contribution. Up to 18 May 1987, 24 Churches, parishes, and religious communities had donated £7086; 20 charitable trusts in Great Britain, together with the European Human Rights Foundation and the Ireland Fund, contributed £26 182; 8 individual contributions and miscellaneous income amounted to £2597. We neither sought nor received funds from any government. The main expenses were for travel, accommodation and meals during residential meetings, usually in religious houses, and office expenses. We are grateful to the British Council of Churches for help with our accounts.

Reference

1. *Coexistence in some plural European societies* (Minority Rights Group Report 72, 1987) (available from 29 Craven Street, London, WC2N 5NT, price £1.80). We wish to acknowledge the help of the authors of these studies: Claire Palley, Antony Alcock, Marc Bossuyt, Dick Leonard, Jonathan Steinberg and Fred Grunfeld.

1 Rights and Responsibilities in Christian Ethics

Human rights are now embodied in international declarations and treaties, sometimes with procedures whereby an aggrieved citizen may appeal to an international body of redress. Human rights are also sometimes a sourse of international tension and recrimination. The language of human rights is so widespread today that it may come as a surprise to some that it is relatively recent.

Of course, the notion of 'right', *jus*, is not new: it has a long history and is basic to any legal system. The 'rights' of individuals include those which they are able to establish by specific claims under the laws of the state in which they live: for instance, disabled people have secured the right in the Republic of Ireland and the United Kingdom to a Mobility Allowance. But the innovation in the past two centuries is that human rights are held to belong to human beings *as such*, regardless of status, nationality, race, religion, or gender. They are widely believed to exist whether or not there are actual laws to enforce them. Indeed, some of their advocates would claim that such fundamental human rights as the right to life, the right to the pursuit of happiness, or the right to freedom of speech, should actually take precedence over any laws of the state which contravene them.

HISTORY OF THE HUMAN RIGHTS CONCEPT

A medieval prince was deemed to have absolute sovereignty over his domains, and a member of an oppressed group within his kingdom had no one to whom to appeal if his interests suffered from the prince's laws. This absolute sovereignty was limited in Christendom, at least in theory, by the authority of the Church. In due course, the influence of the Church declined to the point where it could no longer wield effective authority over the legislation of secular rulers, but people continued to feel the need for some ultimate standard for measuring the justice of the laws of a state. The search for a universally agreed standard of justice was rewarded by the emerg-

12

ence of a theory of 'human rights', a theory which had radical political implications.

Human rights language entered into philosophical writing in the seventeenth century in the work of Grotius and Locke. It was first invoked in practice by the leaders of the French and American revolutions in the interests of creating a new social and political order. The American Declaration of Independence (1776) and the French Declaration of the Rights of Man and the Citizen (1798) formally asserted that certain fundamental rights belong to human beings as such and could therefore be called 'human' rights without qualification.

The concept was in due course to extend to the international plane, and the belief that human beings have inalienable rights wherever they may be is now widely accepted. Since 1945, these universal rights have been incorporated in international treaties which are legally binding on the states which have become parties to them. The phrase 'human rights', therefore, is coming to denote those legal rights established in international law, and it is in that sense that we use the expression. In addition, there are civil rights recognised in national law, such as the right of a person accused of a serious offence in Great Britain to a trial by jury.

There was a vigorous revival of human rights theory after the Second World War, when it seemed a matter of urgency to prevent any recurrence of the type of outrage represented by Nazi atrocities against millions of innocent people. By then, largely as a result of an initiative by religious non-governmental organisations, it was possible to establish the principles underlying the Universal Declaration of Human Rights (1948) and of subsequent international instruments, by reference to a long tradition both of Christian and secular thought: these principles have parallels also in the traditions of other world religions and cultures.[1]

A THEOLOGICAL BASIS FOR HUMAN RIGHTS

Given that both the language and the concept of 'human rights' are a relatively recent phenomenon, it is understandable that it is only in this century that the Churches have felt the need to offer a theological basis for them – or, indeed, to scrutinise their own doctrines and attitudes in the light of them. This has not been a simple task. The Christian tradition cannot be expected to offer direct answers to questions which had not yet been asked when its basic documents were compiled and its basic doctrines formulated. It is rather a matter of discovering how traditional doctrines and new areas of concern may be brought to bear on each other.

The Bible

At first sight, the Bible may seem an unpromising field in which to begin: it appears to condone slavery (which is now universally prohibited in human rights legislation) and on occasion to withhold basic rights from certain subject peoples (the Canaanites were to be slaves simply because of their ancestry).[2] Attempts to derive from the creation narrative 'inherent dignity' or 'equal and inalienable rights', which are features of contemporary human rights law, involve taking biblical texts in a sense that is not their original meaning and intention. Moreover, there is throughout the Bible a noticeable absence of any reference to moral or legal 'rights'.

Nevertheless, it can be argued that some rights are at least implicit in the Bible. The best known eighteenth-century writer on the subject, Thomas Paine, argued that rights and obligations are logically complementary: one person's right implies another person's (or the state's or society's) obligation to respect that right. If this is so, it follows that if we can find obligations in the Bible, we should be able to infer some 'rights' from them.

To a certain extent, this is possible. In the Old Testament, as in any other legal system, many of the obligations imposed by law confer rights upon those to whom the obligations are owed: an aged father who receives no support from his son has a right to redress and may seek it in the courts; a visitor who falls from the roof of a house because of a faulty parapet has a right to compensation and may sue the owner of the house. But this is by no means the case in every instance. A farmer was not permitted to keep all the gleaning for himself; he must leave something for the alien, the fatherless, and the widow.[3] This moral obligation did not confer a legally enforceable 'right' on the poor. A widow or an orphan could not take a farmer to law who left no corn lying in a harvested field: she could only appeal for permission to glean, in the expectation that the owner would respect the obligation laid upon him by law.[4]

This explains the strong element of moral exhortation contained in Jewish law, and why Old Testament law moves so easily between what appear to us to be quite different categories: legislation enforceable in the courts and moral exhortation. A typical example is the juxtaposition among the Ten Commandments of 'Thou shalt not bear false witness' (a punishable offence under Jewish law) with 'Thou shalt not covet' (a moral exhortation). In many instances, the only sanction which would force the rich and powerful to limit their own power was the prospect of legal action brought by the religious establishment or by their own peers; often the poor and the weak were protected only by appealing to compassion, morality, and the fear of God's displeasure – an appeal voiced again and again by the prophets.

The New Testament continues in this tradition: indeed, in some respects it is even less amenable to being invoked in support of a theory of 'rights'. As in the Old Testament, all the emphasis is on duties and obligations: of masters towards slaves, of husbands towards wives, of parents towards children. It would be impossible to infer a corresponding list of 'rights' for slaves, wives, and children, for the same reasons as in the Old Testament. These people had only limited legal redress. Indeed, in New Testament times there were classes of people who were deemed (at least by the Pharisees) to have forfeited their rights at law by virtue of their occupations or origins (tax collectors, prostitutes, and Samaritans, for example), and only moral pressure could secure humane treatment for them if they got into trouble.

Indeed, in many places the New Testament goes a great deal further. In the Sermon on the Mount, followers of Jesus are commanded deliberately to abandon their 'rights' – to turn the other cheek when insulted rather than to seek redress, to waive the repayment of debts rather than to exercise the rights of a creditor, and so forth. The ethic of the Sermon on the Mount is expressed in highly individual terms; it is the response which Christians may be challenged to make to their perception of the demands of God's dawning Kingdom. Moreover, this spirit of self-denial in respect of rights seems immediately to have affected Christian moral thinking. When criticising the members of the Corinthian Church for going to law with each other before pagan magistrates, Paul asked why, in any case, they did not prefer to suffer injustice.[5] In 1 Peter, a positive value is found in innnocent suffering. In general, the emphasis is on willing and sacrificial service rather than on establishing claims and rights.

This emphasis may account for a certain hesitation on the part of

Christians to press for their own human rights: for the individual Christian, the thrust of the teaching of Jesus seems to be elsewhere. The New Testament is a charter for responsibilities – towards the weak, the suffering, the oppressed. But nowhere does it seem to encourage the pursuit of individual rights and entitlements.

But the Christian ethic is not only concerned with the obligations of personal discipleship; it has also had to come to terms with the claims made upon Christians by virtue of their membership of human society in general, and no amount of Christian willingness to waive one's own rights can justify indifference to attacks on the legitimate rights of others.

There has always been an innate tendency for the powerful to dominate, exploit, and oppress the weak. In the Old Testament, the laws made provision for a periodic adjustment of the distribution of wealth (and accordingly of power) in order to check this tendency, and the prophets delivered vehement exhortations to the powerful to discharge their responsibilities to the weak. In the New Testament, the power of pagan governments is respected as necessary to secure social order and peace. But again, rulers are regarded as subject to the standards of divine justice and as receiving their authority ultimately from God, so that they can expect retribution if they abuse their power.

This concern with the realities of power has continued into much subsequent Christian theology, both Catholic and Reformed. Theologians have recognised that all governments have a divinely bestowed authority to exercise power for the common good. This includes coercive power, for human societies cannot always hold together on the basis of consent alone. Nevertheless, although Churches have never been slow to affirm the right of the governments of their own states to exercise divinely given power, they have not always been so quick to recognise the abuses to which state power is liable.

What can curb the tendency of those in power to dominate, exploit, and oppress the people over whom they are set? One answer to that question is given in the slow evolution of modern constitutional democracies, which impose systematic constraints on the power of each organ of government. From this point of view, human rights, legally recognised and enforced, are part of the same movement. They are part of the protection afforded to individuals against the misuse of power. Seen as a means for the protection of the powerless against the misuse of power, the promotion of 'human rights' is clearly something which has the support both of the Bible and, as we shall see, of the Christian tradition.

Christian Tradition

The most widely advocated basis for a Christian doctrine of human rights is probably one derived from natural law. This approach, which has its roots in Aristotle and Stoicism as much as in Christian theology, proceeds from the assumption that the purpose and proper character of human existence can be inferred from human nature itself. And if it can be shown that human nature requires certain conditions in order to realise its potential (such as freedom from slavery, torture, or unjust imprisonment), it will follow that any human society has an obligation to guarantee these conditions to its members, who have a 'natural' right to enjoy them. This approach is characteristic of Roman Catholic thinking and is adopted, for example, in *Iustitia et Pax, The Church and Human Rights*.[6]

This sums up previous pronouncements,[7] and works out the implications of these natural rights in the light of specifically Christian doctrines. Human beings are made in the image of God and have a moral sense imprinted on their consciences by their Creator. Moreover, the Incarnation has opened up for us a new understanding of human nature and new possibilities for human existence. It is the task of the Church to help in the liberation of human beings from those constraints which prevent these possibilities from being realised. This mission impels the Church to promote 'human rights', especially where these are not established by law, as a protection against injustice and oppression.

The Calvinist tradition, on the other hand, has tended to reject the assumptions of natural law. Human reason (it has been argued), like human nature, is corrupted by sin; we cannot rely upon it to infer our moral duties from our natural abilities and potential. Only the grace of God, articulated in his Word, can reveal to us our true vocation and responsibilities.[8] Human beings have rights, not by their own nature, but as a gracious gift from God; and this gives these rights a validity which no human authority can suspend or curtail. It is because of this God-given character that Christian theology has a concern for the humanity of persons, including their rights and duties, which are perceived in the light of our creation in the image of God, our reconciliation through the Incarnation, and our place in that Kingdom of God which has already been initiated by Christ and will come fully into existence at the end of history.

Anglican thinking on human rights can be found in two Reports of 1976 and 1977.[9] There has also been a small ecumenical Report from the Advisory Forum on Human Rights of the British Council of Churches.[10] In all these reports, the dominant theological principle is that man is made in the image of God, 'with all that this implies about his dignity, his sanctity and his destiny'.[11] Any attempt to debase that human dignity and any failure to respect and promote it are incompatible with the Gospel. From this central theological affirmation, a number of practical implications can be drawn.

Examples could be added from other Churches, but these would offer little more than variations on the same themes. Although the approaches have different starting points, their conclusions are remarkably similar, and there is considerable overlap in the specifically Christian insights which are used to establish a legitimate concern for human rights. Christians are broadly agreed that human beings have dignity because God created us in his own image and then restored that image by living, dying, and rising again in Christ. Human life is essentially social because we have been created in the image of God, who combines both unity and relationship within himself. Further, human life, both in its individual and in its social manifestations, is flawed. Christian thinking about human rights must always proceed not only from the dignity and social nature of humanity, but also from the fact that we constantly violate that dignity and those social relationships, and that external constraints are necessary to prevent us from doing so. On the basis of perceptions such as these, Christian theology (in contrast to many lamentable episodes of Church history) offers full support to the reality and the necessity of human rights.

Jews and Muslims also believe that human beings are made in the image of God, and that all have the potential for following the path of righteousness (*halacha* in Hebrew, *shar'ia* in Arabic). This path concerns not only private devotions and communal worship, but a whole way of life in which rights and freedoms are derived from social responsibility and solidarity. Indeed, all the major religions represented in these islands proclaim principles which are wholly consistent with the code of human rights, and all may be said to have contributed to the emerging consensus on human rights and responsibilities. This consensus is thus both international and inter-faith.

PHILOSOPHICAL OBJECTIONS

At the same time, we need to recognise that there are several philosophical traditions which call into question the existence – or, at least, the possible extent – of independent standards of human rights.

According to one of these, which dates from antiquity, no 'right' of any kind can be said to exist until there is a remedy in law against its infringement. Laws come first, and rights derive from them. It follows that it is meaningful to speak of 'human rights' only where there are effective laws which give them force.

Another tradition insists that there are some alleged 'human rights' which could never be universally protected by laws. Take, for instance, the 'rights' to food, work, education, and health care, which now figure in the international code of economic and social rights. These presuppose that the resources exist for them to be enjoyed by all human beings. But in the case of work in the industrialised West, or of food, education, and health care in the Third World, the resources simply are not there. To talk unconditionally of the 'right to work' in cities such as Belfast or Newcastle, or the 'right to food' in some Third World countries, is mere rhetoric.

A different objection is that human rights language implies universality: these rights are to be unconditional, and the documents refer to them as 'inherent . . . equal and inalienable'. But in fact the code itself allows for many of them to be curtailed or even suspended 'in time of war or other public emergency threatening the life of the nation'. Moreover, every state needs to restrict some of the rights of individuals if, for example, they commit crimes, suffer from dangerous communicable diseases, or become insane. Few rights in the code are expressed in entirely unqualified language and are therefore truly universal and unconditional. For the rest – according to those who hold this view – instead of invoking inalienable 'rights' which belong to human beings as such, it would be more accurate (and more realistic) to speak of freedoms or enjoyments which the state has a moral obligation to provide for every citizen, but only to the extent practicable.

Though these positions differ from each other in detail, what they have in common is that they are essentially pragmatic or 'positivist'. Even on their own terms, they can be countered. For example, only a minority of the economic and social rights declared as goals in the international code require the mobilisation of major national resources for their fulfilment, and the principal test for compliance with these obligations is whether the state concerned gives access to what is available without discrimination on grounds such as race, gender, religion, political opinion, and so on. Suspension in cases of public emergency is expressly limited to what is 'strictly required by the exigencies of the situation'. Other limitations on the various rights and freedoms are carefully circumscribed in the code itself and may be said to be designed only to establish boundaries for each such right in order to avoid collisions with other rights protected elsewhere in the code.

In any case, the pragmatic or positivist approach runs counter not only to Christian presuppositions but to a widespread conviction that human rights exist whether or not a legal system is available to enforce them: they are *pre-legal*. Those who speak of human rights are normally appealing to something which is perceived to be moral before it is legal, to something which is of more general validity than 'rights' which flow from particular laws. It is widely believed that every human being has a dignity and worth which confers certain inherent rights, that human life is essentially social, and that society cannot flourish unless certain basic rights are guaranteed. This guarantee is necessary in view of the tendency of all human beings, both as individuals and in organised political groupings, to deny the proper respect due to others. Moreover, the human rights instruments which have been established since the Second World War presuppose a moral belief in 'some common and permanent human characteristics that enjoin certain universally specifiable ways of treating human beings and that prohibit others'.[12] Even though these instruments, which stem from the United Nations Charter and the Universal Declaration of Human Rights, are clearly stamped with a Western philosophical tradition, they have won assent from nations of a wide variety of cultures and ideologies. There is a notable consensus today that human beings *as such* have certain rights, and that these rights need to be protected from the consequences of human selfishness, cruelty, and indifference. These principles may be differently expressed or interpreted according to ideological preferences, but they have nevertheless resulted in a code of human rights which commands a wide measure of respect. This code is expressed in universal and regional treaties, and these are constantly interpreted by the control organs. In addition, new rights are formulated in additional treaties.

DANGERS OF LANGUAGE

It is clear that the language of human rights, framed as it is in general terms and with such a strong moral charge, needs to be used with care. It is important, for example, to distinguish between a 'right' and a 'claim'. Claims are a necessary part of life in any ordered society. A queen may claim her throne, children their inheritance, a visitor his hat and coat in the cloakroom. To do so, each may have to produce evidence to support their claim: in the case of a queen, her royal parentage; in the case of a visitor, his cloakroom ticket. But it is always possible that someone else may have a competing claim. The claimant to the throne may be alleged to be an imposter; the cloakroom ticket may be suspected of being a forgery. In these cases, adjudication is necessary. The strength of competing claims has to be established by an independent authority. But there is nothing morally objectionable in such a dispute. By its very nature, a claim is open to challenge until its validity is established.

Suppose, however, that a claim is upheld by a court or a competent authority. By reason of the adjudication in the claimant's favour, his claim has become something to which he is entitled, and anyone who infringes that entitlement exposes himself to legal action. But such a right is by no means unconditional. I may have established my claim to the ownership of my house, and I may then occupy it without disturbance. But my right to do so may legitimately be overridden in a time of national emergency (if it is required by the security forces) or in the national interest (if it lies on the route of a proposed motorway) or if it is dangerous to passers-by (if I take no action to repair it) or if I go out of my mind and have to be lodged in an institution. Indeed, the rights of every citizen are so hedged with limitations, particularly in respect of the rights of others, that it can be positively misleading to talk of them as necessarily universal or unconditional.

Rights language contains two dangers. The first is that it may be introduced into situations which are in reality ones of conflicting claims, as a result of which one group may seem to gain a moral advantage over the other by claiming a right, and then implying that those who dispute it are necessarily in the wrong. The introduction of the 'human rights' concept does not necessarily simplify the issue or resolve the conflict: it may, indeed, merely exacerbate a sense of injustice. The second danger is that of assuming that simply because something is called a 'right', it must be valid in all circumstances when, as we have seen, virtually every right may be subject to limitations in order to assure the rights of others.

When these facts are ignored, there is a danger of a kind of moral inflation in any dispute. Indeed, in any conflict, people tend to use the most powerful and emotive language they can find to justify and advance their cause, and the language of human rights is ready to hand.

But of course human rights language does not arise only out of abstract speculation: it is elicited by actual situations of conflict, oppression, and injustice. Those who invoke human rights are typically members of a group who are in the minority and are powerless or oppressed, or who speak for them. They see the 'rights' they are claiming as necessary to the dignity and status of human beings, perhaps even to their survival as a people, so that the achievement of these rights becomes a major political objective and a cause worthy of support by all who care for justice and human dignity. But here, too, there are dangers.

It is always necessary to be vigilant so that those who are oppressed and genuinely deprived of their human rights will, when they gain their immediate objectives and the political power that goes with them, preserve the universal character of the rights they have struggled for and guarantee them to their oppressors. Those who rebelled against the Shah of Iran on the grounds of his contempt for human rights have not shown themselves above reproach in their protection of the human rights of their opponents; and when the black people of South Africa achieve their rightful political power, the focus of world attention may well shift to the legitimate rights of the white minority. Human rights are claimed to be inherent, inalienable, and equal for all. By no means all appeals and protests which use human rights language turn out, on analysis, to meet these requirements.

'THE JUSTICE WHICH GOD REQUIRES'

This last point draws our attention to what is perhaps the most serious danger in the excessive use of human rights language: that of reducing the sense of personal responsibility. In the case of specific personal and social rights which are afforded by the law of the land, it is normally true that one person's right is another person's responsibility. My right to walk down the street is matched by your responsibility to drive with due care and attention; your right to drive down the street is matched by my responsibility not to cause an obstruction. But in the case of *human* rights, the situation is often less symmetrical. Claims arising from human rights may be made against governments or public authorities. It is only too easy for people to pursue their human rights against an impersonal entity and to neglect that sense of personal responsibility which we all bear for the specific rights of others, a responsibility normally exercised by individuals through willing co-operation with democratic and judicial procedures.

This apparent erosion of the sense of personal responsibility must be seen in the context of a far-reaching European social change which can be traced back to Renaissance humanism and the political revolutions of the seventeenth and eighteenth centuries. Up to that time, law had been made by the rich and powerful to protect their own interests and regulate their own behaviour for their own benefit. To be sure, there were certain protections for the poor and the weak, but their welfare depended more on goodwill and mutual self-interest than on legal provision. But in the seventeenth and eighteenth centuries, power tended to shift in Europe from the aristocracy to the smaller landowners and merchants, and in the nineteenth and twentieth centuries to the people as a whole through universal suffrage and broadly based democratic institutions. The new perception that power belonged in the last resort to the people themselves – that is, all the citizens of whatever social group or class – fundamentally changed the rationale of law. In theory, it was no longer the few who were making the laws and determining their own responsibilities: it was the people, including the poor and the weak, whose representatives were now the lawmakers.

To this extent, the shift from 'responsibilities language' to 'rights language' is seen as a consequence of a significant shift of power from the few to the many, from the strong to the weak. As such, it is a sign of a change which is strongly to be welcomed. But it is a shift which could go too far, and which carries dangers, both to the harmonious functioning of society and, indeed, to the understanding of human nature itself. In the words of the Archbishop of York, 'There are good reasons to fear that the emphasis on rights, so far from strengthening social cohesion, has in fact reduced it by seeming to justify an individualistic kind of acquisitiveness.'[13]

Current ecumenical theology employs the concept of a 'just, participatory, and sustainable society'. In such a society, certain rights and freedoms must be preserved (such as the freedom to control, to criticise, and to change the government of one's country), and the power of governments to restrict these rights on grounds of national necessity must be strictly limited. But at the same time, the exercise of any freedom involves an answering responsibility. When people are encouraged to claim their rights, there must be a corresponding emphasis on the responsibilities which go with them, so that the power which is yielded by those who were infringing those rights may be responsibly exercised by those who now enjoy them; only so can a proper social solidarity be maintained. Indeed, this sense of responsibility towards neighbour and society, corresponding to the rights and freedoms allowed to the individual, is commended not just in the mainstream of Christian thought but in the teaching of all the great religions represented in Great Britain and the two parts of Ireland.

But the concept of responsibility implies more than this. Its basic and most ancient meaning is *accountability*: to be responsible is to be accountable to someone else for what one does. This meaning is as important today as ever. In the case of some accident or maladministration, people instinctively ask who was responsible, on the assumption that there is someone who can be called to account: and the concept of responsibility is also extremely important in law, where it may be keenly argued whether the defendant may be held responsible for the crime or was subject either to external pressure or to an internal condition such as insanity. But people also recognise a wider sense of the word 'responsible'. A 'responsible' person is not just one who happens to hold a particular position of responsibility. The phrase is one of moral approbation. It describes someone who can be trusted to maintain standards, to take appropriate initiatives, to be alert to dangers and injustices. A sense of responsibility is a highly esteemed moral quality.

Recent theology, both Jewish and Christian, has found this concept of responsibility of great value as a pointer to the relationship which exists between God and humankind. It is not just that human beings are responsible in the sense of being accountable to God – though indeed they are, and this already has profound ethical implications. The word itself suggests 'response', and has led some theologians to stress the initiative of God in addressing his call to us, and the capacity of human beings to respond to God. Human action then becomes a matter of responding to the commands, the call, and the vision which God addresses to us, as well as to the claims made upon us by our fellow human beings; and this can readily be translated into a dynamic model of Christian ethics, understood as a moral response to a personal God who both addresses his Word to us and meets us in the changing situations of life.

That rights imply duties was taken for granted in eighteenth-century discussions of human rights, and was acknowledged (though only in a single article) in the UN Declaration of 1948. The Declaration of the Rights and Duties of Man adopted by the Organization of American States a few months earlier had devoted 10 of its 38 Articles to some of the 'duties' that are correlative to human rights. But it remains true that today responsibilities tend to receive far less attention than rights, and that this must be a cause for concern, both for the long-term future of social and political institutions and for our understanding of the ultimate accountability of human beings for each other and for the environment.

For both social and theological reasons, therefore, it is necessary for us to bring the resources of the Christian faith to bear on the contemporary discussion of human rights in such a way as to correct the shift which has taken place in recent years from responsibilities to rights. But this does not mean that we should be any less zealous in the promotion of human rights themselves. We believe that these rights exist as true moral values, regardless of whether they are yet entrenched in the laws or constitutions of individual states, or in the international code. Though we need to be alert to the dangers of a careless or partisan appeal to the language of human rights, we can recognise certain rights as an essential condition for a harmonious social life. Where they exist, they must be vigilantly maintained; where they are not yet affirmed, they must be unremittingly fought for.

Human rights are a reflection of the justice which God requires in all human societies, and the Christian can have no release from the constant endeavour to see justice upheld. There is, indeed, a strong and simple motive that impels Christians to demonstrate a profound concern for the poor, the weak, and the oppressed. This is prominent in the Bible and has continued throughout Christian tradition. Christians believe that to pursue this concern is to perform the will of God. In previous ages, the institutions of law, for historical and social reasons, were not used for this purpose, and appeal had to be made (as it still is) to human compassion and to the character of divine justice, with its concern for the poor. The modern evolution of law and a widening moral consensus between nations of different cultures, ideologies, religions, and races have caused a new means to emerge in the form of an internationally recognised code of human rights. As members of the main Christian Churches and traditions in Great Britain and the two parts of Ireland, we give wholehearted support to these new legal institutions and the principles behind them, for they stand in the tradition of both Old and New Testaments and also of many centuries of Christian concern. They are a reflection, however imperfect, of the just purposes of God, and are one of the means by which power may be restored to the powerless and justice procured for 'the fatherless, the widow and the alien', the weak and oppressed of today's world.

Notes and References

1. Abundantly illustrated in *The Birthright of Man* (Paris: UNESCO, 1969).
2. Genesis 9.25.
3. Deuteronomy 24.19–22.
4. Ruth 2.7.
5. I Corinthians 6.7.
6. *The Church and Human Rights* (Vatican City: Pontifical Commission, 1975).
7. Such as (i) *Gaudium et Spes* which can be found in Walter M. Abbott (general ed.), *The Documents of Vatican II* (New York: America Press, 1966) p. 199, (ii) the Encyclical Letter *Pacem in Terris* (Vatican City: Polyglot Press, 1963).
8. The implications of this are worked out in, for example, Allen O. Miller (ed.), *A Christian Declaration on Human Rights* (New York: Eerdmans, 1977).
9. *Anglican Consultative Council – Third Meeting* (London, 1977) pp. 28–30, and *Human Rights: Our Understanding and our Responsibilities* (London: Church Information Office, 1977) (GS 324).
10. Roger Williamson, *Christian Concern for Human Rights* (London: Advisory Forum on Human Rights of the British Council of Churches, c.1980).
11. *Anglican Consultative Council – Third Meeting* (London, 1977) p. 29.
12. Article by David Little, in John Macquarrie and James Childress (eds), *A New Dictionary of Christian Ethics* (London: SCM, 1986) p. 279.
13. John Habgood (Archbishop of York), *Church and Nation in a Secular Age* (London: Darton, 1983) p. 42.

2 Rights and Responsibilities in International Law

NATIONAL SOVEREIGNTY

The systems of internal law operating within the United Kingdom and the Republic of Ireland are called national (or sometimes domestic or municipal) laws. We look at them in Chapter 5. But before we do so, we must describe another system of law of particular importance for our study, international law.

The primary function of this system is to regulate the relationships between sovereign states in matters as diverse as the status of their emissaries, the freedom of the high seas, the imposition of customs duties, the carrying on of international communications by post, telegraph, telephone, radio (and nowadays satellite), as well as (so far as possible) what is and is not legitimate when sovereign states are unable to resolve their disputes peacefully and wage war on each other instead. Indeed, the first major treatise on international law, written by Hugo Grotius and published in 1625, was called *De jure belli ac pacis*, Of the law of war and peace.

Because it dealt with the relationships between sovereigns – originally sovereign princes, and only later their successors, the sovereign nation states – international law was much concerned with the concept of sovereignty. Indeed, this concept was central to much of its doctrine. All legal systems operate by ascribing rights and duties to the various entities with which they deal, and correlating these symmetrically with each other, so that whenever *A* has a right, there must be a *B* who has a corresponding duty. (These formal rights and obligations will, of course, often be no more than the legal analogues of the underlying political realities.) The primary right which international law ascribed to a prince (and, later, to a nation state) was his right of sovereignty, and the primary duty of every prince was therefore to respect the sovereignty of his fellow princes. Sovereignty, in this context, meant (and still means) the unfettered exercise of power within the prince's domain – that is, the territory over which

27

he ruled, and the individuals within that territory who owed him allegiance, orginally called his subjects but now more usually described as the state's citizens.

Within his domain, the prince had the right to do as he pleased. In the context of his territory, this was called his territorial sovereignty; in the context of his human subjects, it was called his personal sovereignty. Any infringement of his sovereignty by another prince was, in international law, a wrong inflicted on him, which in turn gave him the right to seek various forms of redress. So, for instance, if one prince invaded the territory of another by armed force, that other would not only have the obvious right of armed self-defence, but also a right to undertake certain reprisals, such as impounding any of the other prince's assets which he found within his domain until the wrong had been righted, in order to obtain just compensation for it and to deter further wrongs.

That being so, international law could, quite logically, have no concern for the rights and obligations of princes and their subjects towards each other. How a sovereign prince treated his own subjects – or, later, a nation state its own citizens – was entirely his own affair.

The notions of civil rights and liberties, which began to be developed in the domestic law of England in the seventeenth century, found their first full flowering, almost simultaneously, in the French Declaration of the Rights of Man and the Citizen in 1789 and the US Declaration of Independence in 1776 and Bill of Rights in 1791. But for a long time, these national statements could find no echo in international law. Private individuals could not be the subjects of that law: they were the subjects of their princes, having only those rights which they were allowed on the level of national or domestic law. There was only one exception to this: how a sovereign prince treated aliens – that is to say, the subjects of another sovereign prince – was a matter for international law, for any maltreatment of them might constitute an infringement of the personal sovereignty of their own prince, who might therefore be entitled to demand compensation for himself, though not for the maltreated subject.

A LEGAL REVOLUTION

Gradually there evolved an international conscience about the humane treatment of individuals, expressed in such ways as the movement to abolish slavery, the development of international humanitarian law applicable in armed conflict, the protection of minorities and the inhabitants of territories under League of Nations mandate, and the conventions of the International Labour Organisation about working conditions. Little of this, however, interfered with the authority of sovereign states over their own subjects. Indeed, this remained the position until as recently as 1945. However, by then it had become plain that this resolute shutting of international eyes to affairs within a sovereign state held grave dangers for the international community of nations. The atrocities perpetrated on their own citizens by the *régimes* of Hitler and Stalin were not only moral outrages which shocked the conscience of mankind; they were a very real threat to international peace and security. And so there was carried through a veritable revolution in international law. Within a single generation, the international community developed a complete code of new law, enumerating and closely defining certain legally protected human rights and fundamental freedoms for all human beings anywhere in the world, which were thenceforth no longer to lie in the gift of the sovereign states whose citizens these human beings were, but were said to 'inhere' in them 'inalienably' and so could not be abridged, denied, or forfeited for whatever cause. In the words of a great international lawyer, Sir Hersch Lauterpacht, in 1950: 'The individual has acquired a status and a stature which have transformed him from an object of international compassion into a subject of international right'.[1] The mechanisms of implementation are still far from perfect, but they are gradually being improved.

The human rights and fundamental freedoms concerned were drawn from several sources: the classical civil and political rights of non-intervention in the lives of private citizens won in the revolutions of the eighteenth and early nineteenth centuries – such as the rights to life, liberty, and security; equality before the law and fair trial; freedom of conscience, belief, speech, assembly, association, and so on – and the economic and social rights developed in the later nineteenth and twentieth centuries, calling upon the state to intervene in order to redress manifest and undeserved injustices suffered by individuals and the groups to which they belonged, such as the right to work, to decent pay and conditions, to housing, health care, education, and the like.

Although these rights and freedoms are derived from several different ideologies and can be classified in many different ways, the new code does not rank them in any order and draws no distinctions of substance between them. As the UN General Assembly has proclaimed more than once, they are 'interrelated and indivisible' or 'indivisible and interdependent'.[2]

THE CHRISTIAN DIMENSION

In the context of our particular study, it is worth drawing attention here to the fact that human rights – and often even the language in which they are formulated – owe much to Christian insights, both before and after the Reformation. As long ago as the eleventh and twelfth centuries of the Christian era, the canon lawyers of Paris and Bologna devised the important maxim *lex iniusta non est lex*, an unjust law is not a law. Such a maxim was highly subversive, since it sought to limit the sovereign right of a prince to make such laws as he pleased: if his laws were unjust (perhaps because they offended against divine law, or what later came to be called natural law), his subjects were entitled to disobey them, and – in an extreme case – even to rebel against him. By this doctrine, the justice of a prince's law could serve as a test of the legitimacy of his rule, and in the measure in which that legitimacy was eroded, so legitimacy was conferred on the claims of those who sought to overthrow him. As the Netherlands States-General put it in their Act of Abjuration from King Philip II of Spain in 1581:

> God did not create the subjects for the benefit of the Prince, to do his bidding in all things whether godly or ungodly, right or wrong, and to serve him as slaves, but the Prince for the benefit of the subjects, without which he is no Prince.

At around that time, in the course of the sometimes barbarous struggles of the Reformation and the Counter-Reformation, the concepts of freedom of conscience, freedom of opinion, and freedom of thought became invested with high values, and these concepts (together with their later derivative, freedom of expression) have all survived into the modern international code.

Likewise, the rights to positive intervention to redress social injustices were not only put forward by the early secular socialists such as Proudhon but were powerfully supported by the Churches. Pope Leo XIII's encyclical *Rerum novarum* of 1891 induced many Catholic countries which were in no sense socialist to include such rights in their social legislation.

However, in both form and content the modern code of international human rights law is avowedly secular. There is no mention of the Creator (as in the American Declaration of Independence of 1776) or even of the Supreme Being (as in the French Declaration of the Rights of Man and the Citizen of 1789). If such a code is to attract the consent of nations of all religions and none, it must not exhibit a bias in favour of any single tradition, the more so as the principles and insights which it enshrines are common to all humanity's major belief systems, religious or humanistic.

The code also seeks to distribute the obligations which correspond to the rights. In the Jewish, Christian, and Islamic traditions, the creature owes to the Creator the obligation to obey his commandments: if I am bound to obey the divine injunction to love my neighbour, my neighbour does not need to rely on a right in order to complain and seek redress if I should injure him. This is why the Judaeo-Christian and Islamic traditions have in the past preferred to use the language of obligations rather than of rights, though in more recent times both Jews and Christians have come to figure among the leading protagonists of human rights.

INDIVIDUAL RESPONSIBILITY

The responsibility for the protection of human rights falls in the first instance on states and their governments, just as (and perhaps largely because) it is governments which have been (and in many places still are) their principal violators. At the same time, international law has not lost sight of the fact that nations and their governments are only convenient abstractions, and that it is sinful human beings and not abstract entities who do both good and evil deeds. Accordingly, part of the post-1945 revolution was the attribution, under what has come to be called the Nürnberg principles, of *individual* responsibility for crimes against peace, war crimes, and crimes against humanity committed in time of war, so adding these offences to the catalogue of other crimes under international law (of which piracy on the high seas was historically the first), and depriving their perpetrators of the defence that they were only carrying out the orders of their superiors.

Since then, several more offences under international law have been added to the list, including the violation of diplomatic immunities, hostage-taking, and the hijacking of aircraft. However,

although these are international offences, there is still no such thing
as an international criminal court to try them. Though it has been
often advocated, many difficult problems would have to be overcome
before such an institution could be established. Instead, therefore,
the international community's current practice is to try to agree, by
multilateral treaties, that the perpetrators of such crimes can be tried
by the national courts of any country in which they are found, even if
they committed the crimes elsewhere, so seeking to ensure that
eventually there will be no safe havens for them.

THE INTERNATIONAL HUMAN RIGHTS TREATIES

In several respects, international law is still weak. Indeed, despite
the sophistication of much of its modern content, some might say
that it is still at a primitive stage. The international community of
sovereign states still has no single international legislative assembly,
nor an international police force to enforce its laws. It does not even
have an international court with compulsory jurisdiction: the
International Court of Justice at the Hague, and the other courts and
tribunals exercising jurisdiction over states (including the human
rights organs which we mention below), can be invoked against a
state only if that state has agreed beforehand to accept that
jurisdiction, either by a general treaty or in the specific case at issue.

The international community can therefore make new laws only by
consensus: that is, by contracting with each other, in the form of
treaties which they agree to regard as legally binding, to accept the
obgligations of a new law. Whenever they do this, they effectively
agree to that extent to diminish or abridge their own sovereignty in
the interests of all of them. This trend has become very perceptible in
recent decades, as the world becomes smaller, more fragile, and
therefore more vulnerable. Indeed, the states which join the United
Nations expressly agree that the obligations of the UN Charter
prevail over their other international obligations (Article 103). The
European Community also represents an ambitious attempt at the
creation of supra-national legislation which is directly applicable in
the jurisdiction of the different member states. As we suggest in
Chapter 3, the increasing internationalism of our time is now steadily
eroding the scope for the arbitrary exercise of national sovereignty in
many fields, and not least in the field of human rights.

The content of the new code of international human rights law which has been developed since 1945 is to be found almost entirely in law-making treaties, all of quite recent date. We have mentioned some of these in the Introduction, and there are a number of others dealing with more specific issues, such as the Supplementary Convention on Slavery (1956, 1957) and the International Convention on the Elimination of all forms of Racial Discrimination (1965, 1969), as well as a large number promoted by the International Labour Organisation establishing minimum employment standards.

Before we consider the obligations of our two states under these treaties, we need to describe the process whereby the treaties themselves come into existence.

The first stage is for all the states concerned to reach agreement on a text. This can sometimes take many years of complex negotiations at a diplomatic conference or in some committee of an intergovernmental organisation such as the United Nations. When the text has at last been agreed, it is formally adopted and opened for signature.

However, that is far from being the end of the matter. Perhaps surprisingly, signature of a treaty alone does not make it binding on the state that signs it. Before that can happen, the state concerned must also ratify it or accede to it. And even then there may be yet one more stage: the treaty itself may provide that it shall enter into force only when it has been ratified by some minimum number of the states that have adopted its text, and this again can take several more years. Accordingly, a state becomes legally bound by a treaty only after it has ratified it and it has also been ratified by enough other states to bring it into force.

Treaties may be called by all sorts of names, such as Charters, Pacts, Covenants, or Conventions. But once a treaty has come into force, it operates just like a contract made between parties who are private persons: that is, it imposes legally binding obligations on the parties who have ratified it. However, these obligations are binding only in *international* law: what effect (if any) a treaty will have on the *national* law of a state – and, in particular, whether the domestic courts of that state can apply it and provide remedies for its breach – is quite a different question, to which we shall return below.

As with all contracts, the parties to a treaty may later decide to amend it or to add to it. This is usually done by means of a Protocol, which is in effect a new treaty supplementary to the original one. So, for example, there is an Optional Protocol to the International Covenant on Civil and Political Rights, and there are now no fewer than eight Protocols to the European Convention on Human Rights.

Not all these have yet entered into force, nor are all the parties to the original treaty also parties to all the Protocols.

The obligations which the United Kingdom and the Republic of Ireland have incurred under the human rights treaties are as follows:

1. The United Kingdom has been bound by the UN Charter since 1945, and the Republic of Ireland since it was admitted to the United Nations at the end of 1955.
2. The two UN Covenants on human rights were approved by the General Assembly in 1966 and came into force in 1976. The United Kingdom ratified both on 20 May 1976; so far, the Irish Republic has ratified neither.
3. The European Convention on Human Rights and Fundamental Freedoms, which was adopted in 1951, came into force in 1953, and now binds 21 sovereign states in non-communist Europe, together with a series of Additional Protocols, of which nos 1, 4, 6, and 7 protect some additional rights. The United Kingdom ratified the European Convention on Human Rights on 8 March 1951, the Republic of Ireland on 25 February 1953; the UK has also ratified Protocol no. 1 to the Convention (dealing with property, education, and elections) but so far none of the others. The Republic of Ireland has ratified five Protocols, including nos. 1 and 4.
4. The European Social Charter, which was adopted in 1961 and entered into force in 1966, now has 18 parties. The United Kingdom ratified the European Social Charter on 11 July 1962, the Irish Republic on 7 October 1964.

What the human rights treaties require is that the state concerned should 'respect', 'ensure', or 'secure' to every individual within its jurisdiction the rights they define, without distinction of any kind such as race, colour, language, religion, political or other opinion, national or social origin, association with a national minority, property, birth or other status; and that in the event of any violation, the person concerned should have an effective remedy.

REMEDIES FOR VIOLATIONS

In many of the world's states, international law is directly applicable, so that once the state has ratified a human rights treaty, its own courts can apply it to give individual claimants a remedy if they have suffered damage through a breach of its provisions. However, both the United Kingdom and the Republic of Ireland have what are called 'dualist' legal systems, under which no part of international law has any domestic legal effect unless and until the parliament legislates to incorporate it into domestic or national law. Although both states are therefore under an *international* legal obligation to protect the specific human rights and fundamental freedoms defined in the treaties they have ratified for all their inhabitants, any of those inhabitants who claims to have had such a right or freedom violated cannot rely on such a treaty obligation alone if he or she complains of that violation in the domestic courts. If there is no redress at home, the victim must seek an international remedy, if there is one.

For the UN Covenant on Civil and Political Rights, the remedy is a communication to an international Human Rights Committee, but only if the state concerned has ratified the Optional Protocol to the Covenant, which the United Kingdom and the Republic of Ireland have not.[3] The Human Rights Committee will investigate such complaints, but it cannot hand down binding judgements; its powers are limited to the expression of views, which any responsible government will of course take seriously but which it is not legally bound to implement. For the UN Covenant on Economic and Social Rights and the European Social Charter, there are no individual remedies at all, either nationally or internationally.

For the European Convention on Human Rights, however, the position is very different. Anyone aggrieved may launch a petition to the European Commission of Human Rights in Strasbourg. If the petitioner succeeds there, and does not reach a friendly settlement with the government concerned, the Commisison will make a finding in the petitioner's favour in the form of a Report. If the government concerned does not accept that Report and act on it, either that government or the Commission may then refer the case to the European Court of Human Rights, also sitting in Strasbourg, and that Court may then (if it agrees with the Commission's conclusions) enter a binding judgment against the defaulting state, ordering it to 'afford just satisfaction' to the injured party, and to put its house in order so that this sort of thing does not happen again. Cases may also be initiated by one state-party against another.

From its establishment in 1955 to the end of 1986, the Commission had registered more than 12 000 applications from individuals. It had issued over 300 Reports, and over 100 cases had been referred to the Court. In 1984, 1985, and 1986, the annual number of applications rose from nearly 600 to over 700 a year; more had been registered in these years against the United Kingdom than against any of the other European states (128, 112, and 140 respectively): the Federal Republic of Germany came close behind; then France, Sweden, and Italy. At the other end of the scale, only 8, 5, and 4 applications had been registered in those years against the Republic of Ireland.

Although this procedure is slow and cumbersome and costs some money (though not as much as most domestic litigation),[4] it can be remarkably effective. For example, though both the United Kingdom and the Irish Republic were doubtless satisfied that their domestic laws and other arrangements adequately met the standards prescribed by the European Convention when they ratified it, both of them have more than once been found in breach of it at Strasbourg. Indeed, by the end of 1985, the United Kingdom had lost no fewer than 12 of 14 cases brought against it before the Court, dealing with such diverse matters as prisoners' rights, freedom of speech, the closed shop, and judicial birching in the Isle of Man; the Republic has so far lost one case, in which a woman who was too poor to bring proceedings for judicial separation in its High Court could not get legal aid.[5] In another case, the Court found that the absence of civil divorce did not infringe the Convention, but that the legal system's discrimination against illegitimate children did.[6] And the Republic itself brought and won a case against the United Kingdom, arising out of the 1971 interrogation procedures in Northern Ireland, which the Court held to be 'inhuman and degrading', but not (as the Commission had found) 'torture'.[7]

Though there are still many countries in the world which blatantly ignore the obligations they have undertaken and continue to commit grave violations of the human rights of their inhabitants, the new international code is beginning to have an effect on respect for the human rights and fundamental freedoms which it so carefully defines, especially where effective remedies exist before international institutions for breach of the treaties concerned, as in the case of the European Convention. As the case law of these institutions develops and their decisions (as well as the treaties from which they flow) achieve increasing publicity, so public consciousness of human rights is raised, and the pressure on governments to respect them mounts in proportion. The treaties are therefore having a perceptible effect in setting effective limits to domestic violations of these rights and freedoms, and are gradually coming to ensure that – at least in respect of such fundamental matters as these – neither the state and its public authorities, nor the law, nor administrative practice, nor any other power-holder, may legitimately violate the fundamental dignity of any human person or discriminate adversely against a person on grounds such as religion, political opinion, or association with a national minority.

INCORPORATION OF HUMAN RIGHTS TREATIES INTO DOMESTIC LAW

Whenever the United Kingdom or the Republic of Ireland has lost a case in Strasbourg, the government concerned has of course taken steps to prevent a recurrence, if necessary by bringing the necessary amending legislation before its parliament. However, all this is a clumsy way of achieving the Convention's objectives, and there has therefore been mounting pressure for those few European countries (including particularly the United Kingdom and the Irish Republic) which have not yet incorporated it into their domestic legal systems now to take this step, in order that their own courts can apply it directly to cases brought before them and so give their inhabitants an effective remedy at home, and not only by the ultimate recourse to an international tribunal abroad. In the United Kingdom, this pressure is increasing steadily, not least from the Standing Advisory Commission on Human Rights in Northern Ireland.

In 1977, that Commission published an important Report called *The Protection of Human Rights by Law in Northern Ireland*.[8] Chapter 6 of that Report began by asking whether it would be desirable to increase the legal protection of human rights in Northern Ireland by the introduction of some form of enforceable Bill of Rights or in any other way; if so, by what method or methods it would be desirable to do so; and whether any change should be confined to Northern Ireland or should apply to the United Kingdom as a whole. Having considered many arguments for and against, the Commission came to the unanimous conclusion that the most appropriate way of increasing the legal protection of human rights in Northern Ireland would be to incorporate the European Convention into the domestic legal system of the whole of the United Kingdom.

Our own area of concern is wider than the Commission's: it extends to the protection of human rights in the whole of the United Kingdom and the Irish Republic. We have therefore considered the same question, but in relation to this larger territory. We too have come to the same conclusion: that is to say, we believe that there would be substantial advantages, and no disadvantages which could not be overcome, for the United Kingdom to enact legislation to make the European Convention part of its ordinary domestic law, and for the Irish Republic to undertake parallel action to the same end.

The arguments on this question are so comprehensively set out in the Commission's Report that we cannot do better than to refer the reader to the extract from that publication in our Appendix 1. Those to which we attach the greatest importance are that:

1. such a step would do much to harmonise the legal protection of human rights in all the parts of the two states and minimise differences between them in matters as fundamental as these
2. it would concentrate the minds of future policy-makers and legislators, and those who advise them, on the continuing need to observe the international obligations to their inhabitants which both states have assumed
3. it would help to remind the populations of both states about the scope and importance of the fundamental values which are shared by all of them and which are reflected in the concept of human rights
4. incorporation does not require anything as revolutionary as the creation of a written constitution for the United Kingdom, or any abridgement of the sovereignty of Parliament, not even to the extent that the European Communities Act 1972 has already done
5. if the ordinary domestic courts in each state were given jurisdiction to interpret and apply the European Convention as part of their own domestic law, taking account of the developing Strasbourg case-law, the inhabitants of both states would be able to obtain redress for any infringements of their human rights at home and would have to seek recourse to Strasbourg only in exceptional cases.

Since the Republic has a written Constitution, it could incorporate the Convention at the level either of constitutional law or of ordinary statute law. If it chose the latter course, it might at some stage need to make some amendments to the Constitution, in order to add some of the rights and freedoms protected by the Convention to those which the constitution already protects – for example, by providing that, in interpreting the provisions of the incorporated Convention and of the Constitution, the courts should favour the interpretation which ensures the greatest protection for human rights.* However, the need for any other changes would not arise in any acute form unless the Strasbourg organs were to find the Republic in breach of the Convention because of some provision of its Constitution, and if this should ever happen it would happen whether or not the Convention had been incorporated into the Republic's domestic law.

In Great Britain, so far only the Liberal Party and the Social Democrats have formally declared their support for incorporation of the Convention, though many other members of both Houses of Parliament – among them a number who hold, or have held, high office – are known to support incorporation also. The House of Lords has now several times passed a Bill which would achieve this objective; Sir Edward Gardner, QC, MP, with wide all-party support, introduced a similar measure in the House of Commons, which was debated for five hours on Second Reading on 13 February 1987. In the event, it was 'talked out' without a division: to abort this manoeuvre would have required 100 votes, and on a Friday afternoon only 96 were available. The issue has not yet been debated in the Dáil in Dublin.

We regard this matter as one of the first importance for all the inhabitants of these islands, and especially for those who are members of minority communities, as well as for the governments of both states. We find it a matter for regret that a question as important but as modest as this has been allowed to drag on for so long without any perceptible progress. Clearly such legislation should not be enacted without a substantial degree of political consensus across party boundaries, and we would therefore urge those of the political parties in the two states which have not yet already done so to make every effort to achieve this by appropriate internal and external discussions, and thereafter to move with all due speed towards the enactment of this important legislation.

We observe that the proposal for incorporation has wide support in both communities in Northern Ireland, including the main political parties and the non-governmental organisations concerned with human rights,[9] and in the Churches in Great Britain.[10] A public opinion poll a few years ago showed three out of four Protestants in Northern Ireland and over 90 per cent of Catholics in favour of a bill of rights for Northern Ireland as soon as possible:[11] the incorporation of the European Convention would provide

*We are much indebted to two of our consultants, Professor Kevin Boyle and Senator Mary Robinson, for sharing their views of this question with us.

citizens with such a bill of rights. Several consultants and members of this Working Party have taken a public stand in favour of incorporation.[12] The Standing Advisory Commission on Human Rights has repeatedly and unanimously advocated this, not as a gimmick for solving the problem of political violence in the Province, but as a measure which would enable aggrieved citizens to secure a more prompt and effective redress than is possible at present. All three options in the report of the New Ireland Forum referred to the need for a bill of rights (paras 5.2(6), 6.2, 7.2, and 8.5), and the Hillsborough Agreement stated that consideration would be given to 'the advantages and disadvantages of a Bill of Rights in some form in Northern Ireland' (Article 5(a)).

The present position is strange. The United Kingdom played a leading role in drafting the Convention and adhered to it more than 35 years ago, and the British and Irish Governments are bound to ensure respect for its provisions. The two Governments have also accepted an optional procedure which allows aggrieved citizens who have exhausted all remedies in national courts to appeal to Strasbourg. As far as the two Governments are concerned, the Convention is an international treaty which they are bound to observe, yet its provisions may not be cited in their own courts. Lord McCluskey argued in his 1986 Reith lectures that it is difficult for judges to interpret the 'vague and imprecise terms' such as are found in statements of fundamental rights: to incorporate would, in Lord McCluskey's view, be 'to abdicate a real measure of democratic responsibility'.[13]

We agree with Lord McCluskey that judges have difficulty if asked to interpret statements drafted in vague and imprecise terms, but it strikes us that the European Convention, as legal documents go, is relatively clear, distinct, and unambiguous.

Robert Alexander, a former chairman of the Bar Council, points out that by incorporating the Convention, the United Kingdom would not be entering an uncharted sea nor pursuing vague or grandiose ideas:

> We will rather be enacting in our domestic law certain basic rights to which we already subscribe by international treaty.[14]

We urge the United Kingdom Government to support the incorporation of the European Convention on Human Rights into statute law, either by promoting a Government Bill or by endorsing and providing parliamentary time for a Private Member's Bill; and we urge the Republic to take parallel action.

As for the two UN Covenants, we have already said that the United Kingdom ratified them both as long ago as 1976. So far, however, the Republic of Ireland has not. In this respect, it finds itself in a minority among UN member states in Western Europe: the only ones – apart from the Irish Republic – which have not yet ratified them are Greece, Malta, and Turkey.[15] We would therefore strongly urge the Republic to repair this omission as soon as possible. It certainly is anomalous that those rights which are in the UN Covenants but not in the European Convention are guaranteed North of the border, but not in the South.

We understand that successive Irish governments have been in favour of ratification once the bureaucratic preliminaries have been completed. Any country which takes its international obligations seriously must examine law and practice with meticulous care before adhering to a human rights treaty. No doubt there are concepts and phrases in the UN Covenants which could cause difficulty in the Republic: the Article dealing with equality of rights of spouses, for example, asserts that this equality shall be ensured 'as to marriage, during marriage and at its dissolution'. It had always been the intention that the words 'at its dissolution' did not imply any obligation on a state to make legal provision for dissolution of marriage, and in any case, it is open to a state to make interpretive declarations or even formal reservations at the time of signature or ratification. The United Kingdom made both declarations and reservations when it signed and ratified the UN Covenants. We encourage Church members and non-governmental organisations in the Republic to urge the Dublin government to ratify the two UN Covenants at an early date, if necessary with interpretations or reservations.

When the Irish Republic has ratified the UN Covenants, both states will be under the same obligations in international law in respect of the main human rights and fundamental freedoms which that law now recognises and seeks to protect. Then, the only remaining question will be the remedies available for any violations of these rights, primarily in the domestic courts – and, if need be, before the competent international organs. In order to ensure the best possible protection, we would hope that both states would ratify what is called the Optional Protocol to the UN Covenant on Civil and Political Rights, which would give their inhabitants the right to use the complaints procedure under that treaty, which operates by the submission of communications to the UN Human Rights Committee. Although that body has fewer powers than the Strasbourg organs, the Covenant protects rather more rights than the European Convention, with the result that although the UK is bound in international law to ensure these rights to all its inhabitants, an international remedy for any violations exists for only some of them. Several of the other state parties to the European Convention (including Italy and all four of the Nordic countries) have already ratified the Optional Protocol, and we know of no reason why the United Kingdom should not follow suit – and the Republic of Ireland, once it has ratified the Covenant.

There are further possibilities which may seem rather technical to non-lawyers. We have already mentioned that the European Convention has some Additional Protocols. Both states have ratified no. 1 which deals with property, education, and elections, and they could therefore incorporate this into domestic law at the same time as the Convention itself. But no. 4, which deals with imprisonment for debt and freedom of movement, has so far been ratified by the Republic of Ireland but not yet by the United Kingdom. We therefore urge the United Kingdom to ratify it, and both states to incorporate it.

That still leaves some other civil and political rights presently protected by the UN Covenant on Civil and Political Rights but not yet by the European Convention. Among these are matters relating to the expulsion of aliens, appeals in criminal cases, compensation for miscarriages of justice, double jeopardy (that is to say, being tried or punished twice for the same offence), and the equality of spouses. In 1984, the member states of the Council of Europe adopted Protocol no. 7 to protect these, but this has not yet entered into force. We would encourage both states to ratify Protocol no. 7 and to incorporate it into domestic law, so making these additional rights justiciable both domestically and, when the Protocol enters into force, at Strasbourg.

In these ways, the same domestic and international remedies could be provided to all the inhabitants of both states for the protection of all the civil and political human rights and fundamental freedoms covered by the international code – a state of affairs which we regard as highly desirable, particularly in the light of the perceptions and strong feelings on these matters prevalent among both the communities in Northern Ireland.

We describe in Appendix 2 how an individual may resort to the complaints procedures at Strasbourg. The process must seem slow and cumbersome to a citizen with a grievance. We encourage lawyers in our two states to familiarise themselves with the Strasbourg procedures, and also the procedure for communications to the UN Human Rights Committee should either state ratify the Optional Protocol to the UN Covenant on Civil and Political Rights. We think that advice on the complaints procedures under human rights treaties, and legal aid for them, should be widely available in both states.

There may well be domestic civil rights and liberties for the protection of which there is a wide national consensus, but which are not reflected in the international treaties. If that is so, then there is of course no reason why these should not also be added to the national statute books.

Notes and References

1. *International Law and Human Rights* (London: Stevens, 1950, reprinted 1968) p. 4.
2. General Assembly resolutions 32/130, 16 December 1977; 40/114, 13 December 1985; 41/117, 18 February 1986.
3. The Republic could, of course, ratify this Protocol only if it first became a party to the Covenant.
4. For a brief summary of the steps which a person needs to take in order to invoke this procedure, see Appendix 2.
5. *Airey* v. *Ireland*, 2 EHRR 305.
6. *Johnston and others* v. *Ireland*, judgement delivered 18 December 1986.
7. *Ireland* v. *United Kingdom*, 2 EHRR 25.
8. London: HMSO, 1977 (Cmnd 7009).
9. Cmnd 7009, Chapter 4.
10. The Roman Catholic bishops of England and Wales supported the idea 'in principle' in November 1985, a majority of the Executive Committee of the British Council of Churches in January 1986.
11. Edward Moxon-Browne, *Nation, class and creed in Northern Ireland* (Aldershot: Gower, c. 1983) p. 142.
12. See, for example, J. E. S. Fawcett, 'A Bill of Rights for the United Kingdom?', *Human Rights Review*, 1 (1976) pp. 57–64; Anthony Lester, 'Fundamental Rights: the United Kingdom isolated?', *Public Law*, 46 (Spring 1984) pp. 46–72; Anthony Lester, *Democracy and Individual Rights* (London: Fabian Society, 1969) pp. 13–15; Paul Sieghart, 'Human Rights and the British Constitution', *Law and*

Justice, 64/5 (1980); 'Law on Human Rights: more than cosmetics', *Daily Telegraph*, 11 June 1981; letters to *The Times*, 4 February 1985, 6 June 1985, 29 December 1986; Colin Campbell (ed.), *Do we need a Bill of Rights?* (London: Temple Smith, 1980); Brian Garrett, 'Bill of Rights: the Revival of the Debate', *PACE*, 16 (3) (1984–85) pp. 3–5.

13.   'An enormous power', *Listener*, 4 February 1986.
14.   'Why Britain needs "a check on growing government power"', *Listener*, 5 February 1987.
15.   All the countries of Eastern Europe except Albania have also ratified the Covenants.

3 Majorities and Minorities

When human beings live in close proximity and social solidarity for several generations, they tend to acquire common ideas and traditions whatever their origins, so that eventually they may come to regard themselves as a 'people'. If other human beings with different ideas and traditions arrive, especially in large numbers in a short period of time, there may at first be difficulties and tensions, but over a period the incomers usually adapt to the style of the majority, at any rate in outward matters. Many of the children of Hindu, Muslim, and Sikh immigrants in British schools dress and speak and eat the same candy bars and watch the same television programmes as the children of those who have lived in Britain for many generations. Indeed, after about a generation, immigrant communities have about the same birth and death rates as the surrounding population.

Because of the political and economic upheavals of recent times, and because long-distance travel is easier than it used to be, there is now more mixing of peoples in these islands than there has been in the recent past, especially in urban areas. Those who live in cities are learning to live alongside neighbours of differing cultures, traditions, and religious beliefs. Things that were taken for granted in the past, such as Sunday observance, now have to be reconsidered in areas where Muslims or Jews predominate and therefore observe Friday or Saturday as a day of rest. Where conflicts between communities are unresolved, the quality of life of everyone suffers: this is true for the majority as well as for minorities, and indeed for those who would attach little importance to communal differences.

THE TYRANNY OF THE MAJORITY

There is much emphasis in public affairs on the rights of minorities nowadays, and rightly so, for majorities can become tyrannical even without realising or intending it. This is one reason why the language of rights is popular with minorities, whereas majorities tend to emphasise responsibilities.

The tendency of majorities to become tyrannical was something which greatly troubled Alexis de Tocqueville, the French political

45

philosopher, when he was writing the first part of his book *Democracy in America* a century and a half ago. The remedy which de Tocqueville believed the Americans had found for this tendency was to have an impartial and independent legal system.

Our own institutions are more sophisticated than those with which de Tocqueville was familiar. We have the modern international declarations and treaties on human rights, and national or regional commissions to prevent discrimination and assure equal opportunities. We review some of these institutions in our two states in Chapters 5 and 6.

It hardly needs saying that majorities have rights as well as minorities; and minorities have responsibilities as well as majorities. There are no rights without responsibilities. This was stressed by Tom Paine in the eighteenth century: 'A Declaration of Rights is, by reciprocity, a Declaration of Duties also'.[1] Mahatma Gandhi, in a letter to UNESCO, wrote that he had learned from his 'illiterate but wise' mother that 'all rights to be deserved and preserved' come from duty well done.[2]

We all belong to majorities in some matters, but to minorities in others. A spinster anywhere in these islands is a member of the minority of women who are unmarried, but at the same time is part of the majority in the population as a whole who are female. A tall red-headed clergyman in Ireland belongs to at least four minorities: of men, of tall people, of red-heads, and of clergy; but at the same time he belongs to a majority, those who profess the Christian faith. This intersecting of majorities and minorities is one of the features which makes for interest and variety in society.

Where the factors which create majorities and minorities coincide rather than intersect, tension can result. In Britain's inner cities, those unemployed blacks who are under-educated and ill-housed belong to the same minority in several important respects: in being black, in being out of work, in being inadequately educated, and in living in squalid housing. This gives them a sense of group identity, the solidarity of mutual misery. They become alienated from the rest of society and especially from those in authority – parents, teachers, police, magistrates, and so on.[3] In situations of this kind, factors which create majority–minority divisions reinforce each other. This reinforcement of communal differences has occurred in Northern Ireland also.

People from Great Britain often fail to understand how complex is the majority–minority situation in Northern Ireland. The unionist-loyalist community, which is mainly Protestant, constitutes a majority in Northern Ireland but a minority in the United Kingdom as a whole, and a minority also in the island of Ireland. The nationalist community, which is mainly Catholic, constitutes a majority in some parts of Northern Ireland but a minority in Northern Ireland as a whole, yet it is part of the majority in the island of Ireland. Moreover, the school population of the two communities in Northern Ireland are now roughly equal, and under plausible assumptions about birth and emigration rates, the communities are likely to be of much the same size by about the middle of the next century. This helps to explain unionist–loyalist fears; whereas the Protestant minority in the Irish Republic could conceivably fall even lower than the present 4 per cent.

In some of the Greek city-states, all adult citizens (or, to be more precise, all free males) played a direct part in public affairs. In our more complex society, with larger units of government, we need representative institutions, but parliaments and assemblies and councils seldom manage to represent every shade of opinion of those for whom they speak. Representative democracy is a rough and ready system, which has traditionally been based on the crude axiom that the minority shall have its rights but the majority shall have its way. This has been acceptable where major political parties alternate between government and opposition, but it may become unfair when minorities are geographically dispersed and never win office or exercise responsible political power under the 'first-past-the-post' system of voting. Minorities not only have moral rights: they need to participate in the processes of government at every level.

Democracy, Winston Churchill once said, is the worst form of government except all those other forms that have been tried from time to time.[4] Just as courts sometimes hand down decisions which accord with law but strike the ordinary citizen as unjust, so parliaments are valued institutions but sometimes make unwise decisions. Moreover, there are some matters (such as those relating to the death penalty or abortion) on which representatives follow their own consciences rather than reflecting the views of their party or their constituents. If citizens are aggrieved when independent courts or representative parliaments seem to act unfairly, they can resort to procedures for redress, but only so long as they recognise that the claim to human rights carries with it duties and responsibilities: even when we are aggrieved, we are not entitled to act in a way that threatens the civil or human rights and freedoms of others.

MORALITY, RELIGION, AND LAW

The common ideas and traditions of a people include a sense of right and wrong. A community's moral convictions are often given expression in legal form: the moral commandment not to kill, for example, is enshrined in the legal prohibition of homicide, including suicide and mercy-killing. Many people who have not thought deeply about the matter may assume that moral and legal codes should be identical, that all sinful acts should be made illegal; but a moment's thought will show that this should not invariably be the case.

> There is ... a clear inter-relation between law and morality, but they are by no means synonymous. It is perfectly possible for the law to be contrary to what most people would accept as natural justice and morality, and there is a whole range of moral teaching which could not possibly be given legal sanction.[5]

In some societies, an attempt is made to distinguish between those moral issues which affect other people and the community as a whole and those moral issues which affect only the individual concerned. A distinguished Muslim thinker has written:

> It is the function of morality to tell us what is right and proper to do, and *it is the function of law to enforce such morals as have a direct bearing on the regulation of the life of man in his relation to his fellowmen.*[6]

Secular law can never entirely coincide with morality. On the one hand, there are some acts which are against the secular law but which are not intrinsically immoral. Most people in the world drive on the right-hand side of the road with clear consciences, but to do so in our two states could lead to a prosecution for reckless driving. On the other hand, there are acts which violate traditional moral teaching but which are not necessarily illegal, such as telling lies or fornicating. It is possible to eliminate discrimination by passing a suitable law, but to eliminate prejudice requires other methods. Not all sins are also crimes, nor are all crimes necessarily sins.

Law in a democracy has to pay heed to the consensus of the community. The Irish Catholic bishops, in their written submission to the New Ireland Forum, stressed that a country where there is a very substantial Catholic ethos and consensus should not feel it necessary to apologise that its constitutional or statute law reflects Catholic values. In another document, they maintained that legislators have to keep many considerations in mind when enacting legislation. 'They have to consider the convictions of those who are not Catholics and those who do not accept the Catholic Church's teaching.'[7] All the Churches want the law to reflect moral values, and all may, if they wish, contribute to the process of law-making.

The moral climate is changing all the time, of course, as old offences fall into disuse and new ones emerge. It is hardly necessary in the United Kingdom or the Irish Republic to have laws nowadays against traditional forms of slavery and the slave trade. Those are practices which have to all intents and purposes disappeared in Western Europe.

But, to take a contrary example, many artists and writers in the nineteenth century were regular users of narcotic drugs. We know more than did our predecessors a century ago about the damage to health caused by drug dependence, and there are now strict controls in both the Republic of Ireland and the United Kingdom on access to dangerous drugs.

How, then, would the authorities in the Irish Republic respond if adherents of a minority religious cult were to maintain that taking a narcotic substance like ganja was a necessary part of their religion because it is alleged to induce mystical states of mind? Should special provision be made for supplying ganja to responsible leaders of such a cult?

That is a hypothetical question, so let us turn to an issue which has arisen in Great Britain and which has raised passionate feelings on the part of two minorities.

There is a council which advises British ministers about the welfare of animals. In 1985, this council issues an advisory report on religious methods of slaughtering livestock, in particular *Shechita*, the Jewish method, and *Halal*, the Muslim method. There are at present two main British statutes governing animal slaughter, but Jews and Muslims are exempt from both of these.[8]

The British council on animal welfare, after a careful review, concluded that religious methods of slaughter, even when carried out under ideal conditions (which is not always the case), necessarily result in a degree of pain, suffering, and distress which does not occur with the usual practice of stunning animals before slaughter. For this reason, the council recommended that the provisions by which Jews and Muslims are exempted from the requirement that animals be stunned before slaughter should be repealed within three years.[9]

Not surprisingly, the Jewish and Muslim communities were outraged by this report, and the Jewish community, for example, issued a 100-page paper of rebuttal. The practice of *Shechita*, they claimed, is a divinely-ordained and integral part of Jewish law. *Shechita* is 'absolutely painless ... at least as humane as any other method'. Jewish slaughterers are expected to show exemplary moral virtues of compassion and kindness. To ban *Shechita* would make it impossible for the Jewish community to eat any meat or poultry. This would represent 'a grave and offensive attack on Jewish law and practice', would deprive Jews of 'fundamental human rights and religious freedoms', and would constitute a 'dangerous erosion of the principle of religious tolerance'. The United Kingdom would be open to a charge of violating the European Convention on Human Rights. Jews would see 'some grave moral defect in a society which places the welfare of animals above that of human beings'.[10]

Some people may find this issue artificial and irrelevant. The concept of causing 'unnecessary suffering' (the prevention of which in relation to human beings is to be found in the Hague Conventions of 1899 and 1907 on the laws and customs of war) is a subjective criterion. How, it may be asked, can we condemn religious methods of slaughtering livestock when many other forms of causing animals unnecessary suffering are allowed? Moreover, there is now a substantial export from both the United Kingdom and the Irish Republic of meat from animals slaughtered by religious methods. If such methods of slaughter were phased out, is it not likely that living animals would be shipped overseas in conditions causing as much if not more suffering and distress than religious slaughter is said to cause?

Whatever view one takes of this complicated issue, we seem to have two conflicting principles: on the one hand, that the infliction of unnecessary suffering on sentient beings is morally deplorable and easily corrupts those who engage in it; on the other hand, that minorities should be free to manifest religious practice and observance, subject only to such limitations as are necessary to assure public safety, order, health, or morals, or to protect the rights and freedoms of others. Is it more important to defend the moral consensus of the majority on the avoidance of unnecessary suffering to living creatures, or the right of two minorities to engage in time-hallowed practices based on religious belief? Can the claims of minorities be met in such a way as not to threaten the integrity or stability of society?[11]

Moreover, this is one of the issues that cannot be resolved solely by reference to the international code of human rights. In 1981, the General Assembly of the United Nations adopted a Declaration on the elimination of intolerance and discrimination based on religion (see Appendix 3). This Declaration goes into considerable detail about such matters as freedom of worship, the right to disseminate religious publications, the right to observe days of rest and to celebrate holidays and ceremonies, and the right to communicate with co-religionists in other countries. We endorse that declaration without reservation, but note that it does not deal with all aspects of religious liberty and that some contemporary problems in matters of religion in our two states are outside its express terms.

There are a number of issues which lie in a sort of 'no man's land' between morality and law. Blasphemy, for example, is a crime at common law in the United Kingdom, prohibiting oral or written statements which are offensive or insulting about the Christian religion. In a case heard by the House of Lords in 1979, Lord Scarman suggested that there was a case for 'legislation . . . to protect the beliefs and feelings of non-Christians'.[12] We doubt whether blasphemy should now be regarded as a criminal offence, but if it is to remain a crime, it would only be equitable to extend it to cover contemptuous or profane statements about the beliefs and writings of Judaism, Islam, and other non-Christian faiths. One way of achieving a change would be by means of a Private Member's Bill in Parliament.

When the people of the United Kingdom took Christian faith and practice more seriously than they do today, it was reasonable to impose a Christian view of the sabbath on the whole community, including unbelievers. Apart from the decline in Christian belief, there are now areas in the United Kingdom in which adherents of non-Christian faiths predominate. We are inclined to favour a system of 'local option' concerning the sabbath, so that days of the week other than Sunday can be designated as days of rest in such areas.[13] We recognise that this is an extremely sensitive matter, for a majority can easily but inadvertently cause offence to a minority (and vice-versa) and so damage community relations.

There are many other issues in the grey area between law and morality: is voluntary euthanasia a moral issue on which religious authorities may properly pronounce, or is it a threat to social stability

on which parliaments should legislate? Should the law prohibit all
dangerous or unhealthy activities, or are all or some of these matters
for personal conscience alone?

INTEGRATION OR SEPARATE IDENTITIES?

Should minorities be encouraged to preserve their distinctive
identities or to merge with majorities? We doubt whether there can
be any general answer to such a question. When the Normans
conquered England in the eleventh century, their presence was
initially resented. Gradually, however, their language was adopted
for most official purposes (and for food!), the feudal system was
extended, royal office-bearers and large land-holders married local
women and learned to speak the vernacular, and by the fourteenth
century the Norman incomers were pretty well integrated and
assimilated.

There has been no violent invasion from outside these islands since
the Norman conquest, though parts of our archipelago have bitter
memories of invasion, depredation, and subjugation from other
parts. But influxes from outside have on the whole been peaceful
since 1066: gypsies in the fifteenth and sixteenth centuries,
Huguenots and the followers of William of Orange in the seventeenth
century, Jews at the turn of the twentieth century and again after
1933, and immigrants from Eastern Europe, the New Commonwealth and Pakistan after the Second World War.

Some of the new arrivals have sought to identify with the natives,
but others have wished to maintain a distinct and separate identity,
by the exercise of religious or communal discipline and by discourag-
ing or banning mixed marriages. Some communities have split on the
issue: many Jews have been adaptable and conformist, entering
public life and holding high office; others have believed that Judaism
and a distinctive Jewish culture can be maintained only by remaining
separate and aloof, speaking Yiddish or even Hebrew at home, and
strictly observing Jewish law and holding to traditional religious
beliefs.

It is in many ways remarkable that the people of the nations of
which the United Kingdom is composed, in spite of cultural
differences, have been able to develop harmonious forms of
coexistence.

In Ireland, successive waves of invaders, up until and including the

Normans in the twelfth and thirteenth centuries, were assimilated to a greater or lesser extent with the people already living there. An exception to this process of assimilation was the Protestant settlement of the sixteenth and seventeenth centuries. From these settlers are descended the Presbyterian and other Protestant communities in Northern Ireland who wish to maintain the union with Great Britain, as an expression of a separate identity from the rest of the people of the island.

Both communities in Northern Ireland wish to preserve their distinctive identities. Strong bonds of history, culture, and religious belief have kept the two communities apart, and it is not helpful when this determination to preserve intact what is precious in a tradition is belittled or opposed. The alternative, as we have seen in the Lebanon in recent years, is chaos and warlordism, causing untold suffering for all.

The concept of the self-determination of peoples has evolved in law and in politics over the past forty years, from a principle to a right. A predicament arises when the exercise of self-determination threatens the territorial integrity of a nation-state. In some societies, land has an almost mystical meaning. 'In the language of my people,' a Cherokee Indian recently told the US Congress, 'there is a word for land: Eloheh. This same word also means history, culture, and religion. We cannot separate our place on earth from our lives on the earth nor from our vision nor our meaning as a people'.[14]

We well understand what the Cherokee was saying, and we have heard the representatives of other peoples make similar assertions – in the Middle East, for example. But our main concern in this Report is with human beings and not with territory, with the human rights and responsibilities of people and, indeed, of 'peoples'. From the point of view of our study, the status of territory is of less importance than the human beings who dwell on it.

We understand the heartache of Catholics in Northern Ireland who yearn for Irish unity or the anxieties of the Protestants when the bond with Great Britain is threatened. Nor are we blind to the role of geography: the island of Ireland, and the cluster of islands which make up our two states, looked at on the map, have a certain territorial cohesiveness. We do not dismiss these considerations as irrelevant, but the focus of our study is the rights and responsibilities of individual human beings and 'peoples', and not the status of the territory on which they live. We believe that, if bloodshed is to be avoided, the status of territory cannot be decided solely by reference to ancient history. At the same time, claims to annex the territory of another state against the wishes of the inhabitants lead to counter-moves, so that the militant people on one side or the other easily slide into violence. That way lies disaster.

Many of our forebears, whatever community we belong to, committed murder, cruelty, and barbaric acts of terrorism. At the same time, all of our communities are the victims of past injustices and wrongs by others. All of our communities have things to forgive, and things for which we need forgiveness.

'SELF-DETERMINATION OF PEOPLES'

The idea that 'peoples' are entitled to self-determination is of quite recent origin. According to one authority, it does not occur in the literature until 1865, when the Socialist First International used it in a declaration on Poland.[15] It did not become widely held until the end of the First World War, when the victorious Allies, with varying degrees of enthusiasm and consistency, applied it when drawing up the peace treaties with the defeated Central Powers. As a result of those treaties, the boundaries of a great tract of Europe from the Baltic to the Adriatic were redrawn more or less in accordance with the principle of self-determination. The concept was still, however, confined to parts of Europe, and the Allies rejected the claim that it should be applied to their existing overseas colonies. However, after the Second World War, the UN Charter in 1945 affirmed 'self-determination of peoples' as a 'principle', that is to say, a legitimate goal for all 'peoples'.

In 1962, the UN General Assembly decided to define the main principles of international law concerning friendly relations and co-operation among states, and 'equal rights and self-determination of peoples' was one of the seven principles thus defined. This declaration of principles was approved by the General Assembly in 1970.

Meanwhile, the process of decolonisation had been proceeding apace, with 66 states being added to the 51 founder members of the UN during the first two post-war decades. Not surprisingly, the new states wanted to use the UN machinery to accelerate the process of decolonisation, and they initiated two steps which were to have important consequences. First, in 1960 the General Assembly adopted a radical resolution on decolonisation: like most resolutions of the General Assembly, this one expressed an opinion and was not legally binding on UN members. Be that as it may, the declaration stated that the self-determination of peoples was not simply a principle, as the UN Charter had affirmed: it was also a right.

Secondly, the newly-independent countries campaigned to include self-determination of peoples in the two UN Covenants on human rights, again not as a principle but as an unqualified right. This effort eventually succeeded. States which become parties to the Covenants have assumed a legal obligation to promote the rights in the Covenants, including the right of 'peoples' to exercise self-determination.

TERRITORIAL INTEGRITY

During the very period in which self-determination has been coming to the fore, other influences have been developing to limit its effect. The first of these has been a parallel stress on territorial integrity. The reason is that there is seldom a neat fit between peoples and international boundaries. The difficulty became apparent as soon as the principle of self-determination was applied on a large scale in parts of Europe after the First World War. The peoples of the regions concerned lived so intermingled that it proved impossible to draw boundaries which would neatly divide them one from the other. In some places, referenda were held to determine the wishes of the people; in others, unwelcome inhabitants were brutally expelled. The new or enlarged states created by invoking the principle of self-determination all contained minorities which would have preferred to be in some other state, but were not allowed to exercise *their* right of self-determination because to do so would create new and larger disgruntled minorities.

The process of decolonisation since the Second World War produced yet more examples of the conflict between territorial integrity and self-determination. Few of the new states created after 1945 were homogeneous: nearly all owed their boundaries to decisions made more or less arbitrarily by colonial powers and contained disparate peoples within their boundaries. The predicament for the anti-colonial countries was how to define self-determination in such a way that it would apply to the overseas colonies of European powers but would *not* apply to those minorities within the borders of Third World countries for whom self-determination of peoples might lead to secession – the Nagas in India, say, or the Kurds in several Middle Eastern countries. Virtually all Third World countries contain minorities of this kind.

It is significant that while the UN declaration on decolonisation affirms that all 'peoples' have the right to self-determination, without defining what constitutes a people, it also asserts the obligation to respect the integrity of the national territory. Any attempt to disrupt national unity and territorial integrity, according to the declaration, would be contrary to the UN Charter. Unfortunately, the declaration says nothing about any possible conflict between the self-determination of peoples and territorial integrity: it simply supports them both.

When we move from law to practice, however, the situation is much clearer. Of 82 cases of self-determination since the Charter was drafted, no fewer than 78 formerly dependent territories have opted for independent statehood and only four for integration or free association with a neighbouring state.[16] The UN Secretary-General has listed 21 additional territories, mainly small and isolated islands, which have not yet exercised self-determination: the only European territory in that list is Gibraltar.[17]

Francesco Capotorti, the UN expert on minorities, wrote in his study that all governments have a legitimate concern to avoid encouraging separatism and to safeguard the integrity of the state. He pointed out that this natural tendency of governments to avoid territorial disintegration 'sometimes presents an obstacle to the adoption of special measures in favour of individuals belonging to minority groups.'[18] Conor Cruise O'Brien goes further, and maintains that secession is 'an evil . . . a breakdown in human relations'.[19]

Conflicts between self-determination and territorial integrity have, in fact, surfaced many times since the Second World War. One of the most noteworthy cases concerned the Falklands/Malvinas issue. Argentina maintained that the islands had historically been part of the national territory of Argentina: the United Kingdom argued that the people had exercised self-determination by opting for British rule.[20]

On the whole, the international community – ex-colonisers as well as ex-colonised – has accepted the desirability of putting a limit on self-determination. Nigeria achieved independence in 1960 amid universal approval; Biafra, attempting to obtain freedom from Nigeria in 1967, secured support from only a handful of states.

MINORITY RIGHTS

Most Western lawyers stress that human rights 'inhere' in individual human beings, but it is sometimes argued that entities like 'peoples', 'groups', and 'minorities' enjoy human rights as collectivities. Whichever view one takes on this issue, it is *individuals* who use the international machinery of petition or complaint if their rights have allegedly been violated. We have already drawn attention to the central anti-discrimination provision in all the human rights treaties. Since discrimination against the members of a minority is inevitably exercised on one of those forbidden grounds (most usually race, colour, language, religion, gender, or national origin), this alone suffices to make such discrimination a violation of individual human rights.

In addition to that, Article 27 of the International Covenant on Civil and Political Rights (by which the United Kingdom but not the Irish Republic is bound) provides that

> In those States in which ethnic, religious or linguistic minorities exist, persons belonging to such minorities shall not be denied the right, in community with other members of their group, to enjoy their own culture, to profess and practise their religion, or to use their own language.

Note that this does not say that 'minorities' have rights: it says that '*persons belonging to* such minorities' have certain specific rights, in addition to the other individual rights which the rest of the international catalogue defines. These can, of course, be exercised only 'in community with the other members of their group', but that is the case for virtually all the individual human rights in the catalogue. The right to a fair trial, the right to freedom of association and assembly, or the right to form or join trade unions, may all 'inhere' in a single human individual marooned alone on a desert island; but he or she cannot begin to exercise these rights in the absence of other human individuals.

A UN expert suggests that, for purposes of self-determination, the following three elements should be taken into consideration in deciding whether an entity constitutes a 'people':

1. The term 'people' denotes a social entity possessing a clear identity and its own characteristics
2. It implies a relationship with a territory, even if the people in

question has been wrongfully expelled from it and artificially replaced by another population

3. A people should not be confused with ethnic, religious, or linguistic minorities.[21]

Some eighty former colonial territories have exercised self-determination during the past forty years, in each case because this was believed to be the wish of the *majority* in each territory. Once a people has exercised self-determination, it is free to make its own laws, subject to the international requirements about respect for the human rights of all the inhabitants of the new state, including those belonging to minorities. But a numerical *minority* (ethnic, religious, or linguistic) can claim only that its members not be discriminated against and that they be allowed to enjoy their own culture, religion, and language. The international code seeks to ensure that everyone within a state is properly treated by that state, and especially that a small but powerful group within it will not dominate all the rest, but not that every disaffected group within its borders will have the right to secede by setting up its own independent state or be able to enforce a realignment of those borders regardless of the wishes of the majority. The problem often is that a community may constitute either a 'minority' or a 'people', depending on the area being considered.

SOME RECENT TRENDS

Partly as a result of the difficulties in the way of applying self-determination without restriction, an alternative method of securing the interests of distinctive groups has come increasingly into vogue. This as we have explained in Chapter 2, is through the legal protection of human rights. An early sign of this trend can be seen in the minorities treaties after the First World War, and we have already described the fully-fledged legal code which has developed since 1945.

Yet another trend of recent times has been a growing recognition of interdependence among nations. Economies have become more open and related: we buy in our supermarkets oranges from Israel, wine from Yugoslavia, calculators from Taiwan, clothing from Thailand. Many large firms (the so-called multinationals) operate across national boundaries and have activities in dozens of different countries. People take their holidays abroad more often than they used to do. Mass culture has become to a great extent homogenised: the people of different countries watch each other's TV programmes and sing each others' pop songs.

This trend has been accompanied by a growth in international organisation. Both the United Kingdom and the Republic of Ireland belong to a considerable number of such organisations: the United Nations, its specialised agencies such as the ILO and WHO, the European Community, the Council of Europe, the Organisation for Economic Co-operation and Development (OECD), the General Agreement on Tariffs and Trade (GATT), and many others. All involve some diminution of sovereignty in return for benefits. The body which modifies sovereignty most extensively is the European Community. In order to promote the political goal of the unity of peoples, as well as the economic goal of prosperity through integration, the member states of the European Community have chosen to renounce their sovereignty in many significant areas of economic and other activity. One particularly striking feature of the Community – which distinguishes it from previous attempts at international cooperation – has been the creation of a supra-national law which is directly applicable in all EEC member states.

The effect of these forces is to dilute national sovereignty in two opposite directions. On the one hand, sovereign states are now constrained by international law to pay more heed to the rights of people within their borders than was true in the past. On the other, they have to some extend pooled their sovereignty in organisations embracing several or many states. Instead of the world being divided into a large number of independent and legally equal states, it is developing a more complex structure, in which some kinds of power are being relinquished upwards to international organisations and some downwards to smaller entities.

These trends seem to reflect the necessary balance between rights and responsibilities. It is not in accord with human dignity that one people should rule over another; it is desirable that peoples should be responsible for their own destinies. But, like other rights, self-determination needs to be balanced by a regard for responsibilities. The majority in any state has a duty to respect the rights of local minorities, and minorities have a duty to respect the democratic wishes of the majority. Moreover, the human family is inescapably interdependent, and states have a duty to cooperate so as to advance their own interests and further the common good of humanity as a whole.

MECHANISMS FOR PROTECTION OF MINORITIES

A variety of constitutional and other devices have been used to assure the rights of minorities, either singly or in combination, depending on the particular circumstances of each case. Before looking at the distinctive problems in Northern Ireland, we thought it might be helpful to look at other countries with communal differences, to see whether any lessons could be learnt from them. Between us, we have had personal experience of a number of such countries or territories, including Malaysia, Sri Lanka, Lebanon, Israel and the occupied territories, Cyprus, South Tyrol, Switzerland, the Netherlands, and Belgium.

As well as relying on our own knowledge, we sought the help of specialists in the field. Here we wish to acknowledge the invaluable assistance of Ben Whitaker, executive director of the Minority Rights Group (MRG) and one of our consultants. The Minority Rights Group commissioned for us papers on several areas of Europe where communal differences appear to have been successfully reconciled, and these studies formed the basis of the next part of this Chapter.

We would warn, all the same, that each country or territory has some unique features, and we cannot assume that because a particular device had the effect of increasing inter-communal harmony in one place, it would necessarily have the same effect elsewhere.

Ten devices have been used, sometimes in combination.

A Bill of Rights

This can be either part of the state's constitution or a separate document. It will enumerate the human and civil rights of all citizens, and perhaps economic and social goals as well. To be effective, there must be some authority to which citizens who believe that their rights have been violated can apply. This may be either the ordinary courts or a special constitutional court or a special commission or commissioner. Such a bill of rights can be designed so that it specifically protects those rights to which a given minority is most sensitive, such as the prohibition of discrimination on religious or political grounds in the Northern Ireland Constitution Act 1973.

Specialised Enforcement Bodies

Over and above the protection given to all citizens by a bill of rights, the interests of particular groups can be given additional protection by specialised bodies such as the Commission for Racial Equality in Great Britain or anti-discrimination commissions in various states of the United States of America. Such bodies can be more flexible than courts of law. A court has to wait till someone brings an action before it can intervene on behalf of citizens' rights; a special agency can take action on its own initiative and can try to achieve a settlement by conciliation.

Proportional Representation

This device is found very widely in those multicultural societies which have successfully assuaged their differences. It is not universal: it does not exist in Canada, for instance, where French–English relations seem to have improved in recent years. But it is to be found in, among other countries, Switzerland, Belgium, the Netherlands, Finland, and South Tyrol. By itself, it gives no more protection to a minority than to a majority; it simply tries to assure that all significant groups in a society are represented more or less in proportion to population. It may help to underpin psychologically a climate of opinion in which proportionality towards all groups in a society is taken for granted as fair.

Qualified Voting

Another method of safeguarding a minority in a legislature is to lay down that, on certain issues at least, more than a simple majority of those voting is required. This prevents one community from pushing through a change which would be unacceptable to a majority of the other community.

Power-sharing in Government

Under this arrangement, representatives of different groups are represented proportionately or by an agreed formula, not just in parliament but also in the cabinet. This has been the situation in Switzerland since 1959. It also applied in Austria between 1945 and 1966. The objection can be made that power-sharing will work only where all groups concerned accept the legitimacy of the state. This is undoubtedly true; but on the other hand, the offer of power-sharing may help a discontented group to accept that legitimacy. The inclusion of a minority veto in power-sharing or weighted voting arrangements has, however, tended to produce instability.

Federalism and Confederalism

In a federal or confederal state, powers are shared between a central authority and regional, provincial, or state authorities. In a federal system, the component units have ceded powers to a central authority, while retaining powers specified in the original document within their own territories. In a confederation, the powers specified in the original document are exercised by the central government, while the component entities retain a high degree of autonomy over residual matters.

Where a minority is territorially concentrated, such devices can be a powerful safeguard of its interests. For instance, most of the French-speaking minority in Canada, and nearly all the French- and Italian-speaking minorities in Switzerland, live within provinces or cantons where they are the local majority and are therefore in a position to safeguard their cultural interests.

Regionalism or Devolution

Regionalism or devolution involves the delegation of some executive powers of government (and perhaps some legislative powers) from the capital to a region. This can be considered a weaker variant of federalism. Under this system, regional or local units are less secure than in a federal system. However, where mutual trust is sufficient, such arrangements can have much the same practical effect as federalism. Regionalism has been used in Italy and Spain to safeguard the interests of culturally distinctive areas such as Sardinia, Sicily, the Basque country, and Catalonia – though it has not brought peace to the Basque country.

An Outside Guarantor

It is common for a minority which feels itself disadvantaged in one state to appeal for support to a neighbouring state with which it has ethnic or cultural links, as the Sri Lankan Tamils look to India and the Turkish-speaking Cypriots to Turkey. The legitimate interest of the neighbouring state has at times been recognised in international law. After the First World War, Germany and Poland signed a treaty providing safeguards for their respective minorities in Upper Silesia. Finland negotiated an agreement with Sweden regarding the status of the Åland Islands, which were under Finnish sovereignty but had a Swedish population. As recently as 1960, the UN General Assembly recognised the legitimate concern of Austria in the fate of the German-speaking population of the South Tyrol, and though that area is under Italian sovereignty, Italy was asked to enter into negotiation with Austria about the future of the area. The current arrangements in the South Tyrol are the result of this negotiation.

Joint Authority

In a joint authority (sometimes also called a condominium), powers of government are vested in two or more states. If there were a joint authority in Northern Ireland (according to the New Ireland Forum), 'the London and Dublin governments would have equal responsibility for all aspects of the government of Northern Ireland'.[22] The Sudan was formerly under joint British and Egyptian rule. The New Hebrides were until recently under joint British and French rule. Andorra is still a condominium of France and of the Bishop of Urgel in Spain. It is true that in all these cases joint authority was adopted more to protect the interests of the sovereign powers than to safeguard the rights of any particular minority within the area concerned. But there is no reason why the device could not be used to protect the interests of an indigenous ethnic group by giving a sympathetic outside power a permanent share in sovereignty. Indeed, the device could be taken further and sovereignty could be shared between outside powers and the population of the area concerned. A precedent can be found in the Moroccan city of Tangier, which was under international control between 1923 and 1956. The legislative assembly of Tangier contained representatives of the local people and of no fewer than eight foreign powers.

International Administration

An extreme form of joint authority occurs when a territory is put under the control of some international body. Danzig between the wars was a free city under the League of Nations. The original United Nations plan for Palestine in 1947 included a provision that the Jerusalem area should be awarded neither to Jews nor to Arabs but be under United Nations control.

We draw three main conclusions from our survey of multicultural societies. The first is emphasised by Professor Antony Alcock in the South Tyrol context: peaceful intercommunity relations, meaningful political dialogue, and economic and social development can be carried out only within a stable framework.[23] The population has to accept that frontiers will not be changed by intimidation or violence.

The second conclusion is that these devices should not be imposed: they will work only if adopted by the free and willing consent of the people concerned.

This leads on to the third conclusion. A fair and responsible attitude of mind is fundamental to the successful resolution of tensions in society. There must be on all sides a willingness to treat other communities with the same fairness as one expects for one's own. Even this willingness may not be enough to defuse all tensions, because groups genuinely differ in what they perceive as 'fair'. The Flemish–Walloon tension in Belgium, for instance, is still not completely resolved because of sincerely-felt differences over the appropriate status to be accorded to Brussels. But in Belgium there is at least agreement on the principle of equal status for the two main linguistic groups. The same agreement on the principle of equality can be found in the other societies covered by the report of the Minority Rights Group: Finland, Switzerland, the Netherlands, and South Tyrol.

On the other hand, where a group in a society (or more than one group) is not prepared to accord equality of treatment, then it does not matter what safeguards are built into a constitution, for resentments will fester and conflict will result. The reasons for this refusal of equality differ from one country to another. In South Africa, many whites claim that inequality is justified because blacks are not civilised. In Israel, many Jews claim that the whole of Eretz Israel has been given to them by God and that the rights of Jews thus take priority over those of non-Jews. In Sri Lanka, many Sinhalese claim that the island is the 'pearl of Buddha', in which Buddhists rightly have priority over others. In the Lebanon, many Maronites claim that the country was created to be a haven for Christians, and they are not prepared to accept the consequences of the fact that it now has a Muslim majority. But whatever the ideological underpinning, the result in all these countries has been the same – turmoil and suffering.

Notes and References

1. *The Rights of Man* (1791).
2. *Human Rights* (London: Wingate, 1949) p. 18.
3. See *Faith in the City* (London: Church House Publishing, 1985) pp. xiv, 9–22, 202, 238–41, 351–2, paras 1.18–1.43, 9.20–9.21, 10.34–10.44; 14.67–14.68.
4. House of Commons, 11 November 1947.
5. J. N. D. Anderson, *Morality, law and grace* (London: Tyndale Press, 1972) p. 66; see also Adrian Speller, *Breaking Out: a Christian Critique of Criminal Justice* (London: Hodder and Stoughton, 1986, for the British Council of Churches) pp. 21, 81.
6. A. K. Brohi, 'The Nature of Islamic Law and the Concept of Human Rights', in *Human Rights in Islam* (Geneva: International Commission of Jurists, 1982) pp. 43–4 (emphasis in original).
7. *Submission to the New Ireland Forum from the Irish Episcopal Conference* (Dublin, Veritas: 1984) p. 19; *Love is for Life* (Dublin: Veritas, 1985) para. 185.
8. In the Irish Republic, *Shechita* and *Halal* are similarly exempt from the provisions of the Slaughter of Animals Act 1935, which is designed to prevent 'unnecessary, avoidable, or excessive pain or suffering'.
9. Farm Animal Welfare Council, *Report on the Welfare of Livestock when slaughtered by Religious Methods* (London: HMSO, 1985) esp. paras 92–3.
10. *Comments by the Jewish community*, available from the Board of Deputies of British Jews (November 1985) esp. paras 4–6, 38, 50–4.
11. Patrick Devlin, *The Enforcement of Morals* (London: Oxford University Press, 1965) p. 16.
12. *R. v. Lemon* (1979) A. C. 658.
13. See the *Fourth Annual Report of the Standing Advisory Commission on Human Rights, 1977–8* (London: HMSO, 1978) para. 31.
14. *Times Literary Supplement*, 21 March 1986, p. 299.
15. K. Rabl, *Das Selbstbestimmungsrecht der Völker*, 2nd edn (Cologne, 1973) p. 32.
16. West Irian chose integration with Indonesia, Ifni with Morocco. The Mariana Islands chose free association with the United States, Niue with New Zealand.
17. Hector Gros Espiell, *The right to self-determination: implementation of United Nations resolutions* (New York: United Nations, 1980) (UN doc. E/CN 4/Sub.2/405/Rev.1) para. 259.
18. Francesco Capotorti, *Study on the rights of persons belonging to ethnic, religious and linguistic minorities* (New York: United Nations, 1979) (UN doc.E/CN 4/Sub.2/384/Rev.1) para. 581.
19. 'What rights have minorities?', in *Minorities: a question of human rights* (ed. Ben Whitaker) (Oxford: Pergamon Press, 1984).
20. Security Council Official Records, 37th year, Supplement for April–June 1982, pp.1, 20, S/14940, S/14973.
21. Aureliu Cristescu, *The right to self-determination* (New York: United Nations, 1981) (doc. E CN 4/Sub.2/404/Rev.1) para. 279.

22. *Report of the New Ireland Forum* (Dublin: Stationery Office, 1984) para. 8.1.
23. Antony Alcock, 'South Tyrol', in *Coexistence in some plural European societies* (Minority Rights Group Report 72, 1987) p. 7.

4 Northern Ireland: A Special Case?

NORTHERN IRELAND IN CONTEXT

The main aim of this Report is to examine human rights and responsibilities in the perspective of developments in two states, the United Kingdom and the Republic of Ireland. But human rights do not exist in a vacuum, but rather in a real world which has many dimensions, of which the religious, social and political are the most important for us. If we look at the economic dimension, we find some common features in the two states which concern us: unemployment, lack of investment, decay of the urban environment and damage to the ecology of the countryside due to increasingly intensive farming, with all the social consequences which ensue. These are common features of society throughout Western Europe. If we turn now to Northern Ireland, the situation has certainly been exacerbated by political conflict, but its economic and social problems are in essence similar to those being experienced in many parts of Europe, even if the particular circumstances of Northern Ireland have caused it to be exceptionally vulnerable to recession in advance of other regions.

Politically, Northern Ireland is not fully integrated into the United Kingdom in the way that Scotland and Wales are. Because the people of Northern Ireland are not agreed on an acceptable form of cross-community regional government, they have been deprived of the benefits of devolution. Since the imposition of direct rule from Whitehall, the powers and effectiveness of local government have been substantially curtailed, and the ordinary citizen has remarkably little opportunity to influence the administration of even local services through democratic institutions. Moreover, citizens of the United Kingdom who live in Northern Ireland are unable to join or vote for candidates of the two main political parties in Great Britain which are expected to form the government of the day. This raises an important constitutional as well as political issue of principle about the character of the polity which operates today.

In the United Kingdom, political parties are treated as voluntary organisations and for most purposes are not subject to any legal controls about where they should organise or who are entitled to become members. A political party can thus decline to admit people to membership or refuse to organise in a part of the country. In the case of the Labour and Conservative parties, this is what happens in relation to Northern Ireland, and people who live there are unable to obtain membership of those parties. The voluntary character of political parties is, of course, an important and valued feature of the British system of politics. Yet it is not without its difficulties. It might be argued that, if unchecked, it would threaten the notion of truly representative government. Governments of the United Kingdom have normally been formed by either the Conservative Party or the Labour Party (or a combination of parties in time of war), but these are not fully representative when citizens of the United Kingdom are denied membership of those parties purely on the ground that they live in Northern Ireland. To make this point is not of course to suggest that there is an overwhelming demand within Northern Ireland for this situation to be changed, nor that the divisions of Northern Ireland would miraculously disappear if the major political parties from Great Britain were to enter the scene. Yet there is a significant number of people in Northern Ireland who do wish to have the right to join one or other of the main parties in Great Britain. Their claim should be respected.

We consider that the political parties concerned should review their policies and accept as a principle that membership should be open to all adults throughout the nation who genuinely subscribe to the party's objectives and who are prepared to be bound by their rules, regardless of where they may live. We must add that we confine this comment to the issue of membership of the major political parties, since issues about where those parties should contest elections ought to remain with the parties themselves. We certainly do not suggest that the law should be changed, simply that the parties themselves should carry out their own reviews of the question.

The system of direct rule in Northern Ireland needs to be set in the context of political developments in the United Kingdom as a whole. Northern Ireland is not the only region where the question of 'home rule' has been a live issue in the past twenty years. There have been moves to create a devolved parliamentary assembly in both Scotland and Wales, and proposals for some measure of devolution are still being canvassed by at least two of the main national parties in Great Britain. Moreover, there has been a tendency to reduce the powers of local government in the past few years, and this has created tension between central and some local governments, and has resulted in a decline in the quality of services provided to ratepayers. It is not only in Northern Ireland that the question of centralised versus local administration has been an important issue, and one that has intimately affected the lives of ordinary people.

Then there is the wider religious dimension. The past thirty years have seen both a growth in ecumenical understanding between the main Churches and the hardening of sectarian positions within those same Churches. On the positive side, there have been a number of significant bilateral and multilateral theological agreements. The progress achieved by the Anglican–Roman Catholic International Commission (ARCIC) and the welcome given to it in many quarters, the visits of the Pope to the Republic of Ireland and Great Britain, and many examples of close local co-operation between the Churches, are all signs of a new and hopeful phase in the relationships between the Roman Catholic, Anglican, and Free Churches. The close collaboration between the leaders of the Churches in Liverpool is a conspicuous example of this co-operation. But this has been accompanied by an increasing intransigence in certain sections of Church opinion. Issues such as the ordination of women, the involvement of the Churches in social and political affairs, and the legitimacy of radical theological questioning and research, have created a polarisation within the Churches that is now a serious setback to the cause of Christian unity. Those in Great Britain who so readily criticise the Churches in Ireland for exacerbating the political conflict need to recall the intransigence and intolerance which has increasingly manifested itself in Church life throughout these islands in recent years. British Christians have no right to demand of Irish Christians a level of forbearance and mutual understanding which they have not yet achieved themselves. They should see themselves rather as called to a common endeavour to repent of their own shortcomings and to enter into the creative possibilities which are open to faith.

The wider perspective is equally important when we consider the problem which is so central in Northern Ireland, but which may seem remote to many people in Great Britain: the relationship between different communities. During the past thirty years, the social scene in Great Britain has been transformed by the arrival of immigrants of Afro-Caribbean or Indian origin, who now constitute 4 per cent of the population of the United Kingdom and who have clustered in certain urban areas, so that there are now districts where the majority of the population is black. These immigrants represent different cultures and often different religions, and the initial expectation that within a generation they would become assimilated into the British culture and way of life has not been fulfilled. Instead, often feeling under threat, they have tended to assert their traditional culture as a way of preserving their distinct identity, and have increasingly pressed for recognition of their 'rights' as substantial minorities within the population as a whole. In response, the British government has introduced legislation to make discrimination on racial grounds illegal, and has set up a Commission for Racial Equality in Great Britain to monitor its effectiveness. Yet few would argue that this has been wholly successful in combatting prejudice and discrimination, and in creating a harmonious multiracial society. Problems of minority rights, particularly in educational questions, constantly arise. There is also growing doubt whether traditional political institutions are any longer adequate to cope with these new circumstances. Black people have virtually no representation at the national level either in Parliament or in voluntary bodies such as Church assemblies, a form of discrimination which we believe demands radical remedies.

In Northern Ireland, the range of legal provisions aimed at protecting human and civil rights is extensive, yet arguments and allegations about the abuse of the rights of citizens, and why they occurred, have been at the centre of much political argument. Today in Northern Ireland the enjoyment of life and liberty is constantly threatened by subversive and sectarian violence and impaired by fear; and attempts by the security forces to control the violence have necessitated curtailment of freedoms enjoyed elsewhere in the United Kingdom.

What are euphemistically known as 'the troubles' in Northern Ireland are best understood against a legacy of history, about which people in Ireland tend to display long and unforgiving memories. Moreover, it is only too easy to let the tribulations of the present colour what is remembered from the past. Certainly the apportionment of responsibility for the legacy – and the history of the British connection with Ireland – remain hotly disputed. There is no wide measure of agreement on when Irish community divisions actually began, nor on what should now be done to heal the wounds. There is no consensus on the nature and degree of Britain's responsibilities, nor of those of Ireland.

We could not hope to offer a universally acceptable, let alone complete, account of the events leading to contemporary problems, and we shall not try. Instead we set out some of the main milestones in the relatively recent history of Ireland. We do so in order to provide a brief *aide mémoire* rather than to give a detailed historical chronicle.

HISTORICAL BACKGROUND*

To understand the identities and tensions of the different communities in Ireland it is necessary to explore the historical background to their emergence. Our purpose is simply to note the key developments which have remained in the memories of the different communities. In this brief account, it is also important to observe that the different communities had at different times to fight for what would now be regarded as their human rights and civil liberties.

Political division in Northern Ireland dates from (at least) the day in 1215 when Pope Innocent III granted Ireland to King John of England and his successors 'as a vassal kingdom' for a yearly fee of 300 marks. In the sixteenth century, Queen Elizabeth of England tried to consolidate this position further by 'planting' English settlers, and Scottish settlers arrived in the reign of James VI and I. Added to the political and social division reinforced by these newcomers, the settlers brought with them their Protestantism, and this intensified the existing alienation between the communities.

During the seventeenth century, Ireland was, ecclesiastically speaking, divided into three main groups: the Establishment (Anglican), the Roman Catholic, and the Dissenter, mostly Presbyterian. These groups were not uniformly present throughout Ireland; the majority of Anglicans and Presbyterians were in the North East.

For the greater part of the eighteenth century, Roman Catholics and Presbyterians were second-class citizens, the former under the Penal Laws and the latter under the Sacramental Test Act 1780. There was a difference in this. The Roman Catholic priest, though considered to be an enemy of the state, was regarded as properly ordained, so that marriages conducted by him were valid, whereas the Presbyterian minister was regarded by the law as a layman, so that Presbyterians married by their own minister were sometimes brought before the Bishops' Courts and put on trial for living in sin. Both Presbyterians and Roman Catholics were unable to take a full

*Professor John Barkley, a member of our Advisory Board, has been good enough to help us with this section.

part in the life of society so that, despite theological differences, they could make common cause in seeking social and parliamentary reform. Throughout the century, military action had reaffirmed the divisions between the communities.

When the Sacramental Test Act was repealed, Presbyterians could take part in public life. By the end of the eighteenth century, the major political problems were parliamentary reform and Roman Catholic emancipation. Grattan's Parliament in 1782 achieved legislative freedom from the control of the English Council (that is to say, control from London) but it remained a Parliament for the Anglican Ascendancy (or Establishment), with no representation from the Roman Catholic or Presbyterian communities.

During the eighteenth century, over a quarter of a million Presbyterians and some 10 000, Roman Catholics emigrated to North America because of economic, social, and political disabilities and religious persecution. The influence of these emigrants led to the affirmation by those remaining in Ireland of ideas about human rights, which were reinforced by the French concepts of the rights of man. The failure of Grattan's Parliament to bring about the necessary reforms led some Presbyterians to band together as the United Irishmen and with Roman Catholics to rise in 1798 – a rebellion which was brutally suppressed.

The failed revolution, however, led to the Acts of Union between Ireland and Great Britain, which ushered in reforms favourable to Presbyterians but not Roman Catholics. However, some Presbyterians and Catholics joined together to struggle for Catholic emancipation and for the repeal of the Penal Laws. In 1829 Roman Catholic emancipation was achieved, as many Presbyterians and the General Synod of Ulster had demanded in 1782 and 1793.

In 1841, Daniel O'Connell made repeal of the Union the central issue. This move was felt by many Presbyterians in Ulster to be an attempt to establish a Roman Catholic ascendancy, and it therefore found little support there. The repeal movement was constitutional in its methods. Further polarisation between the communities was created by the Famine, which affected the Roman Catholic community above all and led to great bitterness. There were those among that community who felt that the only remedy was to try to establish an Irish state by armed rebellion.

The separation of the communities was further intensified by changes in the character of the Irish Roman Catholic Church. Many of the Irish bishops had been Gallican or neo-Gallican in outlook,

seeking freedom from papal control. However, during the domi-
nance of the ultramontane Archbishop Cullen from 1849, with his
stress on the supreme authority of the Pope, other communities
found themselves totally alienated, despite the efforts of some of the
Roman Catholic hierarchy to counter this tendency.

The progressive identification of national consciousness and its
identification with the Roman Catholic community reinforced the
divisions between the communities. This sense of separation was also
strengthened by the Evangelical Revivals in the 1850s and by the
economic divisions created by the industrialisation of the largely
Protestant areas from the 1820s.

Throughout the second half of the nineteenth century, moves for
Home Rule for Ireland played a significant part in the political
agenda of both Great Britain and Ireland. While Presbyterians had
been happy with the Union, they began to make common cause with
the Anglican community to fight Home Rule moves. The final
obstacle to this co-operation disappeared with the disestablishment
of the Anglican Church in Ireland. In this struggle against the Home
Rule movement, the Presbyterian and Anglican communities were
reinforced by the Anglican-dominated Orange Order.

The failure of Grattan's Parliament to deal with the land question
had led to agrarian strife and to the forming of the Orange Society in
1796, with the Crown and a Bishop's Mitre on its early warrants. It
professed belief in civil and religious liberty, but those joining had to
take an obligation of loyalty to the king 'so long as he supported the
Protestant Ascendancy' and to swear that they were not Roman
Catholics or United Irishmen.

It was the Orange Society which founded the Unionist Party in
1886 with the aim of maintaining the union of Great Britain and
Ireland. It presented itself as a bulwark against Home Rule, and
from that period many Presbyterians joined the Orange Order and
began to look to it rather than their Church for religious as well as
political guidance.

Home Rule for Ireland was delayed by the First World War. When
Ireland attained Dominion status, the Protestants, largely concentrated in the North East, faced a country dominated by the Catholic
community.

The combined result of all these events led to the partition of
Ireland in 1920. Protestants were as opposed to the partition of
Ireland as Roman Catholics, except that Protestants were also
opposed to the partition of the United Kingdom. They accepted the

settlement, however, to avoid civil war. As a result of partition, Ireland was divided into Northern Ireland and the Irish Free State (now the Irish Republic), the former being approximately one-third Catholic, under one-third Presbyterian, and over one-quarter Anglican, whereas the latter was then 90 per cent Catholic. The Ireland (Confirmation of Agreement) Act 1925, defining the boundary between North and South, was signed by representatives of the Northern, Southern, and Westminster Governments, and lodged at the League of Nations as an international treaty. In 1937 it was set aside by the South in a referendum. The Constitution of Eire now claimed jurisdiction over 'the whole of Ireland', replacing the liberal–pluralist 1922 Constitution of the Irish Free State.

The conflicting ambitions of the two communities dominated the political complexion and attitudes of the two Parliaments – the Dáil in the Irish Free State and the Parliament at Stormont in Northern Ireland. The Stormont *régime* tolerated various forms of discrimination against Catholics, and the Irish Republic withheld formal recognition of the status of Northern Ireland. While there was no outright oppression of the Protestant minority in the South, the constitution adopted in 1937 contained elements which Northern Protestants found offensive.

The claim of the Irish Constitution of the 'national territory' of the whole island of Ireland further reinforced the determination of the unionists in Northern Ireland to maintain their own identity and government.

The Northern Ireland Parliament for half a century exercised jurisdiction over most internal functions, but taxation, trade, foreign affairs, and defence remained under the control of the United Kingdom Parliament at Westminster, where Northern Ireland MPs had seats. Yet while there was (and remains today) a clear and substantial majority in Northern Ireland in favour of continued association with Great Britain, there also remained a significant nationalist minority holding different constitutional goals. This nationalist mainly Catholic group regarded themselves as Irish; they aspired to Irish unity of a type which would involve ending the constitutional link between Northern Ireland and the rest of the United Kingdom. But it has never been the case that all Catholics are nationalists or all Protestants unionists.

Against this background, it may seem little wonder that religious feeling in Northern Ireland today remains fused with the political and constitutional dispute between the two communities. In 1968 and

1969, a civil rights campaign was mounted which involved large street demonstrations, some of which resulted in violence. This campaign was influenced to some extent by the wider civil rights movements in other Western European countries and the United States. In 1968, the focal point of the demonstrations on the streets in Northern Ireland was the criticism by the minority community of the discrimination organised or tolerated during the years of unbroken unionist rule.[1]

Although since 1968 the scale of the violence has varied, there has been little prospect of its elimination. The dislocation of society has continued, prompting despair about stability and peace ever returning to Northern Ireland. The paramilitaries at both ends of the political spectrum, while enjoying the support of only a minority in their respective communities, are able to cause havoc for ordinary law-abiding citizens.

From 1969 until the end of 1986, 2 525 individuals lost their lives in Northern Ireland as a result of political violence. These figures include over 780 members of the security forces. The worst year was 1972 in which there were some 470 fatalities. But in addition to the violent deaths and murders, there have been many more riots, bombings, and robberies; over 26 000 people have been injured or maimed. These statistics must be understood in the context of a total population in Northern Ireland of approximately 1½ million, and mean that a very high proportion of the people have felt the effects of violence directly or indirectly. Although the scale of violence waxes and wanes, its unceasing pressure should not be forgotten. Nor should we discount the effects of restrictions on daily life and movement, introduced to maintain security. Yet is is sobering to remember that for a generation since the troubles began in Northern Ireland, this disturbed picture is all that the young have known in the course of growing up and entering adulthood.

SOLUTIONS AND INITIATIVES

When the violence and conflict stemming from the 1968 and 1969 protests escalated, attempts by the Northern Ireland Government to control the situation failed. The British army was deployed in the streets to maintain peace (and to protect the threatened Catholic community in Belfast and Derry) when the civil power could not cope. The army has remained ever since.

The first major political consequence of these events was the prorogation (and later abolition) of the Northern Ireland Government and Parliament. Since 1972 there has been a system of direct rule under which executive authority is exercised by a Secretary of State from Great Britain, advised by civil servants in the Northern Ireland Office and Northern Ireland Departments, many of whom at the most senior levels come from other parts of the United Kingdom. Legislation is by Order in Council (a form of statutory instrument) and there is no adequate scrutiny or opportunity for amendment when such Orders are being considered at Westminster. Local government enjoys few powers. The political process is by normal standards in abeyance.

Direct rule was originally introduced as a temporary measure and for only a short time, until the Northern Ireland people had agreed on a constitutional settlement likely to produce stability based on inter-community consensus. But with the exception of a few months in 1974, direct rule has continued.

Direct rule has thus been the form of government for almost one-quarter of the existence of Northern Ireland as a separate political unit. A whole series of special reports have been commissioned from senior judicial figures on various subjects (Lords Cameron, Scarman, Widgery, Diplock, Gardiner, etc.). Yet the complicated and entrenched nature of the difficulties and the seemingly incompatible aspirations of the majority and minority communities have prevented the British Government finding a 'solution', despite a number of attempts to do so.

During this time a large number of legal reforms have been introduced in Northern Ireland, ranging over anti-discrimination and electoral law to improved police complaints procedures and an equal opportunity code. The Standing Advisory Commission on Human Rights has observed: 'These measures amount to a substantial body of legislation to meet grievances and protect human rights in Northern Ireland. As a body of law it is impressive and should not be under-rated'.[2] Against this, measures unparalleled in other parts of the United Kingdom have been introduced into the criminal law of Northern Ireland to counter the threat posed by subversive violence; this has included, at different times, internment without charge or trial, the suspension of the use of juries in terrorist cases, and emergency powers of search and seizure.

A number of political initiatives were taken in the period 1973–82 aimed at achieving a broad consensus across both communities for devolved government. The most significant of these was in 1973–4 when, after an election by proportional representation for a Northern Ireland Assembly, agreement was reached between the leaders of the SDLP, the Alliance Party, and the Faulkner unionists to establish a 'power-sharing' or coalition administration. That administration came into existence in January 1974 following the agreement reached at Sunningdale between the British and the Irish Governments, which also provided for a Council of Ireland. The Council was intended as a forum in which representatives from both parts of Ireland could agree to meet and discuss matters of mutual concern. The 'power-sharing' administration of 1974 marked the first and only occasion when nationalists served alongside unionists in a Northern Ireland executive. The experiment was very short-lived, since it did not enjoy sufficient support in the unionist community. The administration was brought down by the all-out strike of May that year which was organised by sections of the loyalist community opposed to power-sharing and the proposed Council of Ireland.[3]

Between 1974 and 1982 three further initiatives were taken to reach agreement on devolved government: the Convention of 1975–6, the Secretary of State's Conference of 1980, and the Assembly of 1982. The first two of these failed to achieve any progress whatsoever. In the case of the Assembly, although it continued for four years, it too failed to progress because the nationalist–republican parties, the Social Democratic and Labour Party (SDLP) and Sinn Fein, declined to attend. It was therefore impossible to secure the necessary measure of cross-community support to achieve a devolution of functions, so that the Assembly was restricted to a scrutinising and advisory role. This it did through a system of committees which investigated and reported on a wide range of issues.

When the SDLP decided that it would contest seats but not attend the Assembly in 1982, it also decided that it would attempt to persuade the major political parties in the Republic to establish a forum to review the crisis in Northern Ireland with a view to determining the basis upon which constitutional nationalism in Ireland should deal with that crisis. As a result the New Ireland Forum was set up in May 1983 with membership drawn from the three major political parties in the Republic (Fianna Fáil, Fine Gael, and Labour) together with the SDLP itself.

In the words of the Forum's Report, it was established 'for consultations on the manner in which lasting peace and stability could be achieved in a new Ireland through the democratic process and to report on possible new structures and processes through which this objective might be achieved'.[4] The Forum invited and received submissions from many quarters, though the Unionist parties declined to make submissions, and its deliberations lasted nearly a year. Three options for the future were reviewed: a unitary state, a federal or confederal arrangement, and a joint authority for Northern Ireland. The parties in the Forum envisaged a settlement which would recognise the identities and legitimate rights of the two communities (paras 5.2.(4) and 4.16). Cultural and linguistic diversity should be preserved (para. 5.2.(9)), and the unionists had the right to effective expression of their identity, ethos, and way of life (para. 4.15). The parties condemned paramilitary violence (para. 4.11) and affirmed that the goal of Irish unity would be pursued 'only by democratic means and on the basis of agreement' (para. 4.6). Unionists claimed that the tone and substance of the report failed to come to grips with their position, and they considered that the commitment to peace and democracy was meaningless so long as the Constitution of the Irish Republic laid claim to the North.

The report of the Forum was published in 1984. Although Margaret Thatcher declared that the three options in the report of the Forum were unacceptable to the United Kingdom, the report provided a basis for the Irish Government's discussions with the United Kingdom, which led to the Anglo-Irish Agreement in November 1985.

While discussions and new attempts at solutions have continued in the United Kingdom and the Republic of Ireland, there has also been international interest, especially from North America and Europe. In 1983, the European Parliament asked Niels Haagerup, a liberal Danish MEP, to prepare a report on the situation in Northern Ireland. The United Kingdom Government considered that the European Parliament was going beyond its competence in concerning itself with the internal affairs of a member state, and so withheld its co-operation, and the unionist parties declined Haagerup's invitation to co-operate.

Haagerup concluded that there was 'no definite solution' which would satisfy a majority of the two communities in Northern Ireland, so he offered 'no concrete suggestions'. That did not mean that nothing could be done to halt the growing alienation. Catholic aspirations for Irish unity and Protestant uncertainty about the long-term intentions of the UK Government had led to constitutional instability. Nationalist aspiration for unity, shared by all political parties in the Republic, was 'a heavy burden' because the goal could not be fulfilled 'in the foreseeable future'. In these circumstances, it would be desirable for the two communities and British and Irish political parties to seek progress 'within the present constitutional framework without prejudice to possible future changes'. Political reforms in Northern Ireland should be directed towards a system of participation by representatives of both communities, and ways should be sought for 'more legitimate and visible expressions' of the Irish dimension. Those developments would not come about without 'a degree of tolerance'.[5]

Against the background of so many political and constitutional proposals and experiments, there had been further demonstrations, strikes by republican prisoners, and murders. Dirty protests and hunger strikes occurred in prisons, and bombs continued in English cities and Dublin streets as well as in Northern Ireland. The problems which gave rise to and are compounded by the troubles have defied those who search for solutions, whether they be Ministers, constitutional lawyers, political theorists, or Church leaders. What may have had the trappings of a predominantly civil rights campaign in 1968 cannot now be described adequately in such terms: it is a major constitutional crisis.

But if this is a solemn and gloomy picture, it must also be recorded, with admiration, that many people have tried (and tried over and over again) to ameliorate the effects of the situation and to find ways of solving problems as they arise and help bring about peace. There have been high points to such endeavours. At its peak, the Peace People, spearheaded by Betty Williams and Mairead Corrigan, seemed capable for a time of breaking out of the sectarian straitjacket, but the movement was not able to maintain its initial strength and focus.[6]

It would be entirely wrong, however, simply to paint a picture of gloom and doom about Northern Ireland. On the contrary, there are also some remarkably reassuring features about life there. A visitor to Belfast may notice the barricades and fencing, the graffiti and security checks. The visitor will certainly be struck by the presence of armed police and British soldiers in the streets. But he or she will also note that the pubs and clubs, shops and supermarkets, cafés and restaurants, are bustling, and will find a friendly talkative welcome and a rich and warm approach to life. The resilience of those who have lived through so much suffering is obvious and dramatic. There is substantial reason for hope in the very fact that the practicalities of daily life are attended to with so little fuss.

No report on human rights in Northern Ireland would be complete if it did not take account of the Anglo–Irish Agreement signed by the Governments of the United Kingdom and the Republic of Ireland at Hillsborough, County Down, on 15 November 1985 'as a formal and binding Agreement between their two Governments' (joint *communiqué*). While, as we have seen, the attempts to tackle the problems and invent or construct new constitutional solutions have been many, the Anglo–Irish Agreement represents one of the most profound developments in these islands since partition. It is unusal (but not uniquely so) in that it involves a major departure from the usual practice, by providing a framework within which another government is entitled to put forward views and proposals on a wide range of matters. By the Agreement, the British Government has solemnly agreed that the Government of the Republic should be consulted on 'major policy issues' and may make suggestions for legislation affecting the minority community in Northern Ireland (Article 5(c)). The obligation to observe this consultative procedure laid down in the Agreement is binding in international law. The Irish Government supported the declared policy of the UK Government in working for a devolution of functions on a basis which would secure widespread acceptance throughout the community, and accepted that devolved functions would be excluded from the purview of the Anglo–Irish Conference (Articles 2(b) and 4(b)). The two Governments agreed that there is no derogation from the sovereignty of the other, and that both retain responsibility for the decisions and administration within their own jurisdictions (Article 2(b)). In spite of intense unionist objection to the agreement itself and the manner in which it was concluded, the Agreement was approved by very large majorities in the two parliaments, and has been registered at the United Nations.

The text of the Agreement is set out in Appendix 4. Much of the Agreement is outside the scope of this Report, but we highlight those aspects which relate directly to human rights, and draw attention to the impact of the Agreement on community relations in Northern Ireland.

The Agreement consists of a Preamble and thirteen Articles. The Preamble provides a rationale for the Agreement. It highlights the need 'to reconcile and to acknowledge the rights of the two major traditions that exist in Ireland, represented on the one hand by those who wish for no change in the present status of Northern Ireland and on the other by those who aspire to a sovereign united Ireland achieved by peaceful means and through agreement'. The Preamble reaffirms the total rejection by the two Governments of 'any attempt to promote political objectives by violence or the threat of violence', and it emphasises the importance of achieving 'lasting peace and stability'. These are not just high-sounding sentiments – they identify important priorities for all people who have a genuine interest in improved relations in Ireland and who wish to see an end to intercommunity antagonisms and violence. Yet many of those who have assiduously worked for these ideals over the years are opposed to the Agreement.

The Anglo–Irish Conference established under the Agreement is to concern itself with 'measures to recognise and accommodate the rights and identities of the two traditions in Northern Ireland, to protect human rights and to prevent discrimination' (Article 5(a)). Under Article 6, The Anglo–Irish Conference shall be a framework within which the Irish Government may put forward views and proposals on the role and composition of bodies concerned with human rights, equality of opportunity, fair employment, and police complaints. Consideration is to be given to 'the advantages and disadvantages of a Bill of Rights in some form in Northern Ireland' (Article 5(a)).

The first article of the Agreement does three things: it affirms that any change in the status of Northern Ireland would come about only with the consent of a majority of the people of Northern Ireland; it recognises that a majority in Northern Ireland does not now wish to change Northern Ireland's status; and it declares that if a majority should in the future clearly wish for and formally consent to a united Ireland, the two Governments would sponsor and support the necessary legislation in their respective parliaments.

The effect of Article 1 is a matter of controversy. The British Government claims that it represents a recognition of Northern Ireland by the Republic. Unionists point out that the Agreement does not identify the 'status' which the Republic accepts, and that the claim in the Irish Constitution to the territory of Northern Ireland remains intact.

There are widely differing views and much argument about the meaning and effect of other Articles of the agreement. One factor which has impaired its prospects to date, however, stems from the lack of prior consultation with unionists – an omission deeply resented by the unionist community, and exacerbated by the fact that leaders of the SDLP were consulted and now appear to speak authoritatively of their influence on the working of the Anglo–Irish Conference. Furthermore, unionists perceive in the Intergovernmental Conference a scarcely disguised joint authority, and suspect that the reason for their exclusion from the creation and operation of the Conference is because the reconciliation which the two Governments claim to want will be at the expense of unionists.*

The Agreement has become a central focus of controversy in Northern Ireland and has been used by extreme loyalists to justify intimidation and violence. While the authors of the Agreement and its supporters proclaim the Hillsborough arrangements as imaginative and calculated to lead to better relations, unionist opinion in Northern Ireland takes a very different view, and the Agreement is seen by them as weakening the constitutional relationship between Northern Ireland and the rest of the United Kingdom.

THE ECONOMIC DIMENSION†

We have referred to some of the events in the past 19 years and recorded the incidence of deaths and injuries that have resulted from the conflict. But another vital dimension should not be ignored – the economy.

Since its foundation 67 years ago, Northern Ireland's economy has been in difficulty. This had, until the 1970s at least, very little to do with political problems. It was, rather, the result of the general recession in the Western world's economic performance in the 1920s and 1930s. The stimulus provided by the Second World War, followed by further recession, was also mirrored in Northern Ireland. If anything, the problems were larger and the successes smaller because of the local concentration on linen, agriculture, and shipbuilding. The decline of the first (and, more recently, of the last) of these have created significantly larger unemployment figures than those in most parts of Great Britain. The manufacturing base of Northern Ireland has shrunk over three decades; the number

---

*Sean Farren notes that an Agreement between the two governments was necessary, in spite of unionist objections, and that consultation with Unionist leaders during the negotiations would not have increased the acceptability of the Agreement in Northern Ireland.

†We are grateful to Kenneth Whitaker, a member of our Advisory Board, for advice on economic matters.

employed in manufacturing industry has fallen by over 50 per cent. What was a depressingly high unemployment figure has risen significantly since the outbreak of the troubles. The unemployment rate now is around 20 per cent, compared with 18 per cent in the Republic of Ireland and 11 per cent in Great Britain. The public sector now employs 9 in every 20 of the Northern Ireland work-force.

While there has been a slight fall in the number of unemployed in recent months, the prospect for a major change in the depressed state of the economy has not brightened significantly.[7] Northern Ireland, like the Republic, lies on the periphery of the United Kingdom and of Europe. To such natural disadvantage has to be added political difficulties: the troubles are a major disincentive to investment by British, European, or American companies. Continuing efforts by the Industrial Development Board for Northern Ireland to attract investment – and the flexible and imaginative job creation schemes announced in recent years – have mitigated the problems to an extent but have not solved them.

Discussion of the relationship between economic performance and political conflict continues. On the one hand, some commentators criticise the level of subsidy Northern Ireland receives from the British taxpayer (in 1986–7 the figure was £1600 million). It is, of course, difficult to make useful comparisons about the flow of national income and expenditure to or from different regions, and other depressed areas in the United Kingdom also receive assistance. After all, Northern Ireland contributes to tax revenue, and is entitled to the services which are provided throughout the United Kingdom. On the other hand, the immediately adverse economic effects of the Anglo–Irish agreement have been pointed out by Sir Charles Carter, Chairman of the Northern Ireland Economic Council.[8]* We note this view from a distinguished source to underline the symbiotic relationship between intense political unrest and economic stagnation. There can be little doubt that a widely acceptable political arrangement in Northern Ireland would stimulate both external and internal investment and improve the prospect of an increase in jobs and living standards.

To knowledgeable observers in Northern Ireland, many of the local reactions and counter-reactions to particular developments are

---

*Sean Farren does not accept Sir Charles Carter's claim that the immediate effects of the Anglo-Irish Agreement were adverse: he notes that the economic situation of Northern Ireland has been bad for a long time.

predictable. To onlookers in Great Britain, the same events indicate a political style that may seem irrational, xenophobic, almost incredible. Successive British Secretaries of State and Prime Ministers have pursued a range of options for devolution of powers to the people of Northern Ireland, but all have failed. The process has produced a whole new glossary of political terms – 'power-sharing' and 'rolling devolution', for example. The new formulae and proposals quickly attract connotations that have the effect of sucking them into the old traditional dispute.

The nature of the communal divisions underscores the vital importance of the perceptions that members of each community have of the other. Such perceptions influence the behaviour of individuals and their interpretation of events, and perceptions can be as influential as realities. Moreover, accurate perceptions can easily merge into distorted sectarian stereotypes. Thus the Protestant communal view of Catholics often deals with stereotypes rather than with realities, but such a judgement is of little comfort to the Catholic youth trapped in the wrong place at the wrong time by a group of 'Protestant' paramilitary thugs. The converse is also true. Some years ago, a group of Protestant workmen in South Armagh were taken from a van by gunmen, as yet unknown, who killed them simply because they were Protestants. There are all too many such examples. Each community can recite a litany of atrocities directed against their existence.

We all tend to think in stereotypes, but these easily become savage caricatures, and broad brush assessments in Northern Ireland have a degree of salience where people proclaim themselves prepared to fight and die 'For God and Ulster' or 'For God and Ireland'.

We have referred repeatedly to the conflict in Northern Ireland as if it were a dispute between two contestants, but the situation is vastly more complicated than that. We have been helped to understand what is happening by an analysis prepared by one of our number, Professor John Whyte. He has suggested that there are four alternative perceptions about the nature of the basic conflict: Great Britain versus Northern Ireland (the nationalist perception), the North versus the South (the unionist perception), Protestant versus Catholic (increasingly favoured since the publication of the study by Denis Barritt and Charles Carter a quarter of a century ago),[9] and capitalists versus workers (the Marxist perception).[10]

It is sometimes said by outsiders that Northern Ireland is trapped in religious conflict. There is, indeed, a religious dimension, in that much Protestant resistance to change is fuelled by fear of a Catholic-dominated state. The recent outcomes of the Republic's referenda on divorce and abortion will not have reassured the Protestants of Northern Ireland that their human rights and civil liberties would be respected in an all-Ireland state which legislates on the basis of the Catholic Church's social teaching. Nevertheless, the conflict in Northern Ireland is not a religious struggle in the sense of the combatants being engaged in some doctrinal war where substantive points of theology are at issue. The predominant identification of each community with a different religious tradition fuels the troubles by giving to political and cultural hostility the emotional force of religious hatred, and conversely makes that religious hatred more intense where in some other parts of the world it is evaporating. The people of Northern Ireland are trapped in a situation in which religious affiliations have become badges in maintaining community antagonisms.

The situation is in some ways paradoxical. The border between North and South is one of the few in Europe that is disputed, and yet the dispute mainly exists in documents and speeches, and there is no military confrontation between the armed forces of the two Governments on the ground: the parties to the conflict are the two Governments, on the one hand, and armed subversive elements, on the other. And political violence has been prolonged because neither the security forces in the two states, nor the paramilitary subversives, have been able to inflict a decisive military defeat on the other.

It has been said that republican paramilitary violence will end, as did the hunger strikes, when enough members of the Catholic community decide that enough is enough and that terrorists will no longer be given sanctuary. If this analysis is correct, a heavy responsibility falls on constitutional nationalist politicians, who must try to ensure that Catholic grievances are dealt with in such a way that discontent does not escalate to subversion. But it places an equal responsibility on unionist politicians to respond magnanimously to any nationalist overtures at a time when the unionists are feuding with London and Dublin.

RESPONSIBILITIES REVIEWED

Scotland and Wales are two parts of the United Kingdom in which there are movements seeking independence. At present these movements enjoy some support in both countries, but there is no immediate question of having to respond to their demands. But that could change, and we would then have to ask whether the claims were justified. Here, as elsewhere, a balance between rights and responsibilities must be maintained. Peoples who wish to secede have a duty to remember their responsibilities to others: it is not enough to say 'independence is good for Scotland (or Wales)' without also considering the question 'will it do harm to those with whom we have for so long been united?' Conversely it is not enough for a majority of English people to say 'the secession of Scotland (or Wales) is contrary to our interests: therefore we will oppose it': they also have a duty to take equal account of the wishes of the Scots or Welsh.

If a time ever came when a clear and settled majority in Scotland or Wales desired independence, we hope that the issue would be settled amicably. We expect that the Scots (or Welsh) would accept that, as part of the settlement, they would take on their share of the obligations of the hitherto United Kingdom.

There are a number of minorities in the two states which have well-documented grievances but which are dispersed throughout the states. We have in mind the Asian, African, and West Indian communities in Great Britain, and the itinerant people in Great Britain and poth parts of Ireland. Their problems are best met by a generous development of their protection under domestic law, in compliance with the code of human rights.

The most difficult problem is Northern Ireland, to which we now turn.

The constitutional status of Northern Ireland is that it is part of the United Kingdom, and a majority of its population wishes it to remain such. But a minority of the population aspires to unity with the Irish Republic, and a majority in the Republic supports it in that wish. Both groups in Northern Ireland have appealed to self-determination in support of their opposing claims.

To nationalists, Ireland as a whole is the natural unit of self-determination. Until the Acts of Union in 1800, the island had its own parliament. It was that parliament, representing the Anglican Ascendency but acting in the name of Ireland as a whole, which consented to the union with Great Britain. It followed for nationalists, therefore, that a democratic majority of the representatives of the island as a whole had the right to seek and obtain a return of Irish self-government. On these principles, the problem posed by the

Protestant community would be a matter for the people of Ireland to decide among themselves, and in the years before the First World War, when the pressure for home rule reached its peak, nationalist leaders were prepared to offer substantial safeguards to Protestants provided the political integrity of Ireland was not sundered.

Since partition after the First World War, nationalist leaders in both parts of Ireland have argued along similar lines. Most have made it clear that, while they regard the political division of Ireland as wrong, and while they believe that the Protestant tradition would be fully protected in a united Ireland, they accept that partition cannot be ended by force. Unity, they have argued, can come about only by peaceful means and through agreement. In a sense, therefore, it can be argued that while nationalists do not accept the case for unionist self-determination, they recognise that until there is a change within a significant sector of the unionist community, such as would create a democratic majority within Northern Ireland in favour of Irish unity, its present status within the United Kingdom will remain unchanged. A section of republican opinion, represented by the Irish Republican Army and the Irish National Liberation Army (and their political counterparts, Sinn Fein and the Irish Republican Socialist Party), does not accept this view and believes that the partition of Ireland may justly be overthrown by force. However, election results suggest that this view has very little support in the Republic, and only minority support among the nationalist community in Northern Ireland.

Unionists, on the other hand, argue that their community has the right to determine its own status. They argue that they differ from the remainder of the population of Ireland in religion, economic interest, and national identity, and on that ground have the right to a distinct political existence. They claim that, if there is a natural unit in this part of Europe, it is not Ireland but the British–Irish archipelago, and that if Irish nationalists have the right to divide up the archipelago, then unionists have the right to divide up Ireland.

On these conflicting claims, we have two observations. The first is that the merits of the case cannot be decided by appealing to self-determination on its own. As explained in Chapter 3, self-determination cannot be an absolute right. Like other rights, it is accompanied by responsibilities – to deal fairly with minorities within one's own state, and to respect the interests of one's neighbours. Indeed, the recognition by others of one's rights depends on one's acceptance of responsibilities.

The second observation is that we have to start from the situation as we find it. For good or ill, both the archipelago and the island of Ireland have been divided, and Northern Ireland has been in existence for 67 years. We have to start by identifying the rights and responsibilities of the various relevant groups *in this context*.

The constitutional devices reviewed in Chapter 3 could be useful, whether Northern Ireland maintains its present links with Great Britain or opts for some other status. Should Irish unity ever become the choice of the majority in Northern Ireland, minority interests could be safeguarded by a comprehensive bill of rights or weighted representation or a federal arrangement or similar constitutional devices. Indeed, a federal Ireland could form part of a confederal British–Irish archipelago, though that seems a remote possibility at present. In any case, it is not our task to advocate any particular constitutional status for Northern Ireland, except insofar as human rights and responsibilities are involved – though most of us have a preferred option. We would stress, however, that no arrangement in a divided society will bring peace either in Northern Ireland or elsewhere in the archipelago unless there is a willingness on all sides to respect existing frontiers and treat other groups equally.

Uncertainty about the present and future status of Northern Ireland adds to the tension, but we believe that marginal ameliorations are possible whatever the ultimate outcome. Two of the constitutional devices mentioned in Chapter 3 are already in use in Northern Ireland. Proportional representation has been used in elections to district councils and to the Northern Ireland Assembly when it was in existence – though not to Northern Ireland elections for Westminster. There are several specialised bodies to assure human and civil rights: we refer to these in more detail in Chapters 5 and 6.

Other devices have at least been discussed in the context of Northern Ireland. We strongly advocate an enforceable bill of rights for the United Kingdom by incorporating into statute law the European Convention on Human Rights and three of its Protocols, with parallel action in the Republic. Power-sharing in government was tried for five months in 1974, though in the end it proved unsuccessful: it could become a relevant option again. Cantonisation into unionist and nationalist areas, which would be a form of regionalism, has been proposed, though the communities in Northern Ireland are so intermingled that it would be almost impossible to find a way of dividing them territorially. Joint authority was proposed by a majority of the Kilbrandon Committee (an unofficial but prestigious body set up by the British–Irish Association in 1984 to examine the Northern Ireland problem). The arrangement put forward by the Kilbrandon majority was that power should be shared by representatives of the United Kingdom, the Irish Republic, and the two communities in Northern Ireland.[11]

We are convinced that many constitutional arrangements could work, given a sense of responsibility and an attitude of forbearance. Without these, no constitutional set-up would satisfy the immediate and long-term aspirations of the two communities. We are, nevertheless, agreed on the following.

Unionists have the right to remain part of the United Kingdom so long as the majority in Northern Ireland so wishes. This commitment has been enshrined by statute in the United Kingdom and incorporated in an agreement deposited with the United Nations. Indeed, successive governments in Dublin have accepted that there will be no change in the status of Northern Ireland without the consent of a majority – though unionists point out that the territorial claim to Northern Ireland remains in the Constitution. In return, unionists have a responsibility to treat the nationalist minority with absolute fairness and to co-operate with bodies which seek to establish equality of treatment. They also have a responsibility to refrain from activities, such as deliberately marching in sensitive areas, which create ill-feeling. Failure to act with fairness would weaken their own claim to a continued guarantee of membership of the United Kingdom.

Nationalists in Northern Ireland have the responsibility of accepting that the majority in Northern Ireland does not wish to leave the United Kingdom, and of respecting the consequences. This means co-operation with the organs of the state (as has already been pointed out in para. 5 of the report of the inter-Church working party, *Violence in Ireland*, published in 1976, the conclusions of which are reproduced in our Appendix 5). In return, Northern nationalists have the right to expect absolute fairness of treatment.

The Republic of Ireland has the responsibility not simply of tolerating the Protestant minority but of according full respect to those Protestants who are unionists and opposed to the ideology of Irish nationalism. The Republic also has the responsibility of not making demands which make the solution of the problem more difficult. Like Northern nationalists, it has the duty of respecting the current wishes of the Northern majority. In return, the Republic can claim the right to be consulted by the United Kingdom on the formulation of policy on Northern Ireland, for this policy has considerable repercussions on the well-being of the people of the Republic. For instance, because of the violence in the North, the Republic has to spend substantial sums of money keeping troops and police in border areas. Though the United Kingdom spends more in absolute terms on security, the Republic, being a smaller country, actually spends more *per capita*.[12]

Great Britain, as the larger partner in the United Kingdom, has a responsibility for the well-being of all the people of Northern Ireland and the duty of taking every measure possible – political, economic, and cultural – to secure that well-being. It would be quite irresponsible for a British government, in advance of an agreed solution, simply to pull out because it had got tired of the burden. It has the duty of being even-handed towards both communities – in security policy, in economic development, and so on. In return, the British government has the right to expect co-operation from both communities in Northern Ireland and from the Republic of Ireland in its efforts to facilitate or secure a settlement.

Notes and References

1. Brian Faulkner, *Memoirs of a statesman* (ed. by John Houston) (London: Weidenfeld and Nicolson, 1978) pp. 47–9, 59–9, Terence O'Neill, *Autobiography* (London: Hart Davies, 1972) pp. 103, 106.
2. *The Protection of Human Rights by Law in Northern Ireland* (London: HMSO, 1977) (Cmnd 7009) para. 2.19.
3. Faulkner, *Memoirs*, pp. 182, 185, 260–77, Merlyn Rees, *Northern Ireland: a personal perspective* (London: Methuen, 1985) pp. 64, 130.
4. *Report of the New Ireland Forum* (Dublin: Stationery Office, 1984) para. 1.1.
5. European Parliament, doc. 1–1526/83 (19 March 1984) p. 69.
6. Eric Gallagher and Stanley Worrall, *Christians in Ulster, 1968–1980* (Oxford: Oxford University Press, 1982) p. 180.
7. *Annual Report of the Northern Ireland Economic Council, 1985–6* (Belfast: NIEDO, 1986) p. 3.
8. *The Times*, 20 August 1986.
9. *The Northern Ireland Problem* (Oxford: Oxford University Press, 1962).
10. Paper presented at a conference of the British Association for Irish Studies (University of Keele, April, 1986).

11. *Northern Ireland: report of an independent inquiry* (available from 9 St James's Square, London, SW1Y 4LE).
12. A report for the New Ireland Forum calculated that in 1982, the UK spent £9 a head on security costs connected with Northern Ireland, while the Republic spent IR £36 a head: see *The Cost of Violence arising from the Northern Ireland Crisis since 1969* (Dublin: Stationery Office, n.d. but 1983 or 1984) para. 6.3.

5 Law and Constitution in These Islands

THE ROLE OF LAW

Before we embark on a consideration of the laws and constitutions in the United Kingdom and the Republic of Ireland, we need to make some preliminary points about law in general.

First, we should not overestimate the role of law. Simply passing a new law about some perceived mischief will not solve the problem overnight. Before that can happen, many other steps need to be taken. The law must be widely publicised so that people will know that it is in force. People must be educated about it, and it must be explained to them why it has been made, why they should obey it, and above all how they should conduct themselves in order to do that. There must also be effective means for enforcing it, so that anyone who is aggrieved by its breach can obtain an effective remedy at an affordable cost. Without these things, even the best laws will remain empty phrases.

But, equally, we should also not underestimate the role of law. Quite apart from the painful sanctions available for its breach, most people – and most governments – like to be seen to do right and heartily dislike being shown up as wrongdoers. The normal response of human beings, when their conduct is under attack, is to defend themselves by justifying it – that is, by demonstrating that what they did was right. Laws, after all, are the formal and binding rules of conduct which communities agree for their own members, whether those members are the individuals and institutions which constitute the national community of a sovereign state, or the sovereign states which constitute the members of the international community. If you can demonstrate that you have kept strictly within those formal rules, you can readily argue that your conduct was justified, and so hope to escape censure for it.

Finally, many people find the law both pedantic and dull. In order that people can easily foretell whether something they plan to do is or is not going to be lawful, laws need to be precise, to try to foresee all possible circumstances, and to try to make provisions for all of them. That makes laws and legal language notoriously complex, long-winded, and inelegant. And it also makes explanations of the law seem either grossly oversimplified, or else so larded with qualifications as to be boring.

As we point out in Chapter 3, many laws merely set out minimum standards and fall short of a full Christian ideal. Legal precepts may, in most cases, be founded on moral principles (or be related to them), but not all moral ideals can be reflected in law. There are limits to what can be embodied in the law, but it can still be used as a way of influencing *behaviour* in the right direction. It is not possible to compel a person by law to love his or her neighbour, but it may be possible to provide a remedy if the neighbour is harmed.

FOUR LEGAL SYSTEMS

The purpose of this chapter is to outline in very broad terms the protection of human and civil rights for citizens of the United Kingdom and the Republic of Ireland, considering only the law and constitution on these matters. Our review is complicated by the fact that our archipelago contains not merely two legal jurisdictions corresponding to the two separate states, but four: England and Wales, Scotland, Northern Ireland, and the Irish Republic. There are significant differences in the law of these jurisdictions and, consequently, in the protection of human rights. This does not pose as great a difficulty as might be supposed, however, because there is a close relationship between all four. The two Irish jurisdictions are both based on common law, founded on the common law of England. The report by Kevin Boyle and Desmond Greer commissioned by the New Ireland Forum in 1983 demonstrates both the similarity between those systems and their indebtedness to English law.[1]

The Irish Free State on its creation inherited all the existing, mainly British, statute law. As we make clear below, the Republic's legislative development since 1922 has tended to diverge from British models, depending more or less on the subject matter; and the adoption by the Republic of Ireland of a written constitution has led to many significant differences.

In 1921, Northern Ireland inherited the same statute book as the Irish Free State, but the laws of Northern Ireland have remained much more closely related to those of England and Wales, partly because the Parliament at Stormont was restricted in its legislative competence, and partly because Stormont governments deliberately adopted a step-by-step policy on most matters. Since the introduction of direct rule, the legislative differences between Northern Ireland and England and Wales have been further reduced. With regard to judicial decisions, 'in both jurisdictions ... the major source of influence remains the decisions of the English courts'.[2] The result is that while there are differences between the three common law jurisdictions, English and Irish lawyers generally talk the same language, employ the same concepts, appeal to the same principles, and refer to the same cases and statutes.

The position in Scotland is quite different. Scottish law is not based on common law, but on civil or Roman law, and consequently has much more in common with continental legal codes. Of course, the fact that since 1707 Scotland has had the same legislature as England and Wales has meant that there has been a considerable intrusion of common law concepts into the Scottish legal system, particularly where social policy and political considerations have been critical. Nevertheless, Scottish law remains distinctive, and this produces the curious position that in some areas of law, English and Irish lawyers could be said to have more in common than English and Scottish ones.

CONSTITUTIONS

From the point of view of the protection of human rights, the most important difference between the jurisdictions concerns the presence or absence of a written constitution. All countries have a constitution in the sense of a body of rules concerning such matters as the institutions of government; the powers of those institutions and the relationship among them; the courts; and the procedures for the adjudication of disputes. Rules dealing with these matters do not have to be in a formal written document: they may be embodied in legislation, in case-law, or merely in convention, custom, and practice. Many countries 'entrench' some or all of these rules so that they cannot subsequently be changed by ordinary legislation, but only by a special procedure. This may involve a special weighted parliamentary majority or a popular referendum. There are also cases where certain rules are declared to be unalterable.

The existence of a written constitution with entrenched provisions has important consequences. The entrenched provisions operate as restrictions on the freedom of action of government and legislature.

They may also transfer power from the government to another body – for example, to a supreme court. Where provisions relating to human rights are entrenched, those particular rights will have a high degree of protection. On the other hand, if the human rights in question are not entrenched, they may be changed by ordinary legislation and may be vulnerable to the actions of the government of the day. The human and civil rights in the Constitution of the Irish Republic are entrenched and can be changed only by constitutional amendment; those in the constitution of the United Kingdom can be changed by ordinary legislative or judicial process.

The United Kingdom is unusual in not having a formal document setting out the rules of its constitution. Whether there is any 'fundamental law' in the United Kingdom is a disputed question. On one view, the only fundamental rule is the supremacy of parliament, which is said to be capable of enacting any law whatsoever, on any subject, and of being incapable of binding itself with regard to future legislation. On this view, it would be impossible for the United Kingdom to entrench a bill of rights with the same effect, say, as the equivalent provisions of the US constitution. Indeed, those statutes thought of as being fundamental to the liberties of British subjects – such as Magna Carta and the Bill of Rights of 1688 – are capable of amendment and repeal. Only a few clauses of Magna Carta now remain on the statute book: these are of no practical significance and are retained largely for sentimental reasons.

Yet there are certain enactments in the United Kingdom that could be regarded as containing fundamental law. The union of England and Scotland was effected by two Acts of Union, one passed by the English and one passed by the Scottish Parliament. These Acts, which abolished the separate Parliaments of England and Scotland and created a new Parliament of Great Britain, state that the Scottish legal system and the system for the government of the Presbyterian Church were to continue for all time, and the system of church government was also declared to be 'fundamental and essential'. English lawyers usually take the position that the new parliament inherited or acquired the sovereign characteristics of the English Parliament, so that the 'fundamental' provisions of the Acts of Union are no more unalterable than those of Magna Carta. Some Scottish lawyers – and, significantly, some Scottish judges – have taken the view that these provisions are 'fundamental'.[3]

Similar arguments might be made about the Irish Acts of Union, but while parliament appears to have been relatively scrupulous in its observance of the Scottish Acts (with the result that there have been no authoritative decisions on the scope of the relevant sections of the Scottish Acts of Union), the same care has not been shown about those provisions of the Irish Acts of Union which appeared to create 'fundamental' law. This issue has led to litigation, but on the two occasions when judicial challenge to alleged departures from the Irish Acts were made (concerning the disestablishment of the Church of Ireland and the Anglo–Irish Agreement), they failed.[4]

Consequently, it is the orthodox view that there is no 'fundamental' law in the United Kingdom, and therefore no special constitutional protection for human rights. There appears to be no limit to the extent to which Parliament can change or abolish rights which in many other countries are regarded as fundamental. Sovereignty is said to reside in the Queen in Parliament, that is, the Queen acting 'by and with the advice and consent' of the Lords and Commons. In practice, power now rests almost entirely in the House of Commons, for it is a firm convention that the sovereign would assent to any Bill passed by the two Houses, and the House of Lords can, in virtually all cases, eventually be over-ridden by the House of Commons – a situation which has been described by Lord Hailsham as 'an elective dictatorship'.

In Britain, rights such as freedom of the press, of speech, and of assembly are not guaranteed by statements of general principle: instead they are said to be 'residual' – that is, they are the residue left after the restraints of civil and criminal law, including the powers available to the executive, have been defined. Freedom of assembly is thus simply the freedom to gather with others – except in so far as another person or body is legally entitled to prevent such an assembly on the grounds, say, of trespass or obstruction of the highway. Again, liberty of the person is protected by the writ of *habeas corpus*, but this writ is not available if detention can be justified by a statute.[5] This residual freedom has relevance for governmental bodies. Thus in a case on telephone tapping, Sir Robert Megarry (vice president of the Chancery Division of the High Court) said:

> If the tapping of telephones by the Post Office at the request of the police can be carried out without any breach of the law, it does not require any statutory or common law power to justify it: it can lawfully be done simply because there is nothing to make it unlawful.[6]

The judge went on to hold that the tapping was lawful, as there had been no trespass to the plaintiff's premises. The plaintiff complained to the European Commission of Human Rights, which referred the case to the European Court of Human Rights, which held that there had been a breach of Article 8 of the European Convention (right to respect for private life). As a result, legislation was brought forward to regulate such tapping.[7]

There have been occasions when judges have talked about rights as a matter of general principle, but these have been few, and often the comments are part of a dissenting judgement.[8] More frequent, perhaps, have been the occasions when the courts have been prepared to apply a general principle of this nature as a presumption to assist in the interpretation of a statute, as has happened over the right of access to the courts,[9] and the right not to be deprived of property without compensation. But these are merely presumptions which must give way to the clear words of a statute. International treaties, such as the European Convention on Human Rights, although they are not directly applicable in the courts, can sometimes be referred to as an aid to interpretation: there is a presumption that a statute ought to be construed so as to avoid, if possible, a breach by the government of its international obligations.[10]

LEGAL PROTECTION FOR HUMAN RIGHTS IN THE UNITED KINGDOM

We do not have space here to attempt a comprehensive survey of the major issues in human rights law in the United Kingdom today, but some of them can be briefly mentioned.

We begin with race relations. The first Race Relations Act was passed in 1965, and further Acts were passed in 1968 and 1976. None of the legislation against racial discrimination extends to Northern Ireland. The first two Acts made discrimination in housing and employment illegal, and the latter Act extended the meaning of 'discrimination'. It also created the Commission for Racial Equality, which replaced the Race Relations Board and the Community Relations Commission, which had been created under the earlier Acts. The 1976 Act defines 'discrimination' as treating a person less favourably on racial grounds than another person might be treated. It also states that segregation amounts to treating a person less favourably and so amounts to discrimination. The legislation in Great Britain provides for some 'positive discrimination' so that the particular needs of racial groups may be catered for. The provision of special educational and employment facilities is lawful if the preferential treatment is because the proportion of persons in a particular group in the field concerned is less than the proportion of those belonging to other groups.

One matter which is not clear is the extent to which the legislation may be used to protect cultural and religious traditions. Historically the legislation was concerned with equal treatment for individuals (usually immigrants), so that they were on a par with other people in the country. However, the role of the Commission is to promote good race relations and is capable of a fairly broad interpretation, and latterly there has been more emphasis on the cultural and religious practices of the various immigrant communities. Remedies may be obtained either by the individual or the Commission taking action in the courts, though in certain cases action can be taken only by the Commission, including indirect discrimination where there is no actual victim, and discriminatory advertisements.

The law on sex discrimination has followed a similar pattern. Legislation on equal pay was enacted in 1970, but did not come into operation until 1975 when the Sex Discrimination Act was also passed. The 1975 Act is on broadly similar lines to the Race Relations Act 1976. Discrimination on grounds of sex is prohibited in the fields of employment, educational opportunities and training, facilities for goods and services, and the disposal of premises. The enforcement machinery is similar to the 1976 Act, and the Equal Opportunities Commission has a similar function to the Commission for Racial Equality. In 1982, the European Court of Justice (not to be confused with the European Court of Human Rights at Strasbourg) held that the United Kingdom had failed to comply with EEC law regarding equal pay. Subsequently the United Kingdom introduced amending legislation to ensure compliance with EEC law.

The Scandinavian office of Ombudsman was the model for the creation of the office of Parliamentary Commissioner for Administration (Ombudsman).[11] A separate Parliamentary Commissioner for Northern Ireland was created in 1969 to investigate complaints of maladministration by government departments causing injustice. Complaints are submitted through a member of the Northern Ireland Assembly or, when the Assembly is in abeyance, through a

Westminster MP. There are a number of limitations on the powers and role of the Commissioner. He may not act on complaints directly from a member of the public. The Commissioner is also limited to investigating 'injustice as a consequence of maladministration': the terms are not defined, but any question of the policy or the merits of an administrative decision are firmly excluded. If he finds that there has been maladministration, the Commissioner may make a report to the department concerned and to parliament, and may in that report recommend action such as the payment of compensation; but his decisions cannot be enforced in law against the departments. The establishment of this office was a very cautious step. Parliament wished that the Commissioner should be an aid to MPs, and not to displace them. It was also anxious to ensure that the Commissioner did not have a political role.

Nevertheless, the example of the Parliamentary Commissioner has been followed, and a series of other Commissioners have been created. Bodies have also been created to give a remedy to the citizen who has suffered from the actions of more powerful bodies. The other Ombudsmen include the various Commissioners for Local Administration to inquire into complaints of maladministration in local government, with powers and procedures similar to those of the Parliamentary Commissioner,[12] and the Health Service Commissioner established in 1973.[13] A new Police Complaints Authority, whose members are not and have not been policemen, has been created,[14] and while in many cases the police will continue to investigate complaints against themselves, the new Authority will be responsible for supervising a range of serious complaints, and will also be involved in determining (in some cases) whether a report should be made to the Director of Public Prosecutions.

There has thus been a series of enactments designed to give a remedy to citizens who believe that their rights have been infringed. Despite this there is still concern about the adequacy of the protection of human rights in the United Kingdom. Most of the measures mentioned above are of an administrative character. They create bodies which stand between the aggrieved citizen and those who he or she claims to have caused injustice, and while they can act for the aggrieved person, their impact is limited because of their limited powers and the discretions built into their procedures.

Another major area of concern has been the possible abuse of discretionary powers. The development of government services has resulted in a considerable growth in discretionary powers given to central government, local government, and various statutory bodies. The traditional British approach to civil liberties cannot cope with this danger, and in the absence of specific legislation aimed at combatting discrimination (such as the Race Relations and Sex Discrimination legislation) there are only two other remedies. The first is the Ombudsman, and the other is the rapidly expanding field of judicial review of administrative action. This remedy enables judges to review administrative discretionary decisions in the light of general principles of reasonableness. This remedy (developed by the courts themselves, initially without any legislation) enables the judges to review the decisions of the administration in the light of the general principles of reasonableness (which are sometimes also referred to as rationality).

Until comparatively recently, there was little systematic consideration of human rights in the United Kingdom. Human rights had been protected, not through a coherent and comprehensive code of laws, but by the mores of society. Such protection continues to be effective in most cases, but not all. The litany of successful cases brought against the United Kingdom at Strasbourg shows that the traditional approach no longer affords sufficient protection.

NORTHERN IRELAND

These general observations on the constitution and legal protection of human rights in the United Kingdom apply equally to Northern Ireland. However, as Northern Ireland, along with the United Kingdom, had for many years a devolved Parliament and Government, its position differed. Devolution stemmed from the Government of Ireland Act 1920, which provided for Parliaments in both Southern and Northern Ireland. The Northern Ireland Parliament and Government operated until 1972. It was commonly referred to as Stormont, after the place where it met. It had extensive powers over most (but not all) internal matters but remained subject to the overriding powers of the Government and Parliament at Westminster.

The fact that the Stormont Parliament and Government operated in accordance with a written constitution (namely, the Act of the Westminster Parliament which created it[15]) was potentially significant for the protection of some aspects of human rights, for certain provisions in that Act were intended to prevent discrimination. The best known of these was Section 5, which prohibited legislation which discriminated (positively or negatively) on the grounds of religious belief. This section also protected the property of religious denominations and concluded with words of more general ambit ('or take any property without compensation'). There was also protection against discriminatory legislation affecting certain universities (University College, Dublin; Trinity College, Dublin; The Queen's University, Belfast).

In addition to these prohibitions on discriminatory legislation, Section 8 related to the discriminatory use of executive powers, and provided that in the exercise of 'any prerogative or other executive power of His Majesty'

> no preference, privilege, or advantage shall be given to, nor shall any disability or disadvantage be imposed on, any person on account of religious belief, except where the nature of the case in which the power is exercised itself involves the giving of such a preference, privilege, or advantage, or the imposing of such a disability or disadvantage.

This section did not extend to the exercise of local government powers, a limitation which was to prove significant, as most of the complaints of discriminatory treatment that were subsequently made by Catholics in Northern Ireland concerned the exercise of such powers, rather than actions by the Stormont Government.

As we have already noted, the 1920 Act was originally intended to apply to both Northern Ireland and to Southern Ireland. However, the Act failed to operate in the South which became a Dominion (as it was then called) in accordance with a treaty.[16] That treaty also contained a provision (Article 16) relating to discrimination, on the same lines as Section 5 of the 1920 Act. Article 16 was embodied in the Constitution of the Irish Free State, and can even be traced into the Constitution adopted in 1937.

The remarkable thing about these fundamental provisions in the Northern Ireland constitution which, so far as the Northern Ireland Parliament was concerned, were firmly entrenched, is that they gave rise to very little litigation. The general protection of property rights at the end of Section 5 gave rise to 9 cases in which the validity of legislation interfering with property rights was challenged.[17] However, in only one case was religious discrimination alleged, and that was an action brought by a Protestant challenging state aid for Catholic schools.[18] It was acknowledged in the Northern Ireland Parliament that one Act it had passed was unconstitutional,[19] and amending legislation was introduced.

The question may be asked why Catholics in Northern Ireland, who believed that they were discriminated against on religious grounds, did not take advantage of the broad constitutional guarantees contained in Sections 5 and 8 of the 1920 Act. There might have been problems with regard to lack of knowledge and lack of financial resources for litigation, which would certainly be prolonged. But there were those, including those who held strongly nationalist viewpoints, who were learned in the law and who might have been expected to challenge controversial actions. Boyle, Hadden, and Hillyard suggest that the failure reflected a lack of confidence in the legal system, yet as the authors point out, the actual performance of the Northern Ireland judges in 'civil rights' cases should have dispelled the fear of judicial bias.[20]

The failure may have been caused, as the authors also suggest, by an absence of laywers with fire in their bellies, or it may be that lawyers trained in the common law approach were slow to appreciate the potential which the constitutional guarantees represented. It may be significant that the constitutional guarantees in the 1937 Constitution of the Irish Republic did not give rise to a large volume of litigation until the late 1960s. It seems that it needed a new generation of lawyers familiar with a written Constitution and with entrenched guarantees before cases were brought in any number.

The guarantees in the 1920 Act were repealed in 1973 and were replaced by a number of provisions aimed at the prevention of religious and political discrimination.[21] This is another example of a significant difference in the legal protection of human rights in Northern Ireland and Great Britain: there is no specific legislation against religious or political discrimination in Great Britain.

The 1973 Act provides that any discriminatory legislation is void. This provision applies only to measures of the Northern Ireland Assembly, which is currently in abeyance, and to Orders in Council made under the Northern Ireland Act 1974 – the main form of legislation under direct rule – but not to other Westminster legislation. The 1973 Act also prohibits discrimination by public bodies.

The 1973 provisions are an advance on those of 1920 as they include discrimination on political grounds, but they omit the specific provisions in the 1920 Act relating to education and the property of religious and educational bodies. To date there has been only one case under the 1973 Act, where it was held that a district council discriminated against the Gaelic Athletic Association in refusing to lease facilities to them.[22] In contrast, there has recently been a stream of cases relating to the conduct of the campaign against the Anglo–Irish Agreement. These cases do not turn on the above constitutional provisions, they instead rely on the common law principle of rationality.

The 1973 Act also established the Standing Advisory Commission on Human Rights, which has the task of advising the Secretary of State for Northern Ireland on the adequacy and effectiveness of the law in force relating to discrimination, and informing him on the extent of discrimination by public bodies. Unlike the European Commission of Human Rights in Strasbourg, the Northern Ireland Commission does not investigate individual complaints: it conducts or commissions research as a basis for advising the Secretary of State. While we have been at work on this Report, studies by or for the Commission have dealt with such matters as emergency provisions arising from the Northern Ireland (Emergency Provisions) Act, electoral abuse, delays in criminal justice, composition of Crown Courts, supergrasses, police complaints procedure, strip searching, the UN Convention against torture, education about human rights in schools, and the question of incorporating the European Convention on Human Rights into domestic law. The Commission is at present conducting a major review of existing laws and institutions in securing freedom from discrimination and equality of opportunity.

Of the Commission's recommendations to the Secretary of State during the three years we have been at work on our Report, several coincide with our own independent studies. Among the others, the following seem to us to be of interest:

1. In preparing young people for life, schools should be encouraged and supported with appropriate resources to enable them to teach the fundamental values needed for young people to combat the prejudice there is in society
2. Steps are needed to heighten public awareness of the work of the Police Authority
3. There should be an independent review of the law on the use of fire-arms by the security forces
4. The justification for the present seven-day maximum period of arrest should be carefully examined

5. The British government should ratify the UN Convention against
   Torture without reservation or interpretative declaration which
   would detract from the force of the Convention.

In addition there have been a considerable number of legal and
administrative reforms affecting human rights introduced in Northern
Ireland since 1969. The Standing Advisory Commission's special
report lists fourteen of these, and concludes:

> These measures amount to a substantial body of legislation to
> meet grievances and protect human rights in Northern Ireland. As
> a body of law it is impressive and should not be underrated.

The Commission continued:

> But the blunt fact is that what might have succeeded at another
> time or in different circumstances has not been sufficient to change
> a situation where violence has become a way of life for some and a
> perpetual terror for others. As Lord MacDermott has pointed out:
> 'Most of the long-term damage, of the scarring and the misery, is
> due first and last to the terrorist.' The continuing state of
> emergency has not only seriously impaired the effectiveness of the
> substantial legislative and administrative reforms which have been
> made since 1969 for the better protection of human rights but has
> also inevitably resulted in the restriction of certain basic rights and
> freedom in Northern Ireland.[23]

Some of these measures had the effect of bringing Northern Ireland
into step with the rest of the United Kingdom without any significant
change, as in the case of the Parliamentary Commissioner (Ombudsman). In other cases, the models from Great Britain were followed
with slight modifications, as in the case of the Commissioner for
Complaints whose decisions can be enforced in the courts. Other
measures were entirely unique.

One of the latter measures is the Fair Employment Act 1976,
which extends the prohibitions on discrimination in employment
contained in the Constitution Act 1973 to cover the private sector.
Employers and others have a duty to afford equality of opportunity
in employment to persons of differing religious beliefs (including
those of no belief). Employers are invited to subscribe to a
declaration and be registered as equal opportunity employers.
Failure to register or removal from the register may affect the
prospect of obtaining government contracts and assistance. The Fair

Employment Act also creates the Fair Employment Agency, which has extensive investigative, quasi-judicial, conciliation, and enforcement functions, conducts research, monitors recruitment and promotion practices, undertakes education, and examines complaints. It promotes conscious and systematic affirmative action programmes to achieve equality in employment, but it does not advocate quotas or measures of reverse discrimination which simply transfer disadvantage from one community to another.

A person who believes that he or she is the victim of unlawful discrimination may make a complaint to the Agency, which must then investigate it. For this purpose the Agency is given the same powers of compelling witnesses to attend and requiring the production of papers as the High Court. If unlawful discrimination has occurred, the Agency may order employment, reinstatement, or compensation, and these orders are legally enforceable, appeal lying to the County Court.

Employment as a clergyman, as a teacher, and in a private household are specifically excluded from the Act, as is any other case where the essential nature of the employment requires a person of a particular religious belief or political opinion. There is also an exception for national and public security reasons, and a certificate from the Secretary of State that a person was excluded from employment for these reasons is conclusive evidence that the exclusion was for those reasons. Because no evidence is given for such exclusions, they have given rise to controversy on some occasions, and have led to one successful application to the European Commission of Human Rights, which in turn led to successful litigation in Northern Ireland. On the other hand, some believe that this power has not been used frequently enough, thus permitting the employment of persons who then 'set up' the killing of fellow-workers who are members of or have connections with the security forces.

Another measure unique to Northern Ireland was the introduction of proportional representation for local and regional elections, the single transferable vote being the particular type chosen. This was of considerable political significance, assisting political minorities within each community.

Whatever else may emerge from the above summary, one thing seems clear: the approach to the protection of human rights in the United Kingdom has not been systematic but piecemeal, reflecting the typically British empirical tradition. However understandable this may be, it does raise some questions. In particular, should there not within a single state be common legal provisions on fundamental aspects of the citizen's rights? Is there not something fundamentally wrong with a system where it is lawful to discriminate on grounds of race or colour in Northern Ireland, but not in the remainder of the United Kingdom; and where it is lawful to discriminate on grounds of religion and politics in Great Britain, but not lawful to do so in Northern Ireland?

What might be done? One obvious answer is to consider the incorporation of an international catalogue of human rights, such as the European Convention, into United Kingdom law, which we recommended in Chapter 2. But is it enough? Are the rights protected by the Convention co-extensive with what might be regarded as citizens' basic civil rights? Are not such matters as the electoral system and anti-discrimination laws part of what should be common throughout the state, and which are not now common to all the citizens of the United Kingdom? It can be argued that the absence of such commonalty has contributed to the troubles which now beset Northern Ireland.

THE REPUBLIC OF IRELAND*

The Republic of Ireland is distinctive among the jurisdictions of these islands in having a fully elaborated written Constitution containing clauses protecting fundamental rights and giving the judiciary explicit powers to declare legislative and executive acts invalid.

It has often been said that Irish constitutional law is the British constitution written down. The system of parliamentary democracy, cabinet government, and independence of the judiciary attest to the truth of that observation. But in other respects, the constitutional experience of the Republic of Ireland since independence has meant a radical departure from its British origins. This finds reflection in the rejection of British theory as to the source of political authority. The constitution of 1922, according to Irish legal theory, reflected a republican philosophy. The source of governmental power derives from the people; the state and its organs are institutions created by popular will and cannot claim any immunity or prerogative similar to the Crown in the United Kingdom. Sovereignty is not a characteristic

---

*We acknowledge with thanks the help of Kevin Boyle, one of our consultants, in drafting this section.

of parliament but of the people: the concept of parliamentary supremacy, the lynchpin of the British constitution, is foreign to the Irish constitutional system.

The 1937 Constitution, or *Bunreacht na hEireann* to give it its official title, added something new to this notion of popular sovereignty. Largely the work of Eamonn de Valera and his religious and lay advisors, this document attempted to unite republican principles with Roman Catholic social teaching. The Constitution, enacted bilingually with the Irish text having precedence, reflected also the Gaelic ideal.

The 1937 Constitution is firmly based on natural law and on a vision of moral order in which all institutions of positive law are subordinate to Divine authority. The Preamble invokes the Most Holy Trinity 'from whom is all authority and to whom . . . all actions both of men and States must be referred'. In adopting the Constitution, the people are said to acknowledge their obligations to 'Our Divine Lord Jesus Christ', and all powers of government are declared to derive 'under God from the people' (Article 6).

The Constitution, particularly in the clauses dealing with fundamental rights (Articles 40–43), emphasises the superiority of natural law. Thus in Article 41, the family is described as 'a moral institution' possessing 'inalienable and imprescriptible rights antecedent to and superior to all positive law'. Private ownership of property is described as a 'natural right' antecedent to positive law.

The significance of these provisions was trenchantly summarised by Mr Justice Walsh in 1974:

> [These Articles] emphatically reject the theory that there are no rights without laws, no rights contrary to the laws, and no rights anterior to the law. They indicate that justice is placed above the law and they acknowledge that natural rights, or human rights, are not created by law but that the Constitution confirms their existence and gives them protection. The individual has natural and human rights over which the State has no authority.

Justice Walsh went on to say that natural law is the law of God promulgated by reason and is the ultimate governor of all the laws of men:

> In view of the acknowledgement of Christianity in the Preamble and in view of the reference to God in Article 6 of the Constitution it must be accepted that the Constitution intended the natural human rights I have mentioned as being in the latter category

rather than simply an acknowledgement of the ethical content of law in its ideal of justice.[24]

In practice, these theological underpinnings of the Irish Constitution have been more background than central to the development of constitutional jurisprudence. There was a general belief that the courts over time could successfully harmonise the attitudes of the 1930s to meet different circumstances of the present day. To a considerable extent that has been achieved, but recent developments, including the rejection of any recognition of homosexual privacy[25] and the referenda in 1983 and 1986 on abortion and divorce, have led to some unease.

But the Constitution was in many respects a progressive document for its time. It not only proclaims protection of the classic personal rights, including personal liberty, freedom of expression, freedom of conscience, and the free practice of religion, but it provides recognition and protection for the family and for the educational rights of parents in language that anticipated the provisions of the Universal Declaration of Human Rights of 1948. In addition, Article 45 contains 'Directive Principles of Social Policy', which outline the economic and social goals of government, again anticipating the post-war recognition of economic and social rights.

The clauses dealing with fundamental rights did not take on immediate significance. It was not until the 1960s that the judiciary, led by the then Chief Justice Cearbhall O Dalaigh, seriously addressed their significance for government and people. The courts not only upheld the content of the Articles dealing explicitly with fundamental rights, but went beyond them in declaring that the Constitution guaranteed other rights that were implied by a general guarantee clause (Article 40). This reads:

> The State guarantees in its laws to respect and as far as practicable by its laws to defend and vindicate the personal rights of the citizen.

In a case in 1965, Mr Justice Kenny, while holding against a plaintiff challenging the compulsory fluoridation of the Dublin water supply, accepted that a right to bodily integrity was guaranteed by this clause.[26] In subsequent decisions, the courts have held in a wide variety of circumstances that legislation or administrative acts of government contravened human rights implied in Article 40.

Without cataloguing these rights exhaustively, it may be useful to list some of them:[27]

1. to maintain an action in the High Court
2. to free legal aid
3. to earn a livelihood
4. to work
5. to a passport
6. to freedom from torture and inhuman and degrading treatment
7. to privacy in marital relations.

Finally, it should be noted that the rights of the individual are to be found not only in the Articles of the Constitution dealing specifically with fundamental rights but are also contained explicitly or implicitly in other provisions. Thus Article 34 guarantees the right to trial by jury on a serious criminal charge, and the right to join a trade union in Article 40 has been held to include a right not to be compelled to join.[28]

The Constitution does not, however, directly recognise the presence of any distinct minority in Ireland, hence the absence of any explicit set of minority rights which it might be the function of a written constitution to provide. It would be a mistake, however, to assume that some of the internationally recognised minority rights are not protected to some extent. The Constitution is very explicit on the matter of individual freedoms (Articles 40, 41, 42, 44). Under the terms of these, members of minorities could seek legal protection should they feel that rights affecting their status were being violated – for example, the right to have their children educated according to particular beliefs and values, the right to freedom of religion, the right to freedom of expression, and so on.

A major criticism of the Constitution of the Irish Republic is that these civil rights are based on Roman Catholic social teaching of the 1930s and ignore the fact that the whole island of Ireland, to which the Constitution lays claim, contains a Protestant minority of approximately 25 per cent. Even viewed within the context of the 26 counties which form the Republic, with its Protestant minority of less than 5 per cent, this complaint is well based.

The contribution of the judiciary to the meaning of the Constitution since the 1960s has been to make government and administration conscious of constitutional principles, and in particular the need to respect the rights of the citizen. The Irish experience undoubtedly demonstrates the positive values of a Bill of Rights. In a sense unknown in the United Kingdom, the Irish political system functions within a set of constitutional checks and balances that has given stability and continuity to the state during periods of intense internal and external conflict and change.

But the judicial activism in the courts, and rapid social and economic change, have also highlighted problems in the constitutional document itself. Despite the signal contribution of the judges in adapting its provisions to changed circumstances and new challenges, the evidence is clear that constitutional review is needed.

It is perhaps significant that the fiftieth anniversary of the Constitution's adoption is not being specially marked. The continuing Northern Ireland conflict and recent bitter constitutional referenda over divorce and abortion have made the fundamental law a document that provokes controversy rather than consensus. In a nutshell, the problem is one of harmonising a document imbued with Catholic social and religious thinking of the 1930s with the pluralistic expectations of the international code of human rights and at least a section of the modern Irish electorate.

The tension generated by the clash of traditional and new thinking in the country is likely to find a focus in the immediate future in the gradual impact of external influences deriving from the state's involvement outside its frontiers.

The Northern Ireland crisis has had a profound impact on the Republic, which found its most important expression in the Report of the New Ireland Forum in 1984. The all-party agreement in that Report on the acceptance of consent as the only moral basis for a united Ireland also implied that a united Ireland would need a new constitution devoid of confessionalism. Such a position bears on the adequacy of the present Constitution, and in particular its approach to the protection of minorities. The author of the 1937 Constitution, Eamonn de Valera, believed that it would serve as fundamental law that one day could unite all Irishmen. There is no one who would seriously maintain that position today, although there is a significant (and perhaps majority) opinion that would place attachment to the existing Constitution and its Catholic ethos before the goal of a united Ireland.

The part of the Constitution which outrages Northern unionists is the definition of the national territory as consisting of 'the whole' island of Ireland. Article 2 of the Constitution states that the national territory consists of the whole island of Ireland, its islands, and the territorial seas. Defenders of the text might say that the national territory is the territory of all Irish people, North and South.

The next Article of the Constitution (Article 3) may make sense to constitutional lawyers, but the man or woman in the UK street cannot be blamed for failing to understand it. To simplify, it limits the effect of legislation to the 26 counties of the Republic, 'Pending the reintegration of the national territory'. A committee was set up in 1966 to review the Constitution of the Republic. No change was suggested in Article 2, but a new version of Article 3 was suggested as follows:[29]

1. The Irish nation hereby proclaims its firm will that its territory be re-united in harmony and brotherly affection between all Irishmen.
2. The laws enacted by the Parliament established by this Constitution shall, until the achievement of the nation's unity shall otherwise require, have the like area and extent of application as the laws of the Parliament which existed prior to the adoption of this Constitution. Provision may be made by law to give extra-territorial effect to such laws.

In 1981, Garret FitzGerald launched what he called a constitutional crusade so as to produce a revised document 'such as might have emerged in an independent all-Irish State containing a twenty-five-per-cent Protestant minority'.[30] But neither in opposition nor in government was FitzGerald able to proceed very far down this track, partly because of the pressures of other problems, and partly because a constitutional amendment is not effective unless passed by both houses of parliament and approved by a majority of votes in a referendum (Articles 46 and 47(1)).

At Sunningdale (1973), the Republic of Ireland had solemnly accepted the fact that there could be no change in the status of Northern Ireland until a majority of the people of Northern Ireland desired a change in that status, and in Article 1 of the Anglo–Irish Agreement (1985), the Republic entered into a formal commitment to recognise the present status of Northern Ireland so long as this is the wish of a majority of the people there.

In an ideal world, the United Kingdom and the Republic would negotiate an agreed formula which could replace both Articles 2 and 3 of the Constitution in the Republic and the Northern Ireland Constitution Act at Westminster. That is the course recommended by Tom Hadden and Kevin Boyle.[31] This would not, of itself, resolve the question of Northern Ireland's future, but it would eliminate a Unionist grievance and remove one uncertainty about future procedures.

The Republic of Ireland, along with the United Kingdom, joined the European Community in 1973 and received a further source of fundamental law in the form of the European Community treaties. In addition, the Republic has been a party to the European Convention on Human Rights, having accepted indefinitely the right of individual petition and the compulsory jurisdiction of the European Court of Human Rights. The European Convention, however, as is the case for the United Kingdom, is not part of internal law and may not be directly pleaded in the courts. If anything, the Irish judiciary, with few exceptions, have been less prepared to take note of the Convention and its implications for the protection of human rights than their British counterparts. The status of the Convention, as a source for the interpretation of fundamental rights clauses in the Constitution or of the terms of ordinary legislation, remains unresolved by the Irish courts, a gap which is increasingly anomalous.

A further anomaly at the international level is the fact that the Republic of Ireland has yet to ratify the major UN treaties on human rights. The Convention against racial discrimination and the two UN Covenants have been signed by the government, but a decade has been allowed to pass without final ratification. Successive governments have failed to give any substantive reasons for this failure, and indeed have claimed that ratification was imminent. It is hard to avoid the conclusion that the problem lies in potential conflict between the international standards on human rights and those upheld in Irish law. Something of this concern has emerged recently in the debate over the referendum required in Ireland as a result of the successful constitutional challenge to the Single European Act, the proposed amendment of the European Community treaties. Along with fears that closer European union may jeopardise Ireland's traditional military neutrality, opponents of the Single European Act have claimed that it may mean that Ireland will be required to permit divorce and abortion. One professor of law has urged renegotiation of the measure before the Republic accepts it, so as to allow recognition of 'Ireland's different attitude to some fundamental human rights'.[32]

However, it should be said that this opinion was regarded as a minority view during the referendum campaign and was not taken seriously by mainstream political or legal thinking in the Republic. (Indeed, the earlier Supreme Court judgment on the Single European Act had explicitly rejected the claim.)

The extent of this 'different attitude' to human rights is reflected in the referendum decision of June 1986, when the population voted to reject an amendment permitting divorce in certain circumstances. In the earlier vote on abortion, a constitutional statement positively recognising the right to life of the unborn was adopted in an initiative intended to preclude absolutely abortion in any circumstances. The European Court of Human Rights has found that the divorce prohibition does not violate the European Convention, although it did find that the Republic of Ireland's illegitimacy laws were in violation of the non-discrimination clause of the Convention.[33] The issue of the abortion clause may also be ultimately referred to Strasbourg. A recent decision of the High Court, based on the new constitutional amendment on abortion, has declared counselling, advice, and information given by women's centres in Dublin on the availability of lawful abortions in the United Kingdom to be unlawful.[34] This decision is under appeal to the Supreme Court. The European Commission of Human Rights has already held that any prohibition on abortion which did not clearly provide for the primacy of the mother's right to life in any conflict with that of the foetus is incompatible with the Convention.[35]

The existence of a remedy, even a constitutional remedy in court, is often academic from the point of view of the ordinary citizen, not least because of expense or the relatively minor nature of complaint. As in other countries, the Republic of Ireland has felt the need to supplement court-based remedies with additional provision for the protection of rights. An Ombudsman institution, largely modelled on the British one, was established in 1980, but the first holder of this post did not take office until 1984. His role is to investigate complaints about administrative decisions, delays, and inaction of government departments, local government authorities, and the telecommunications and postal services.

A new system of dealing with complaints against the police was legislated in 1986.[36] Although the Republic has not had the scale of complaint and controversy over police actions that Northern Ireland has experienced, the 1970s in particular saw periods of serious concern over the treatment of arrested persons and led to the demand for some mode of independent supervision of complaints against the *Garda Síochána*. The 1968 Act provides for a Complaints Board independent of the *Garda*, but with representation of the *Garda* Commissioner, and this will be operational in 1987. It has supervisory powers over complaints which, however, will continue to be investigated by the police; but in certain cases it may itself also investigate complaints. The central role in the new machinery will be played by a Chief Executive Officer appointed under the Act, who has to be notified of all complaints and may intervene in investigations. The Complaints Board will also have jurisdiction to institute and adjudicate on disciplinary infractions by the police. The machinery is linked with new and detailed regulations governing the treatment of arrested persons in custody. These changes represent a major strengthening of protections available to arrested persons in the Republic.

The Employment Equality Agency has been in existence since 1972, and was established under the Employment Equality Act of that year, with similar functions to the Equal Opportunities Commission in Northern Ireland. The Agency carries out an active investigatory and educational role. The Agency reports that

> Women form a large part of the part-time workforce which is traditionally likely to suffer lay-offs and low pay ... It is only through measures of positive action in schools, training agencies and the workplace itself that we can hope to see visible change from a sex-segregated and sex-imbalanced distribution of paid and unpaid work.[37]

The Role of the Employment Equality Agency is to promote equality of opportunity between men and women, and the elimination of discrimination in the work-place. The agency has formal powers to investigate alleged discriminatory practices and to take court proceedings in the case of discriminatory advertising and discriminatory work practices. In an important step in 1985, the Republic ratified the UN Convention on Discrimination against Women.

While the Republic has established machinery to combat sex discrimination, it remains of concern that protection against racial discrimination is non-existent, and it is known that British-based political groups have operated from addresses in Dublin to produce and disseminate racist literature within the United Kingdom. Moreover, concern has recently been expressed about evidence of racial discrimination against members of the Republic's small non-white community, and demands have been made for the introduction of legislation to counter any development of racial discrimination. The absence of such legislation has been one reason why the Republic has not yet ratified a number of international treaties such as the Convention on the Elimination of all Forms of Racial

Discrimination. We have heard that legislation in this field is planned by the government, but with what priority is unknown.

Explicit religious discrimination is not a major problem in the Republic of Ireland. Unionists would say that this is because those Protestants who were most vulnerable to discrimination have left the country, so that the Protestants who remain are from privileged sectors of society. Leaving aside disagreements over questions such as divorce, the minority Churches have frequently expressed their satisfaction with the practical enjoyment of full religious and educational freedom. On the other hand, the rights of non-believers are hardly guaranteed. Since education at the first and second levels is effectively controlled by the Catholic and Protestant Churches, a non-Christian has a slim chance of obtaining appointment as a teacher in these schools. The Rules for National Schools (1965, as amended) permit a board of management 'with the approval of the appropriate Ecclesiastical or other Religious Authority' to refuse 'on the ground of faith and morals to appoint a particular teacher from an approved panel to a . . . vacancy for which he is eligible'. The need to respect theistic belief other than Christian, and agnostic and atheistic beliefs, is a debate that has hardly begun in the Republic of Ireland.

The Constitution of the Irish Republic demonstrates the value of a bill of rights, but we believe that a major constitutional and legislative review is now needed in the Republic. Unbelievers and adherents of non-Christian faiths undoubtedly suffer disabilities, and members of minority Churches are not always able to follow their own informed consciences in matters of family law; yet public debate on some aspects of this has barely started. The basic problem is how to harmonise the social teaching of the Catholic Church which is enshrined in the 1937 Constitution with the more pluralistic concepts at the heart of the modern code of human rights. We welcome reports that race discrimination is to be outlawed, so that the Republic will be in a position to ratify the UN Convention against racial discrimination. As UN organs are now giving major attention to measures to implement the Declaration against intolerance and discrimination on grounds of religion or belief (see our Appendix 3), it would make sense for the Republic to outlaw religious discrimination at the same time as making racial discrimination illegal.

People in both the United Kingdom and the Irish Republic may have something to learn from the US experience, where public commissions exercise considerable powers of intervention so as to require employers to redress any imbalances in their work-force.

What are called 'class actions' can be taken to eliminate unlawful practices which affect whole groups such as ethnic minorities. Not all United States practice would be acceptable or appropriate in these islands, but greater public determination is needed if discrimination is to be eliminated.

In the 'Little Red Schoolbook' case (*Handyside* v. *UK*), the European Court of Human Rights defined the European vision of a democratic society, founded on respect for human rights, as having the hallmarks of 'pluralism, tolerance and broadmindedness'. These standards require further development and acceptance in Ireland, North and South, and in the social and educational process, to institutionalise them further. In the Irish Republic, ratification of UN instruments on human rights and the incorporation of the European Convention on Human Rights into domestic law will have a major role.

Notes and References

1. *The Legal Systems, North and South* (Dublin: Stationery Office, 1983).
2. *The Legal Systems, North and South* p. 47.
3. See *MacCormick* v. *Lord Advocate* (1953) s.c. 396.
4. *Ex parte Canon Selwyn* (1872) 36 J. P. 54, on the disestablishment of the Church of Ireland; and *ex parte Molyneaux* (1985) unreported, on the Anglo–Irish Agreement.
5. Such as the Prevention of Terrorism (Temporary Provisions) Act 1984.
6. *Malone* v. *Metropolitan Police Commissioner* (1979) Ch. 344.
7. Interception of Communications Act 1985.
8. See *Cheall* v. *Association of Professional, Executive, Clerical and Computer Staff* (1983) Q.B. 126, Lord Denning dissenting, on freedom of association; and *Home Office* v. *Harman* (1983) A.C. 280, Lords Scarman and Simon dissenting, on freedom of communication.
9. *Pvx Granite* v. *Ministry of Housing and Local Government* (1960) A.C. 260.
10. *Central Control Board* v. *Canon Brewery* (1919) A.C. 744.
11. Parliamentary Commissioner Act 1967.
12. Local Government Act 1974.
13. National Health Services Reorganisation Act 1973.
14. Police and Criminal Evidence Act 1984.
15. Government of Ireland Act 1920.
16. Embodied in the Irish Free State (Agreement) Act 1922.

17. Education Act (Northern Ireland) 1930.
18. *Londonderry C.C.* v. *McGlade* (1929) 47, an action brought by a Protestant challenging state aid for Roman Catholic schools.
19. Education Act (Northern Ireland) 1930.
20. Kevin Boyle, Tom Hadden, and Paddy Hillyard, *Law and State* (London: Martin Robertson, 1975) pp. 11–13.
21. Northern Ireland Constitution Act 1973, Part III.
22. *Purvis* v. *Magherfelt D.C.* (1982) N.I. 20.
23. *Report of the Committee to consider, in the context of civil liberties and human rights, measures to deal with terrorism in Northern Ireland* (London: HMSO, 1975) (Cmnd 5847, Gardiner) p. 57.
24. *McGee* v. *Attorney General* (1974) I.R. 284, 310.
25. *Norris* v. *Attorney General* (1984) I.R. 36.
26. *Ryan* v. *A.G.* (1965) I.R. 294, 313.
27. The case law is extensively discussed in the leading textbook on Irish constitutional law, J. M. Kelly, *The Irish Constitution*, 2nd edn (Dublin: Purist Publishing Co., 1984).
28. *Educational Company of Ireland Ltd.* v. *Fitzpatrick and Others* (*No. 2*) (1961) I.R. 345.
29. *Report of the Committee on the Constitution* (Dublin: Stationery Office, 1967) (Pr 9817), para. 12.
30. *Irish Identities* (London: BBC, 1982) p. 15.
31. *Ireland: a positive proposal* (Harmondsworth: Penguin, 1985) pp. 44–52, 98; see also 'Hopes and Fears for Hillsborough', paper presented to the British Irish Association Conference, (1986) pp. 8–9.
32. *Irish Times*, 23 April 1987: 'McAleese says SEA would let EEC impose abortion'.
33. *Johnson and Others* v. *Ireland*, judgement delivered on 18 December 1986.
34. *The Attorney General at the relation of SPUC* v. *Dublin Well Woman Centre Ltd and Open Line Counselling Ltd*, High Court decision, unreported, 19 December 1986.
35. *Application No. 8416/78, Paton* v. *United Kingdom*, decision of the European Commission of Human Rights, 13 May 1980:

    The 'life' of the foetus is intimately connected with, and cannot be regarded in isolation from, the life of the pregnant woman. If Article 2 were held to cover the foetus and its protection under this Article were, in the absence of any express limitation, seen as absolute, an abortion would have to be considered as prohibited even where the continuance of the pregnancy would involve a serious risk to the life of the pregnant mother. The Commission finds that such an interpretation would be contrary to the object and purpose of the Convention (*paras* 19, 20).

36. The Garda Siochána (Complaints) Act 1986.
37. *Annual Report of the Employment Equality Agency for 1984* (Dublin, 36 Mount Street, 1984) p. 6.

6 The Protection of Minority Rights[*]

The concept of 'responsibility' has several quite different meanings in religious and philosophical discourse. Responsibility as response to God and to that of God in other people is crucial in the writings of some Jewish and Christian theologians (Martin Buber, Dietrich Bonhoeffer, Richard Niebuhr, and Joseph Fletcher, for example).

Responsibility in the phrase 'the responsible society' (derived from Max Weber) was popular in ecumenical circles in the first two decades after the Second World War, but its meaning was sometimes fuzzy.

Human responsibility, in the context of this Report, has both moral and legal connotations. Its primary meaning is respect for the civil and human rights and fundamental freedoms of others, of which a crucial element is to refrain from all acts of discrimination on grounds of race, religion, gender, national origin, and the like. The responsible citizen not only respects the rights of others in personal life: the responsible citizen stands for the active promotion of such respect. Human responsibility in some societies may mean resistance to demands – whether from governmental authorities or from individuals – which are incompatible with international human rights law – or, in time of armed conflict, with international humanitarian law.

Refusal to discriminate is essential in our increasingly plural world, with different ethnic groups and religious traditions existing side by side. Most of us find little difficulty in tolerating neighbours whose private beliefs differ from our own, but private beliefs are sometimes manifested in overt actions, such as the methods of religious slaughter of livestock to which we refer in Chapter 3. We see no general principle which will enable society to resolve issues of this sort. We would, however, stress that tolerance is not weakness. To co-exist harmoniously with those whose beliefs are fundamentally different from our own is one aspect of human responsibility and in no way endangers our own beliefs: the effect, indeed, may be to strengthen them.

*We are grateful for the help of Anthony Lester, QC, one of our consultants, in preparing this chapter.

Great Britain, Northern Ireland, and the Republic of Ireland are each administered under a different constitutional system, and in each the phrase 'minority rights' has a different connotation. Scotland and Wales, forming part of Great Britain, contain large indigenous minorities whose cultures have experienced considerable erosion as a result of the process over several centuries of assimilating their peoples into the dominant Anglo-Saxon mould. Celtic culture in Ireland suffered a similar fate, but this was to be overlaid by the religious prejudice which still vitiates community relations in Northern Ireland today.

Successive legislative measures from the late eighteenth century gradually dismantled many of the legal expressions of this cultural erosion. By the early twentieth century most, but not all, civil disabilities affecting these minorities had been repealed – though assertion of their cultural rights, in particular for language, still gives rise to a sense of grievance in some sections of the Celtic communities.

In England (and to a lesser extent in Scotland and Wales) there have been other identifiable minorities such as the Jews, and these have suffered from racial or religious prejudice and discrimination. In the absence of a written constitution and bill of rights in Great Britain, these minorities have not had any formal legal protection until recent times, other than that available to any citizen in the United Kingdom.

Growing concern for minorities in Great Britain followed the massive immigration from the Caribbean and the Indian sub-continent after the Second World War. A series of Acts was passed between 1965 and 1976 which made certain forms of racial discrimination unlawful, and which set up agencies to assist in the enforcement of the law and to promote better community relations. The question has been raised at the United Nations, however, as to why British legislation to bar race discrimination has not been extended to Northern Ireland, and the UK representative could only say, rather feebly, that he would transmit to his Government the concern on this matter at the United Nations.[1] We shall return to this issue below.

At the same time, there has been a growing recognition of the disadvantages suffered by women in British and Irish society, and parallel but not identical legislation was introduced in Great Britain, Northern Ireland, and the Republic of Ireland during the 1970s.

CULTURAL IDENTITY

Cultural imperialism may be deliberate or it may be unintentional. Many majority–minority conflicts the world over are exacerbated by attempts on the part of a majority to stifle the cultural identity of a minority. Such attempts may include measures against a minority's language, its religion, or other features of its traditions and culture.

Promotion of a community's culture can be used as a weapon in a political dispute, or it can be a genuine search for distinctive roots and identity. If the nationalist minority promotes Gaelic culture in Northern Ireland merely to wrong-foot the unionist majority, it is not surprising that the unionists should react with hostility. On the other hand, any minority is entitled to ask others to respect its own culture and traditions.

While English is the first language of most people in Northern Ireland, the Irish language, or Gaelic, holds a special place in the cultural life of the nationalist community. It is taught in Catholic schools and promoted by cultural groups. The result has been that Gaelic has become a symbol of Irish nationalism. The BBC has now begun to transmit Irish-language programmes on radio and television, but using Irish to conduct official business is still effectively denied.

Until the late 1950s, little mention was made of Gaelic games on radio or TV programmes, despite their large following within the nationalist community. We are glad to record that there have been considerable changes in recent years, reflecting a recognition of the need to serve all tradiions. Further evidence of this more positive attitude is to be found in the unionist document, *The Way Forward*, which argues for the need to respect and support the legitimate cultural traditions of all sections of society in Northern Ireland.[2]

The Anglo–Irish Ministerial Conference has indicated that the position of Gaelic culture in Northern Ireland is being reviewed as a matter of urgency.

In the Republic of Ireland, controversy over cultural rights of the kind experienced in Northern Ireland has not arisen on any considerable scale. The small size of the Protestant community in the state (now about 4 per cent), the limited cohesion among its scattered population except on a number of very specific matters like education, and its general acceptance of the political *régime* go far towards explaining the absence of conflict. Some Protestant educationists objected in the early decades of the state to the pace of efforts to increase the use of the Irish language within the school system, because Protestant schools by and large had not included Irish in their curricula before the establishment of the state. The effects of this policy, it was alleged, were making Protestants feel unwelcome. After 1922, it became compulsory to include Irish in school curricula, and most Protestant schools complied. A number, however, considered that the speed with which the new *régime* was promoting the Irish language was putting Protestant students at an educational disadvantage. Such views were not, however, confined to Protestant educationists. Successive governments were criticised by people from different sections of Irish society because of the stress laid on the Irish language. Today there are no exclusively Catholic or Protestant views on such cultural matters. Some features of the Gaelic revival in the early decades of the Irish Free State contained strident anti-British sentiments, implying that Ireland should turn away from cultural links with its neighbour, but this has to a large extent disappeared.

Events in Northern Ireland do occasionally affect community relationships in the Republic, especially in the border counties where the largest concentrations of Protestants are to be found. An example of this is the fact that at the beginning of the troubles in the North the Orange Order in County Donegal felt it necessary to cancel its annual parade at Rossnowlagh for fear of counter-demonstrations.

In Great Britain, the Celtic minorities in Scotland and Wales had to struggle long and hard to obtain formal recognition of their languages. Not until 1967 did the Welsh Language Act provide recognition and protection for Welsh-speakers. There is no similar legislation in either Scotland or Northern Ireland for Scots-, Gaelic-, or Irish-speakers.

Recognition and respect for the cultures of Great Britain's recent ethnic minorities is developing only slowly and unevenly.

THE FAMILY

It sometimes happens, the human heart being unpredictable, that persons of different religious traditions or ethnic origins fall in love and wish to marry and have children. Some religious faiths have a complete ban on marriage with persons of other Churches or other faiths. In the nineteenth century, for example, Quakers were disowned for 'marrying out', as it was then called. In the Jewish community, children of a Jewish mother are regarded as Jews unless they expressly change their religion, even if the father is Gentile.

While we were at work on our report, a Muslim man and a Sikh woman in London fell in love and then committed suicide because both sets of parents disapproved of marriage to a person of another faith.

In considering matters related to family life, a distinction needs to be made between those moral issues which are matters for the guidance of the religious community and personal conscience, and those issues affecting the common good of society which are properly subject to constitutional or statute law. We regret the erosion of traditional Christian teaching on the sanctity and monogamous nature of marriage ties; at the same time, law and social services have to deal with the consequences of marital breakdown and illegitimacy.

Sometimes the law has to compromise with the moral sense of the community. British law makes no provision for contracting polygamous marriages within the national territory, but it recognises the validity of polygamous marriages contracted elsewhere for such purposes as divorce, judicial separation, and alimony.[3]

The constitution of the Irish Republic provides protection for the family (Article 41), and also contains a prohibition of any law 'providing for the dissolution of marriage' (Article 41.3.2). This latter provision denies a right to remarry to those whose first marriage has irretrievably broken down.

This is an exceedingly complex issue. What is the responsibility of the state if the majority of citizens are adherents of a religion which takes the line that certain rules are needed for the common good and should be universally binding, even on adherents of other religious traditions and on persons having no religious beliefs at all? The Constitution and laws of the Irish Republic in regard to the family reflect the teaching of the Roman Catholic Church, to which the great majority of its citizens belong, so that certain practices which are legal in the United Kingdom, such as procedures for dissolution of marriage and divorce, are contrary to Constitution and law in the Irish Republic. The Irish Catholic bishops believe that legislators have to take seriously the teachings of the Catholic Church in this regard, but that they should keep four other considerations in mind. First, the conviction of non-Catholics. Secondly, maximum freedom for citizens, consistent with the rights of others and the common good. Thirdly, the creation of a body of laws which favours reconciliation between citizens and communities. Fourthly, the good of society as a whole.[4]

Applying these considerations to the issue of divorce, the Irish Catholic bishops believe that the moral issues raised by breakdown of marriages affect the whole of society. They argue that the legalisation of divorce inevitably leads to an increase of marital breakdown:

A divorce mentality spreads through the community. Divorce becomes socially acceptable, even fashionable.

In such a society, spouses have no incentive to overcome marital difficulties. The bishops teach as a matter of faith and morals that valid marriages of Catholics should in no circumstances be dissolved, but they go further: divorce is contrary to the common good and should not be tolerated by the state either.[5]

The Catholic bishops thus have a two-fold attitude to divorce – and, indeed, to similar moral questions. To the Catholic faithful, their pastoral guidance is based on natural law; but when they address the wider community, they proclaim what they believe serves the common good of the whole of society. A person who does not belong to the Catholic Church might well maintain that one of the considerations stressed by the bishops is the need for reconciliation between persons and communities, so that any action which might be divisive and hinder reconciliation should be avoided. It would follow that the secular authorities should hesitate before imposing the consensus of the majority on minorities. The minority in the Republic of Ireland might argue that the Roman Catholic Church is fully entitled to give authoritative guidance to its own members on matters of faith and morals, but that members of other Churches, and indeed members of the Catholic Church also (or, indeed, of no Church) should be free to follow their own informed consciences, that the laws of the Republic should not be allowed to constitute what we have called in Chapter 3 'the tyranny of the majority' or to interfere with the basic human right to privacy in home and family. During the recent referendum campaign in the Republic, which we discuss below, a number of priests who spoke in favour of the amendment on divorce were forbidden to speak further on the matter.

While divorce is not included as an express right in any of the human rights instruments, it is widely available in the world today as a means of regularising marital breakdown and the remarriage of previously married spouses. Pressure for the legalising of divorce increased in the Republic throughout the late 1970s and early 1980s.

In 1986, the Government decided to hold a referendum to amend the Constitution in order to allow the introduction of divorce legislation. The Protestant Churches were consulted by the Government prior to the referendum, and all declared themselves to be in favour of a change so as to allow divorce legislation. Social workers and family lawyers were not consulted at that time, however. The Catholic Church alone remained resolute in its opposition to any change. The result of the referendum was decisively against an amendment to the Constitution.

So the Republic's prohibition on the dissolution of marriage remains, though complex and unanswered problems persist, not least because of the wide gap which has emerged between Catholic and state law on nullity. Ironically, the situation now is one in which the position of the Catholic Church on nullity pleas is much more liberal than that permitted by the state. The result is that many couples have had their marriages annulled by the Church and are thereby free in the eyes of the Church to enter second unions which are regarded as bigamous in the eyes of the state. By not invoking its law against the partners of such unions, the state seems to be accepting the less rigorous position of the Catholic Church, while maintaining on paper only the unconditional ban in the Constitution.

It is not surprising that the constitutional and legal position in the Republic should have become such a sensitive indicator of attitudes towards minority rights, particularly for Protestants in Northern Ireland. Many Northern Protestants regarded the divorce referendum as a test of the Republic's capacity to accommodate a plurality of views on marriage and other moral issues, a test which they judge the Republic has failed.

One grievance of the Protestant community in Ireland has been the insistence of the Catholic Church that the children of mixed marriages be brought up as Catholics. Before 1900, it was the practice in some parts of Ireland that sons were brought up in the Church of their fathers and daughters in the Church of their mothers. This ended with the Catholic *Ne temere* Decree of 1908 which required that both parties of a mixed marriage should give a written undertaking that their children would be brought up as members of the Roman Catholic Church: this became part of the 1918 Code of Canon Law. Although this provision seems not to have been applied uniformly, it caused much unhappiness and conflict. Many Protestants regarded the Catholic requirement as in part responsible for the decline of the Protestant population in the Republic of Ireland and, moreover, as evidence of an unwillingness of the Catholic Church to treat other Christian communities with the respect due to 'separated brethren', as Pope John XXIII called them.

Following the Second Vatican Council, the 1918 legislation concerning mixed marriages was replaced by a document issued by Pope Paul VI entitled *Matrimonia Mixta*: this new legislation was later incorporated into the 1983 Code of Canon Law, replacing the 1918 Code. According to this legislation, only the Catholic party was now obliged to give an undertaking to do all in his or her power to have the children brought up as Catholics. Although no undertaking was required of the non-Catholic partner, it was nevertheless required that the non-Catholic be fully informed of the promise made by the Catholic. Catholics were still required to marry in a Catholic church, but if serious difficulties stood in the way of this in mixed marriages, the Bishop now had the power to grant a dispensation to enable the marriage to take place in the church of the non-Catholic spouse. It was for the local Bishops' Conference to determine norms according to which such dispensations would be granted uniformly throughout all the local dioceses. In Ireland, the practice is now increasingly that the marriage takes place in the church of the bride.

Some variations in practice did arise among the dioceses in Ireland. In 1983, the Irish Bishops issued new directives and guidelines (*Directory on Mixed Marriages*). This Directory incorporated the Church's legislation as contained in the 1983 Code of Canon Law, and included as well some local norms for Ireland. For example, in future the Catholic party could give the required promise orally rather than in writing. The Bishops stressed that the religious upbringing of the children was the joint responsibility of both parents: 'the obligations of the Catholic party do not, and cannot, cancel out, or in any way call into question, the conscientious duties of the other party' (p. 19). The Bishops went on to remark: 'It is precisely because of this basic principle that each party, before deciding to marry, must be satisfied that he or she is not entering a situation in which the parties' obligations in conscience cannot be reconciled' (p. 19). The stress in practice has been that the religious upbringing of children is seen as a joint decision to be taken in the practical circumstances of the marriage, where it is understood that the non-Catholic partner may also have obligations to his or her Church.

The Bishops laid great stress on the need for joint pastoral care of a couple entering a mixed marriage, to be undertaken as far as possible in consultation and co-operation with the minister of the other religious denomination. This, they said, was especially important in the case of a genuinely 'inter-Church' couple, that is, where each partner was deeply committed to his or her own Church (p. 9).

While we have heard of instances of the new guidelines not being followed, the Catholic Bishops affirmed to the New Ireland Forum their commitment to them.

The development of joint pastoral care for intending spouses has lessened the tension which this issue had previously caused. In the Dublin area, for example, a pre-marriage course is sponsored by the four main Churches, organised by the Association of Interchurch Families. The Churches urge inter-Church couples to attend these courses, and they provide the personnel to lead the sessions. This has led to the conviction on the part of the Churches and the couples themselves that an inter-Church marriage is not a second best.

Problems of inter-Church marriages in Ireland are not confined to those between Catholics and Protestants: they can also arise in marriages between members of different Protestant Churches. The problem is usually dealt with nowadays by the new family adopting the husband's Church affiliation.

EDUCATION

The available resources for education in our two states are never enough; but within that inevitable constraint, education should be provided for all without discrimination on grounds of race, sex, religion, political opinion, and the like. This is not only a human right: it is essential for the development of a full sense of human responsibility.

We have to admit to some indecision about human rights and responsibilities in matters of education, and so we start this section of our Report with three principles, which we derive from the international code of human rights:

1. Subject to the maintenance of minimum educational standards, religious communities or other groups should be free to establish and maintain, at their own expense, schools in which children are educated in accordance with their own beliefs, and parents should be free to send their children to such schools
2. The state is free to contribute financially to the maintenance of such schools, but it is under no obligation to do so

3. The state should ensure that neither its own schools, nor those established by religious communities or other groups, will promote or sustain divisiveness: indeed, it has an obligation to ensure that all schools, and not only its own, will be so established and run as to promote understanding, tolerance, and friendship among different groups, including religious ones.

It seems to follow that, if there were cogent evidence that schools maintained by religious communities or other groups in any part of the two states promoted or sustained divisiveness, the government concerned would come under a positive obligation to bring this state of affairs to an end.

When we turn from principles to facts, we find a paradoxical situation. The Churches were often first in the field both with good academic education and, in some cases, with educational experiments. We would not want to recommend anything which interfered with good education or with educational experimentation, or with the freedom of parents or guardians to choose a particular kind of school for their children. On the other hand, a fragmented educational system can undoubtedly contribute to the fragmentation of society. In some of the multi-ethnic areas of Great Britain, and perhaps elsewhere in these islands, there are demands for special 'black' schools, and also for single-sex schools for Muslim girls. On what basis could we defend the right of Christian Churches to establish their own schools but deny that right to other groups? The tolerance and mutual understanding which we expect others to manifest towards us requires that we should respect the integrity of the beliefs, cultures, and traditions of other communities. Those communities may well claim that they cannot maintain their identities without their own schools.

Moreover, a new factor has recently entered the situation in Northern Ireland, the establishment of half a dozen integrated interdenominational schools, usually established on parental initiative, and pioneered by Lagan College in Belfast. We think that this is a welcome rejection of the narrow sectarianism which formerly disfigured some schools in the other two systems, and sometimes still does. We welcome integrated schooling in Northern Ireland for those who want it. Before this development, there were in Northern Ireland two main sets of schools, those established by the Catholic Church principally for their own members, and state and non-Catholic voluntary schools attended largely by Protestants. The latter are Christian to the extent required by the Education Acts, but are non-denominational. The existence of two types of school was part of the segregation of the two communities, which extended also to other aspects of life such as residence and employment. While the majority in both communities seem to be satisfied with this dual system of education, we believe that the progressive lessening of segregation in education, as well as in housing and jobs, will in time make for more harmonious relationships between the two traditions. It is for this reason that we welcome these integrated schools *for those who wish this form of education* for their children. We think it likely that the demand for such schools will increase. It hardly needs saying that integrated schools should be required to reach a general standard not lower than that set for other schools by the statutory authorities. Admission of pupils should be non-discriminatory, possibly subject to the requirement that the proportion of children from either community should not be allowed to fall below a prescribed figure (say, 30 per cent). Selection of staff, decisions about the curriculum, and the style of teaching should be handled in such a way as to foster respect for all human beings irrespective of religious belief, ethnic origin, or gender.

We greatly regret that some of the opposition to the movement for integrated education has come from within the Churches. These schools are an expression of a clear desire from within both communities to challenge religious and political sectarianism. In taking up this challenge, the schools deserve the support of the Churches and the secular authorities. We look forward to the time when the Catholic and other Churches will appoint chaplains at integrated schools so as to provide pastoral care for staff and pupils.

There are now a number of inter-Church or ecumenical schools in Great Britain. There is a joint Anglican–Catholic primary school in the Sunderland area, and we know of five Anglican–Catholic secondary schools. There are also about 25 Anglican–Methodist schools in Great Britain.

The initiative for these ecumenical schools has sometimes come from the Church authorities, sometimes from the teachers, some-times from parents.[6] All had to overcome major obstacles in getting established, and many still face difficulties. One headmaster told us that all school assemblies and non-Eucharistic services are fully integrated, and that there have been 'no complaints from the Archbishop'. Another head teacher noted that there is good Roman Catholic support for the school over a wide area, but that Anglican and Free Church support comes mainly from outside the deanery. A variety of syllabuses for religious instruction are used. One lower school uses for morning assembly once a week a form of worship based on that used by the Taizé community. Attendance at Mass or Holy Communion at that school has been voluntary, but parents are beginning to question this, so the school is experimenting with two compulsory joint Eucharistic services a term, held in local Anglican and Catholic churches. Admissions policy at ecumenical schools in Great Britain varies. In two cases, preference is given to pupils whose parents are practising and committed members of the two founding Churches, then to pupils whose parents are members in good standing of other Churches, then to younger sisters or brothers of children already in attendance. One of these schools also considers applications from children who live near the school and children who have a long or difficult journey to another school. The other school gives priority to children where there is a pressing medical, social, or family need. Two schools try to operate a quota system, though in one case it is difficult to keep up the Catholic quota, partly because of a major decline in the birthrate in Catholic families. The head teacher of one of the schools with a quota system added, 'we are determined to provide a welcoming and caring religious environment for pupils of all faiths, classes and races'. Another head teacher wrote of the attempt at his school 'to promote a common Christian outlook' and of the enthusiastic support of the two Bishops. A third wrote, 'All who work at ... feel privileged to be part of Britain's pioneering ecumenical school'.[7]

It is natural that parents or guardians should wish their children to go to schools in which religious instruction accords with their own beliefs. While the religious education of children is primarily the responsibility of the home and the religious community, we believe (as is stated in the principal international instruments) that no child should be compelled to receive religious instruction at school inconsistent with the convictions of his or her parents. If parents object to religious instruction which is at variance with their own convictions, they should have the right to arrange for their children to opt out of religious instruction or to seek an alternative school.[8]

In practice, of course, it is not always possible to respect parental wishes. We heard of a survey in Inner London, for example, which showed that the majority of parents wanted their sons to go to co-educational schools and their daughters to single-sex schools.

Many schools in Great Britain have pupils from more than one religious faith, and the number of these will probably increase. The 1944 Education Act, enacted for Northern Ireland in 1947, provides that schools shall have a daily act of collective worship, and also requires the provision of religious intruction. Although the Act did not specify that the worship and instruction should be explicitly Christian, that was undoubtedly the intention; parents are entitled to withdraw their children from the school's act of worship. In the Republic of Ireland, primary schools are required by ministerial order to provide daily religious instruction, with provision for opting out. Secondary schools are not required by the secular authorities to provide religious instruction, though virtually all do so.

In Scotland, when the two large Presbyterian Churches gave over their school buildings and training colleges to the state, there came to be two kinds of school in the state system: non-denominational and denominational schools, the latter overwhelmingly Roman Catholic. The state, through the local authority, is obliged to provide a denominational (Catholic) school where the population justifies it and to bear all of the building and running costs: but the Church controls the appointment of staff and can veto unsuitable appointments. Although the clear intention of the Education Acts was that all schools were to be Christian schools, the non-denominational schools have increasingly been seen as secular, and 'religious education and observance' required by law have tended in the past to be neglected, and today to be seen in terms of 'World Religions'. In the light of the secularisation of the other sector, which the national Church has been powerless to prevent, Catholics have been understandably reluctant to yield any of their exclusiveness, resisting even any proposals to have schools with shared facilities, and resisting the closure of Catholic schools when required by falling rolls. Yet the Churches were able to co-operate effectively in response to the recent teachers' dispute, and closer and continued co-operation in education might provide a counterbalance to the secularism which the Churches deplore. In this, the Catholic Church might see a responsibility to the community as a whole, rather than simply to its own members.

We commend those schools in Great Britain with pupils drawn from different communities which have experimented with ecumenical and inter-faith worship and have provided instruction in comparative religion. The Swann Committee reported that one multi-ethnic school draws the material for daily assembly from a variety of sources. Festivals from the major faiths are looked at as 'parables'. Prophets and teachers are quoted and discussed, and issues such as tolerance, love, prejudice, jealousy, and war are dealt with. Pupils themselves are encouraged to submit suitable material.

As for the question of parental choice in the matter of religious and moral education, we already have the benefit of two important decisions by competent international human rights organs. The first was the judgement of the European Court of Human Rights that states are free to impart knowledge of a directly or indirectly religious or philosophical kind, and that parents may not object to the integration of such teaching in the school curriculum – provided that the state takes care that knowledge included in the curriculum is conveyed in an objective, critical, and pluralistic manner.[9]

In a parallel decision under the UN Covenant on Civil and Political Rights, the Human Rights Committee said that, if parents objected to religious instruction at school, it was permitted for instruction to be given instead in the history of religion and ethics, provided that this was done in a neutral and objective way and respected the convictions of parents and guardians who did not believe in any religion.[10]

In all schools, whether under public or private auspices, whether in Great Britain or the two parts of Ireland, the curriculum and style of teaching should be designed to foster a tolerant and compassionate attitude to human differences. At its best, religious education includes an understanding of the religious dimension of human experience, of the plurality of faiths that children will encounter, and an appreciation of the diverse and sometimes conflicting values involved, so that the children will be better able to determine their own religious position.[11] Education should be directed to a recognition of the dignity of all human beings, to the growth of respect for the rights of others, and the avoidance of stereotyping.

In Northern Ireland, a number of programmes have been developed to encourage mutual understanding, respect, tolerance, and co-operation. Some of these programmes are sponsored jointly by the Irish Council of Churches and the Irish Commission for Justice and Peace. Curricular and other kinds of projects have been initiated for both the primary and the post-primary sectors of schooling, and the Department of Education has formally adopted a policy of 'education for mutual understanding'.[12] Most of the projects enjoy support from both sections of the community. The effects are difficult to assess at this stage, but the fact that they give priority to harmonious community relations and fundamental issues affecting human rights must in the long run lead to a greater awareness amongst young people about how problems in these areas might be tackled.

In the Republic of Ireland and in Great Britain, some projects of a similar kind have tried to bring the question of human rights into sharper focus. The term 'human rights' may not always be explicit in these projects, but where they aim to foster understanding and respect for members of different cultures and traditions, and in particular for minorities, they are dealing with issues of human rights.

In order to disseminate more widely the lessons of these projects, what is required is a teaching force fully aware of basic human rights and of the problems and needs of plural societies, so that they can foster respect and understanding for differences, for the greater good and cohesion of the whole of society.

Where children from different communities go through different educational systems, we would encourage schools from one tradition to engage in joint activities (whether scholastic, athletic, or social) with schools of other traditions, even within the limitations which are inevitable in diverse patterns of school ownership and management.

We conclude this review of secondary education by drawing attention to a statement drawn up by the Commissioners of Education in Ireland, and published in 1835 (see facing page). It was re-issued by the Department of Education in 1986.

Higher education in the two states is almost entirely integrated, with the notable exceptions of teacher training. We particularly welcome the fact that theological education is now conducted ecumenically in the University context, where staff and students from the different Churches study together the different insights from their traditions which inform Christian witness and theology today.

In some instances, however, we note that ministerial training, which in some colleges and seminaries encompasses all theological education, does not include facilities and encouragement for ecumenical contacts. We strongly urge that the Churches should try to ensure that all ministerial candidates receive direct experience of and reflection on the insights and life of Christian traditions other than their own.

In the Irish Republic, the organisation and financing of education is quite different from the system in Northern Ireland and Great Britain. The primary school structure has remained basically unaltered since pre-partition days, except for the introduction of boards of management for schools: this has given parents and teachers a voice

General Lesson.

CHRISTIANS should endeavour, as the Apostle Paul commands them, to live peaceably with all men (Romans, c. 12, v. 18), even with those of a different religious persuasion.

Our SAVIOUR, CHRIST, commanded his Disciples to love one another. He taught them to love even their enemies, to bless those that cursed them, and to pray for those who persecuted them. He himself prayed for his murderers.

Many Men hold erroneous doctrines; but we ought not to hate or persecute them. We ought to hold fast what we are convinced is the truth; but not to treat harshly those who are in error. JESUS CHRIST did not intend his Religion to be forced on men by violent means. He would not allow his Disciples to fight for him.

If any persons treat us unkindly, we must not do the same to them; for Christ and His Apostles have taught us not to return evil for evil. If we would obey CHRIST, we must do to others, not as they do to us, but as we would wish them to do to us.

Quarrelling with our neighbours and abusing them, is not the way to convince them that we are in the right, and they in the wrong. It is more likely to convince them that we have not a Christian spirit.

We ought, by behaving gently and kindly to every one, to show ourselves followers of CHRIST, who, when he was reviled, reviled not again. (1 Peter, c. 2, v. 23.)

Issued,
November, 1863.

DUBLIN, PRINTED FOR HER MAJESTY'S STATIONERY OFFICE.
By Alex Thow & Co. (Limited).
527 10000 4 91

Issued from 1835 onwards by the Commissioners of
National Education in Ireland with the requirement:

'that the principles of the Lesson be strictly inculcated
in all schools admitted into connexion with them'

in running schools. Most primary schools and many second-level schools are still provided by voluntary agencies, usually associated with one of the Churches. All schools recognised by the Department of Education are in receipt of considerable public funding.

In recognition of the needs of the Protestant community for boarding facilities at secondary level, there is a special financial arrangement for assisting schools under Protestant management. This arrangement is in line with an earlier one introduced in the 1930s, which subsidised school transport for Protestant pupils in rural communities 30 years before a similar scheme was introduced on a general basis.

It is difficult to establish non-denominational schools in the Republic. We understand that Irish-language and multi-denominational schools in the Republic experience difficulties which those under the auspices of the more traditional education agencies do not encounter. For example, evidence of viability of a more stringent kind than is required of Church-sponsored schools is often demanded by the Department of Education before financial assistance is made available. Government departments have an obligation to allocate public monies wisely, but they also have an obligation to ensure that civil rights are not infringed.

RELIGION AND THE CHURCHES

The law about religious discrimination in Great Britain is different from what it is in Northern Ireland, in that it is now entirely negative. At different times in the historic past, there were laws which discriminated specifically against Catholics, Dissenters, and Jews. Over the past century and a half, these have all been repealed, most recently by an Act in 1974 which made it possible for the Lord Chancellor to be a Roman Catholic. Today, only the monarch has to be a Protestant.

However, this has some curious consequences. Although Great Britain (though not Northern Ireland) now has legislation – in the form of the Race Relations Act – which make it unlawful to discriminate on grounds of race, there is no law which makes it unlawful to discriminate on grounds of religion in England, Scotland, or Wales. When a Sikh complained that he was discriminated against by being required to wear a crash helmet when riding his motorcycle, while his religion required him to wear a turban, the English courts held that the discrimination was not unlawful because it was on the grounds of religion and not of race, and that was permitted. Had that case been brought in Northern Ireland, its outcome might well have been different.

On the general principle that fundamental human rights should be equally protected in all parts of the United Kingdom, we think it would be highly desirable for the existing laws which forbid discrimination on any of these three grounds (race, gender, and religion) to have their extents enlarged so that all of them are equally applicable in all parts of the United Kingdom. We would also like to see a law against racial or religious discrimination in the Republic and ratification of the relevant UN instruments.

Article 44 of the original Constitution of the Irish Republic recognised 'the special position of the Holy Catholic and Apostolic Church as the guardian of the Faith professed by the great majority of the citizens' and the existence of other named denominations: the main Protestant Churches, the Society of Friends, and the Jewish Congregations. Although the Article conferred no actual privilege on the Catholic Church, it nonetheless was regarded as offensive to other Churches. Because of this, the Government proposed the removal of the paragraphs in question in 1972, and this was carried in a referendum during which virtually no opposition to the proposal was expressed by the Churches concerned.

Today, therefore, there is complete separation of church and state in the Republic, in contrast to the situation in England and Scotland where there are established Churches which enjoy privileges and discharge responsibilities in the life of the nation.

As far as Northern Ireland is concerned, the Churches are quite separate from the state. The Government of Ireland Act 1920 prohibits state endowment of religion.

POLITICAL REPRESENTATION

Societies which consist of communities divided in their fundamental loyalties pose considerable challenges when the question is posed of how to achieve just and equal representation in political institutions.

In Northern Ireland, the method of political representation until the early 1970s was the first-past-the-post system, which still operates in Great Britain. Single-member constituencies and wards returned representatives to local councils, to the Northern Ireland Parliament, and to Westminster. Except in a small number of local councils, this resulted in unionist control of all major political institutions, so that nationalist representatives were in permanent opposition. Changes in the 1970s brought proportional representation and multi-member constituencies for elections to district councils, the Northern Ireland Assembly, and the European Parliament. Furthermore, the principle of 'cross-community support' was adopted by the British Government as the only one under which devolved government would be restored to Northern Ireland.

In Great Britain the demand for the special representation of minorities in political bodies is beginning to be heard. If ethnic minorities are to play a full part in public affairs, new methods of representation may be needed in political bodies and, indeed, in Church assemblies.

The UN Covenant on Civil and Political Rights affirms the right and opportunity of citizens to take part in public affairs, to vote and be elected by universal suffrage and secret ballot, and to have access to the public service of the state. This right is to be exercised without discrimination (Article 25). We note that both communities in Northern Ireland are minorities in the United Kingdom, and both claim that they are denied fair representation in the state's executive and legislative institutions.

One anomaly in the franchise in Northern Ireland is that residents who have not acquired residential qualifications may vote in elections to the Westminster Parliament but may not vote in elections for the Northern Ireland Assembly or for district councils.[13] It is not certain how many people there are in this category, but it is probably around 6000.[14] We understand that the law in this matter may be repealed soon.

There is said to be a considerable amount of personation and other electoral abuse in Northern Ireland elections. 'Vote early, and vote often', is a well-known slogan. The very high turn-outs for parliamentary elections in Northern Ireland, often 85 per cent or even more (compared with an average of around 75 per cent in Great Britain) suggests that there may be a degree of illegal voting. The right of free election is a precious human right. The Standing Advisory Commission on Human Rights has prepared a detailed set of recommendations to prevent electoral abuse: we do not reproduce them here, but they have our full support.[15]

STATUTORY AGENCIES CONCERNED WITH HUMAN RIGHTS

There are, broadly speaking, three groups of functions performed by statutory human rights agencies in the United Kingdom: the investigation of specific complaints, the monitoring of performance, and studies and research. All three functions have an important educative effect. Three agencies in Northern Ireland undertake only the first task, the investigation of complaints: the Police Complaints Board (to which we refer in Chapter 8), the Parliamentary Commissioner for Administration (Ombudsman), and the Commissioner for Complaints. Two Northern Ireland agencies conduct all three functions: the Fair Employment Agency and the Equal Opportunities Commission. The Standing Advisory Commission on Human Rights is limited to the third function, studies and research.

Standing Advisory Commission on Human Rights (SACHR)

Like the Constitution of the Republic of Ireland, the Northern Ireland Constitution Act 1973 contains no direct reference to the existence of a minority within its jurisdiction. The recognition of minority rights is implied in Part III of the Act, entitled 'Prevention of Religious Bias and Discrimination'. This was included in response to concerns about discrimination against the Catholic minority in such reports as that of Lord Cameron (1969).[16] The Act prohibits bias and discrimination on religious and political grounds, and established the Standing Advisory Commission on Human Rights (SACHR) to monitor implementation.

The Standing Advisory Commission on Human Rights is charged with advising the Secretary of State on the adequacy and effectiveness of the law in preventing discrimination. As the Commission is only advisory, the British Government is not obliged to implement its recommendations, and many of its major recommendations have not been acted upon. It is not surprising, therefore, that a major criticism of the Commission is that too many of its recommendations have fallen on deaf ears.

We have heard criticisms of the work of all the statutory agencies concerned with human rights in Northern Ireland, though some of those from opposite ends of the political spectrum cancel each other out. We also know that the Standing Advisory Commission has at times been restive that the boundaries of its mandate are so restrictively drawn. We also realise that the activities of these bodies constantly impinge on the work of ministers and officials. A system of checks and balances easily leads to occasional tension, perhaps needlessly so: but we consider that this tension is a small price to pay if it helps to create a more humane society.

We therefore recommend that similar advisory commissions on human rights be established in England, Wales, Scotland, and the Republic of Ireland, to conduct studies and research. We understand that the official view in the United Kingdom is that such bodies are not necessary, that they use up scarce resources, and that they delay efficient administration; and we can imagine that such views will be echoed in the Republic. We disagree with the first point: we believe that such bodies *are* useful. We accept the second point about the use of scarce resources, but we think that experience in Northern Ireland over a decade has shown conclusively that there is useful work to be done, even over such matters as the rights of travelling people (gypsies) which are unrelated to the basic conflict between the two traditions. As for the fact that such bodies may interrupt the work of ministers and officials, we cannot deny this possibility, but we consider it a necessary price as part of a general educative process within and outside government.

If such commissions are established, we hope that there would be a sharing of information and experience among them, both formally and informally.

Parliamentary Commissioner for Administration (Ombudsman) and Commissioner for Complaints

The Parliamentary Commissioner for Administration (Ombudsman) considers complaints of maladministration. Of 165 complaints received in 1985, none alleged that there had been political or religious discrimination, but one complainant contended that he should be allowed to use the Irish language in correspondence with government departments. The Parliamentary Commissioner found no evidence of maladministration in this case.[17]

The Commissioner for Complaints investigates complaints from persons who claim to have suffered injustice because of maladministration by local authorities or other public bodies in Northern Ireland. The Ombudsman usually acts also as Commissioner of

Complaints. If a complaint is within the Commissioner's mandate, he seeks to establish the facts and, if he considers that maladministration has occurred, to effect a settlement of the grievance. The Commissioner has the power to award damages. In 1985, 398 complaints were received, of which all except 10 were either outside the Commissioner's jurisdiction or no maladministration was found to have occurred. Four of the complaints alleged religious or political discrimination: one of these was outside the Commissioner's mandate, one was referred to the Fair Employment Agency, and two were still being investigated when the Commissioner's report went to press. [18]

We fully support these two Commissioners and we consider that they are useful means for dealing with a range of grievances about maladministration. At the same time, we note that they have restricted mandates and so are not able to deal with some of the more deep-rooted causes of prejudice and discrimination in Northern Ireland.

Fair Employment Agency (FEA)

The Fair Employment Agency began work in 1976 to promote equality of opportunity in employment between people of different religious beliefs and to eliminate discrimination. The Agency maintains a Register of employers and organisations who support the principle of equality of opportunity by signing a Declaration of Principle and Intent: there were 7919 names on the Register in 1985, including nine of the 26 local authorities, all of the boards for health and social services, and all but one of the boards for education and libraries.

On 1 April 1985, 80 Fair Employment Agency complaints were outstanding from previous years, and 81 complaints were received during the following 12 months. Three complaints were excluded from the Agency's jurisdiction on grounds of national security, 27 were withdrawn, and 86 were still outstanding at the end of the year. Of the remaining 45, the Agency found that there had been unlawful discrimination in five cases and no discrimination in the remaining 40.

Three complaints in 1984 raised the question whether discrimination is unlawful only when a Catholic discriminates against a Protestant and vice-versa, or whether it is unlawful to discriminate against someone of *the same* religious tradition. [19] The Agency's view was that if discrimination *within* the two major religious groupings were to occur, it would be unlawful.

In the eight years up to 1985, the Agency had made findings, of which about two-thirds followed complaints from Catholics and one-third from Protestants. Critics maintain there there are a number of weaknesses in the existing anti-discrimination legislation, as well as inadequacies in the Agency's own procedures. One cause for concern is the fact that few of the complaints were against employers in the private sector, where even the Agency's own monitoring investigations have revealed serious imbalances. Some victims of discrimination in employment are reluctant to complain and to pursue a complaint for fear of victimisation. Moreover, the hidden and indirect nature of discrimination (for example, arising from the siting of industry) means that victims may be unaware of its existence. There is also a widespread feeling in the nationalist community that the Agency uses an over-strict definition of discrimination: unionists, on the other hand, suspect that the Agency is biased against Protestants. Moreover, to give the two communities equal opportunities does not necessarily ensure that they will be equally represented in the workforce.

The Agency's reports suggest that recruitment for many jobs is now non-discriminatory, though it may take decades before this works its way through to the senior levels. Although there have been significant improvements in the employment rate of Catholics in the Northern Ireland civil service, these improvements are slow to have significant overall effect on employment patterns. The Agency's studies reveal that most employers do not operate 'employment equity' or 'affirmative action' programmes which set out how equality of job opportunity is to be achieved.

The question of fair employment opportunities is a sensitive one for both communities in Northern Ireland. Representatives of the unionist community deny that there is wide-scale job discrimination. They claim that the under-representation of Catholics in the workforce is to be explained by such factors as the traditional absence of certain trades within the Catholic community and the reluctance of Catholics to apply in sufficient numbers for positions in the public service, a reluctance deriving from their political attitude to the Northern Ireland set-up. Lower educational attainments by Catholics in the past and large Catholic families have also been quoted as negative factors affecting Catholic opportunities. Sometimes there have been job vacancies, but not in areas where Catholics are concentrated. On the other hand, the perception of the nationalist community is that discrimination continues, and it demands that the Government should tackle the problem through the Fair Employment Agency with greater energy and a firmer commitment to the elimination of discrimination.

In addition to investigating individual cases, the Agency has published several reports detailing the religious composition of the work-force in various enterprises (public and private), including the Northern Ireland civil service and the major banks and building societies. Most of these reports have revealed a bias against Roman Catholics. It is clear from the Agency's research papers that there has been and continues to be job discrimination against Catholics who, at the time of the 1981 census, constituted just over 39 per cent of the population of Northern Ireland.[20] In the past, this has to some extent reflected the different academic achievements of Protestants and Catholics. Protestants achieved more O-levels than Catholics in mathematics and science in 1979 and 1982, whereas Catholics did better than Protestants in languages, the arts, and religious education.[21] More than 80 per cent of the top posts in the non-industrial civil service are still held by Protestants, and more than 60 per cent of the lower grades.[22] These figures are confirmed by the Continuous Household Survey, which showed that more than twice as many Protestants as Catholics held professional or managerial jobs in 1983–4, whereas twice as many Catholics as Protestants were unemployed.[23] Given current employment trends, the prospect of this gap narrowing does not appear likely in the immediate future.

Race Relations in Great Britain

In Great Britain, equality of job opportunity is one of the aims of the Race Relations Act 1976. In spite of the fact that the 1976 Act was the third piece of legislation in 10 years aimed at eliminating racial discrimination, it is still subject to considerable criticism from ethnic minorities, who continue to suffer discrimination in the work-place.

The problems experienced in Great Britain are similar to those in Northern Ireland. For example, the burden of proof in complaints about job discrimination lies with the applicant, and so the number of successful cases brought before industrial tribunals is still very few. As in the case of affirmative action programmes in Northern Ireland, many employers in Great Britain have not adopted 'equal opportunities' policies, and few of those who have such policies take the trouble to monitor them regularly. The Commission for Racial Equality has urged several changes in the 1976 Act in order to achieve adequate protection for minority rights. These changes include formal investigations without waiting for evidence of discrimination; the creation of a separate discrimination division within the industrial tribunal system; the simplification of what is meant by 'indirect' discrimination; and the keeping of ethnic records by employers.

Equal Opportunities for Women

While women constitute a majority, their role in society has left them sharing many of the characteristics of minorities which have suffered from prejudice and discrimination. In this respect, women in both parts of Ireland and in Great Britain have much in common. Legislation in Great Britain in 1976 made discrimination on the basis of sex illegal, established the legal principle of equal pay for equal work, and set up an Equal Opportunities Commission with powers to monitor work-forces and to investigate complaints. In spite of some progress, traditional attitudes and patterns of employment for men and women are only slowly being changed.

The Equal Opportunities Commission was created in Northern Ireland in 1976 to promote equality of opportunity between men and women, and to eliminate discrimination. The Commission undertakes a wide range of educational and promotional work, initiates research, and enforces the law regarding equality of opportunity. The Commission receives 'a consistently high level of complaints of alleged discrimination in employment': research which the Commission has sponsored showed that nearly a quarter of a female sample had been subjected to some form of sexual harassment during their working lives. The Commission received 103 complaints and enquiries from men during the year to 31 March 1986, and 331 complaints from women, the largest category being of discrimination in employment (mainly relating to appointments and promotions or sexual harassment).[24]

Because of a longer experience of industrialisation which gives women opportunities to work outside the home, Great Britain (and to some extent Northern Ireland) contrasts with the Republic of Ireland regarding women's role in the economy. Furthermore, because of the strong emphasis in Catholic teaching on the family, on an exclusive role for women as mother and spouse with primary responsibility for children, traditional attitudes towards women in both parts of Ireland have lasted longer than in Great Britain. Despite these differences, it was only in the 1970s that legislation was enacted in both states outlawing discrimination on the basis of sex and establishing agencies to promote equality of opportunity.

In 1986, the Northern Ireland Office published a consultative document proposing a new Fair Employment Commission to promote equality of opportunity in both public and private sectors on the basis of religion or sex, but adding two additional dimensions: marital status or disability.[25] This followed a comment of the Standing Advisory Commission on Human Rights in 1980–1 to the effect that handicapped people suffered material disadvantage and a variety of threats to human rights.[26]

THE NEED FOR CONSISTENCY AND COHERENCE

Our review of the constitutional and statutory forms of protection of minorities and of measures taken to prevent discrimination in Great Britain, Northern Ireland, and the Republic of Ireland reveals a patchwork of provisions. The existence of a written Constitution in the Republic and of a constitution forming part of statute law in Northern Ireland would, at first sight, appear to offer considerable protection against discrimination. Fundamental law of this kind, however, cannot address all the specific demands for protection which are made, nor can it resolve all conflicting claims when, as is the case with the Republic's Constitution, fundamental law explicitly reflects convictions of the Catholic Church whose adherents form the majority in the state. Nonetheless, fundamental law is of great significance because it provides the individual with a basis on which to judge the more specific measures of statute law and administrative action. This has been frequently demonstrated in the Republic of Ireland, particularly during the past 15 years as more and more people have become aware of the protection which the Constitution provides and have resorted to it in order to challenge statute law and administrative action.

The absence of fundamental law in the United Kingdom has meant that British citizens have had to go elsewhere to find a legal basis for challenging what they regarded as encroachments on their human rights by the legislature or by administration. The European

Convention on Human Rights has provided that basis, with the result that the British Government now has had more cases brought against it for breaches of the Convention than any other party. A further consequence has been that British courts dealing with cases alleging discrimination have at last begun using the Convention and the law of the European Community to interpret British law.

Our review, therefore, firmly points towards the need in the first instance to strengthen fundamental law. This means actually providing an entrenched bill of rights in Great Britain and Northern Ireland, and reviewing the provisions of the Constitution in the Republic. Great Britain, Northern Ireland, and the Republic of Ireland are plural, multicultural societies, in which the beliefs, values, and attitudes of one group must not cause detriment or disadvantage to others. This is not an argument for separateness, but a conviction that respect for diversity is the basis for social cohesion.

It will be a difficult task, especially in Northern Ireland, to reconcile the demands that will arise once such an approach to law-making and administration is adopted. We do not claim that the courses we recommend will eliminate the tensions and conflicts which now disfigure human society in these islands, but we do believe that better procedures for adjudicating claims and protecting human and civil rights will improve the quality of life for everyone.

We cannot make people equal by law. We cannot eliminate prejudice by governmental edict. What the law *can* do is to assure equal opportunities and deter discrimination. We recommend an urgent review of the law in the United Kingdom so as to provide a more comprehensive and consistent barrier to discrimination.

Notes and References

1. General Assembly Official Records, 40th session, Supplement 18, paras 290, 300.
2. A discussion paper, presented by the Ulster Unionist Assembly's Report Committee (1984).
3. Matrimonial Proceedings (Polygamous Marriages) Act 1972. There is not a comparable statute in the Republic of Ireland, so that if the issue were to arise, the courts would decide the case on common law principles.
4. *Love is for life* (Dublin: Veritas, 1985) para. 185; see also the

statement of the bishops on the proposed constitutional amendment on divorce, 11 June 1986 (mimeo).

5. *Love is for life*, paras 190, 195, 209–10.
6. Phil Dineen, 'The shared school', *Tablet* (21 May 1983) pp. 480–2. We are grateful to Miss P. Chadwick for allowing our Chairman to see a copy of part of her M.A. thesis on curriculum development in an ecumenical school.
7. Letters dated 29 October 1986, 11 November 1986, 1 December 1986 and enclosure dated 20 November 1986, and 2 December 1986.
8. *Education For All: the report of the committee of inquiry into the education of children from ethnic minority groups* (London: HMSO, 1985) (Cmnd 9453, Swann) p. 480, para. 3.8; p. 518.
9. *Kjedsen et al. v. Denmark.*
10. *Hartikainen v. Finland.*
11. *Education For All*, pp. 465, 468, 475, paras 1.2, 2.3, 2.11; see also pp. 468–70, paras 2.4, 2.5, 2.7, 2.8.
12. Circular 82/81, 'The Improvement of Community Relations: The Contribution of Schools' (Belfast: Northern Ireland Office).
13. Electoral Law Act 1961.
14. *Twelfth Annual Report of the Standing Advisory Commission on Human Rights, 1985–6* (London: HMSO, 1987), Chapter 11, para. 12.
15. *Tenth Annual Report of the Standing Advisory Commission on Human Rights, 1983–4* (London: HMSO, 1985) appendix D, para. 38.
16. *Disturbances in Northern Ireland*, (London: HMSO, 1969) (Cmnd 532, Cameron).
17. *Annual Report of the Northern Ireland Parliamentary Commissioner for Administration for 1985*, paras 2, 6, 43–4. The Ombudsman received 150 complaints in 1986, 67 against the Department of the Environment and 51 against the Department of Health and Social Services.
18. *Annual Report of the Northern Ireland Commissioner for Complaints for 1985*, paras 5, 12. The Commissioner for Complaints received 370 complaints in 1986, many against the Housing Executive.
19. *Tenth Report and Statement of Accounts of the Fair Employment Agency for Northern Ireland* (London: HMSO, 1986) pp. 11–12, 40–2, 53–4. (Cases 330–1, 387).
20. David Eversley and Valerie Herr, *The Roman Catholic population of Northern Ireland 1981: a revised estimate* (Belfast: Fair Employment Agency, 1985) (research paper 17) pp. 10–11.
21. Robert D. Osborne and Russell C. Murray, *Educational qualifications and religious affiliation in Northern Ireland* (Belfast: Fair Employment Agency, 1978) (research paper 3) pp. 23–4, 40–2; Robert D. Osborne, *Religion and educational qualifications in Northern Ireland* (Belfast: Fair Employment Agency, 1985) (research paper 8) pp. iii–iv, 64, 66, 72, 74, 79; *Equality of Opportunity in Northern Ireland: future strategy options – a consultative paper* (Belfast: HMSO, 1986) p. 65.
22. *Report of an investigation . . . into the non-industrial Northern Ireland*

civil service (Belfast: Fair Employment Agency, 1983) (research paper 13) p. 19.

23.   *PPRU Monitor no. 2* (June 1985), Continuous Household Survey, pp.16, 18; *Equality of opportunity in Northern Ireland: future strategy options – a consultative paper* (Belfast: HMSO, 1986) p. 47.

24.   *Tenth Annual Report of the Equal Opportunities Commission, year ending 31 March 1986* (London: HMSO, 1987) pp. 17, 22, 25–6 (Tables F and H).

25.   *Equality of Opportunity in Northern Ireland: future strategy options – a consultative paper* (Belfast: HMSO, 1986).

26.   *Seventh Annual Report of the Standing Advisory Commission on Human Rights, 1980–1* (London: HMSO, 1987) paras 27–33.

7 The Responses of Christians to the Conflict in Northern Ireland*

We have been appointed by leading members of the Churches in our two states and so it is right that we should look critically at the role of Christians regarding human rights and responsibilities, especially since the onset of the troubles in Northern Ireland in 1968. We do not undertake this task in any judgemental spirit: there are events in the history of every Church of which its members are rightly proud, but also events of which they should be ashamed. Because God has reconciled the world to himself and has committed to us the ministry of reconciliation, no Christian in these islands can be satisfied so long as communities remain unreconciled.

Nowhere in the world has it been easy to develop those genuine forms of ecumenical dialogue and partnership which discover tasks which Christians may undertake together creatively, while respecting differing traditions of belief and worship. The Churches are not immune to the problems of power and the struggle for survival. Where one Church has a dominant position, it may abuse its power. Where two Churches face a common threat, they make common cause. But where one Church sees the other as a threat, when they fear that their continued identity and existence is at stake, each easily perceives the other as a permanent enemy. In situations of political tension and frustration, where fear and hostility have bred violence, Christian people, while not approving the violence, may remain silent rather than condemn those who use it. It takes considerable courage to do otherwise; and we have been continually impressed by the silent courage of those from both communities in Northern Ireland who, in spite of threat, intimidation, and violence, have sought to build bridges of trust and friendship across the Protestant–Catholic divide.

*One member of the Working Party has informed the editor that he disagrees with the basic thrust of this Chapter. In his opinion, the Working Party should have described the social function of the Churches and assessed their responses as institutions to events in Northern Ireland. He does not find it helpful to distribute praise and blame, for he is sure that there are sincere Christians in all the Churches. He believes that it is wrong to identify Christianity, as distinct from particular Churches, with any particular nationalism or political approach to the conflict.

There are quiet heroes on the pews and benches of all the Churches, as well as among those who never go to a place of worship.

One reason why all of the Churches need to review their policies regarding other Churches is that attitudes inherited from the past may no longer be adequate for contemporary problems. The rules about inter-Church relations are changing.

Religion can bring the sword as well as peace. Religious convictions are, and ought to be, deeply held. But whether serious doctrinal differences between Christians have the effect of dividing communities depends partly on the tendencies in ourselves which we allow to become dominant. For there are two ways in which we may deal with our anxieties. One is to seek security in a system of certainties, to build a citadel against whatever seems to threaten our deeply held beliefs. The other is to find faith in the unconditional grace of God which enables us to venture out in faith, hope, and love. The first tendency exists in each of us, for no one can live without some securities. But there is no doubt that religion can be organised and taught in such a way as to intensify anxieties, to increase the attractions of an exclusivist and intolerant dogma. At its extreme, this becomes fanaticism – religion organised on the basis of fear and hostility rather than on the basis of faith and love.

A significant religious division in these islands is not between Catholic and Protestant but between these two tendencies in each individual, Church, and community. The one fuels conflicts and erects barriers: the other defuses tension and builds bridges. Means have to be found to encourage more trusting and open attitudes, while dealing creatively with the real anxieties of each community. This challenge is more difficult for Churches than for individuals. Churches must have a pastoral concern for all their members and the danger is that the anxiety and hostility of some may permeate the whole, so that it evolves into an institution of unyielding hostility.

Moreover, Church structures can become corrupt and heretical. Although leaders may have the courage and strength to resist this tendency, not all Church members may be prepared to follow. The leadership may then find that those who have the courage and faith to work for peace are accused of betraying the cause.

The dynamic which gives rise to these tendencies is rooted in the theology and doctrine advocated by ultra-Protestant sects, drawing their strength from a narrow interpretation of Christianity, yet finding resonances within the main Protestant Churches. Sects have proliferated, and these maintain a tradition of exclusivity and sectarianism. Because of the small cockpit in which they operate, these sects have to some degree influenced the major Churches, as well as the smaller groupings like the Quakers, the Salvation Army, and the Baptists.

One cannot read the sermons or the writings of ultra-Protestants without realising that what inspires much unionism is not primarily a love of Great Britain but a rejection of a monolithic Catholic Church dominating public life in the Republic. To describe the Pope as 'the whore of Babylon', or the Catholic Church as the instrument of a foreign power determined to subvert the British crown and ultimately to reverse the Protestant Reformation, can easily be used to encourage paramilitary violence as a means for resolving differences. Protestants are understandably determined to reject a united, Catholic Ireland; but their case loses credibility when it is maintained by bigotry and propagated by violence.

Religion is by no means the only element in the civil strife in Northern Ireland, but it is often a crucial element. What has influenced some unionist politicians, and inspires Protestant extremism at the present time, is a rejection of Catholic supremacy. The way in which the Republic of Ireland maintains its territorial claim to the whole island and shapes its laws relating to marriage, divorce, contraception, and censorship, has had the effect of encouraging the growth of Protestant extremism in the North. Each feeds off the other.

There is, of course, a Catholic counter-reaction to the fixity of purpose of Protestant extremism, often exacerbated by a romantic view or Irish culture and nationhood. For some Catholics, death at the hands of the security forces may be a form of patriotism and martyrdom. At the funeral of one of the republican paramilitaries who was killed at Loughgall in 1987, the priest denounced the 'gross injustice' of the British presence in Northern Ireland, and praised the dead man as 'upright . . . [a man who] loved his family, Irish culture, his faith and his country'. Language of that sort does nothing to bring the peace for which both communities long. In the South, a few misguided people have countenanced and supported paramilitary violence to secure political objectives. Some months ago, a member of the Fine Gael-led coalition described the leaders of the Protestant Churches as 'the enemies of the people' who 'believe themselves to be your masters rather than your servants'. That this view did not represent Fine Gael policy is shown by the fact that the person concerned was repudiated by her party leadership and lost her nomination as a party candidate in the ensuing election, and then her seat, but it is such inflaming of community differences that is exploited by the people with guns

We have referred to a stratum of romanticism and patriotism in the Catholic community, but all the main Churches in Ireland have, at different times, added this stratum to the conflict. This has tended to distort political debate. Increasingly during the past decade, however, attempts have been made by Church leaders, North and South, to emphasise a more Christian version of patriotism; but the traditions of centuries cannot be altered overnight.

Religious affiliation for both Protestants and Catholics can thus be used to provoke and justify evil deeds and so ensure the continuation of the conflict. Such 'religion' is inconsistent with the teachings of Jesus of Nazareth.

In the wider perspective of Church history, none of this is surprising. For centuries Christians, though professing a gospel of mutual love, reconciliation, and peace have fallen lamentably short in promoting human rights and responsibilities, have persecuted their fellow human beings on grounds of race or false doctrine, and have often contributed to the polarisation of communities and the erection of barriers between individuals.

The tendency to polarise has occurred not only in the social and political actions of the Churches in Ireland, but also in their way of doing theology – of trying to understand the nature of God and of humankind. Too much theology has emphasised differences, an approach evident in some catechisms, pamphlets, Bible study books, and works of theological scholarship. This approach has helped to define Christian communities and aided their self-identity, but it has also reinforced a sense of opposition to other communities. Such Christian theology has developed a rationale for the separation of communities in Northern Ireland and their alienation from each other.

But in many parts of the Church, this situation has been changing in the past 50 years. There has been significant progress in toleration, mutual understanding, and ecumenical co-operation, so that in many places the Churches have been able to witness effectively to the resources of the Christian faith for promoting reconciliation and overcoming old prejudices. It is against this background that we have to observe that in Northern Ireland some of the Churches are in danger of becoming an intractable part of the problem rather than an agency that could contribute to a solution.

Yet, as we have stressed in Chapter 4, today's polarised division between the Catholic and Protestant communities has not always been a feature of Irish history. There was a time when the division was between the Church of Ireland (which was allied to Anglo–Irish Ascendancy interests) and the Roman Catholic, Presbyterian, and dissenting Churches, which were largely denied access to political power. In particular, we noted the common cause of Roman Catholics and Presbyterians in the past. Presbyterians provided the first Catholic chapel in Belfast and attended the first Mass. Today's divisions are not immutable.

As we consider the role of Christians in furthering human rights and responsibilities during the past two decades, we can distinguish between the witness of individual Christians and the contributions of institutional Churches. The individual Christian can rarely be effective without the nurture and support of a Church in the background, but often the individual Christian has launched an initiative without waiting for institutional support. So we look first at the acts of Christian men and women, clergy and laity, in their individual and unofficial capacities in Ireland. We then turn to the role of the Churches.

THE WITNESS OF INDIVIDUAL CHRISTIANS

John Habgood, Archbishop of York and President of this Project, has written that 'Decisions made by individual Christians, and at local church level, do as much, if not more, to determine the character of a church as do those of designated leaders'.[1] We therefore start with those Christians in Northern Ireland whose primary witness has been to participate in secular organisations dedicated to peace and justice, including trade unions, political parties, and civil rights movements. Christian witness manifests itself in numerous ways, including sacrificial commitment, catalytic action, and dedicated leadership.

It is, perhaps, invidious to refer to individuals and organisations by name, and to do so would be unfair to anonymous people in both communities who were faithful to Christian ideals in circumstances of tension and danger. Some Christians were active in the civil rights movement of 1968–9, but their witness was eventually vitiated when the movement came under the influence of a small but militant faction which wanted a dramatic confrontation with the police.[2]

Other Christians were active in the New Ulster Movement. Both these movements aimed to recruit across the sectarian divide, and both stood for a community devoid of sectarian bigotry. This is not to argue that either movement was unique, for there were other non-sectarian parties and organisations which advocated similar ideas. Concerned Christian men and women, Protestant and Catholic, were trying to act in ways that were peaceful and non-threatening to traditional Protestants and Catholics on both sides of the Irish border. They advocated change on the basis of common humanity, peace between communities, and justice for all.

In the Peace People movement of the mid-1970s, not only was the sectarian divide breached by women of conviction, but so was the sex divide. While Ireland has always thrown up remarkable women leaders, only a few have emerged since 1945. The feminist movement has still to make headway in many Protestant and Catholic communities throughout Ireland. The media gave the Peace People massive coverage, and for a time it mobilised large numbers of people who were weary of bigotry and bloodshed. This recognition contributed, ironically, to their decline.[3]

These initiatives demanded considerable courage, for those who work for cross-community harmony may be subjected to massive intimidation in the form of threatening telephone calls and letters, physical abuse or discrimination at work, common assault on the public highway, the public burning of effigies of those who seek to cross the divide, the assembly of hooded men and women who march up and down the road outside the family home, the 'kneecapping' of those deemed to have offended, and a range of similar pressures ending with bullets, incendiaries, and bombs designed to destroy and kill. Ultimately, over the years, this pressure forces people to leave the country, move to the relative security of a sectarian ghetto, or desist from their attempt to work for a united community.

We must not underestimate the cost of personal Christian discipleship. A small group like 'Witness for Peace' was started by a clergyman and his wife when their young son was killed by a bomb on the streets of Belfast as he went about the family shopping. The couple appealed for no retaliation and advocated non-violence. But such is the power of the sectarian extremist that many, including the founders of 'Witness for Peace', have left the country of their birth. Some are tormented and pressurised intolerably by bully boys and terrorists. Some are broken mentally and spiritually by their daily encounter with evil. Some die for their faith. Others lose home and business in bombings and burnings, being made bankrupt in the process.

It has been a feature of life in Northern Ireland that a small number of paramilitaries can exert pressure out of all proportion to their numbers. Through the bomb and the bullet, they try to make governments and communities dance to their tune. That is the real challenge. It is to the credit of many ordinary Churchgoers that they seek to create Christian homes, decent lives for their children, excellence in education and public services, modest prosperity for the community as a whole, and the opportunity to grow old with dignity. We should not forget that there is much constructive activity which goes unreported by the media. It is not only social and political success which manifests the Christian spirit or witnesses to the Kingdom of God in our midst. It is the 'failures', too: the attempts by men and women to demonstrate the vigour of their faith by trying to shape, reshape, and shape yet again the social and political framework.

Because extremists have been able to use fear to coerce the divided community into mental and spiritual as well as physical ghettos, the dreary and costly conflict continues, and will continue, until those outworn and self-defeating categories are displaced and a different type of leadership wins the support of the community. Human rights legislation can set standards, but unless people want to live according to those standards, little can change.

THE ROLE OF THE CHURCHES

We turn now to Christian initiatives which were sponsored by or organically related to Church life. Some of these initiatives are well documented. One of the first was the Churches' Industrial Council, established in 1956. All the main churches – Roman Catholic, Church of Ireland, Methodist, Presbyterian, and others – formally appointed their representatives to a body concerned for the need to increase employment and distribute wealth more equitably, to decrease discrimination in employment and in the location of industry, and to encourage the growth of an industrial society in Ireland neither exploitative nor destructive of the traditional and authentic Christian gospel. The single most important achievement of this group of lay and clerical representatives was in helping to secure recognition of the Irish Congress of Trades Unions by the Stormont Government. This gave rise directly to a host of positive policies in the economic development of Northern Ireland, including the training of its labour force in new skills, the promotion of productivity, and the distribution of industry.

During the past two decades, all the main Churches have been active in supporting or initiating moves to improve social and economic rights, especially in relation to employment and housing. Since 1978, there has been in existence the Human Rights Forum of the Irish Council of Churches. This has produced a number of pamphlets on human rights issues in Ireland, and these have been widely discussed in the Churches. The Forum has also collaborated with the Catholic Church's Commission for Justice and Peace on an examination of prisons in Ireland. Meanwhile, the Corrymeela Community in the North and Glencree in the South have tried to act as creative forces for new ideas. Their purpose – and that of other initiatives identified below – is not to reconcile people to repression or injustice, but to stress the imperatives of human rights, justice, and peace. Like the Columbanus Community, they give witness to the ecumenical and spiritual dimension of life which is vital to the witness of individual Christians and the institutional Churches.

Here we would like to commend those in the various Churches who have been pioneers of bridge-building, including such bodies as the Irish School of Ecumenics in Dublin; the sponsors of the talks held jointly at St Anne's Cathedral in Belfast and the Servite Priory in Benburb; the clergy and laity who sustain the ecumenical prayer and study groups at the Redemptorist Monastery in Clonard Street, Belfast; Catholic and Protestant Encounter (PACE); the Cross Group, started by the bereaved relatives of those killed in the troubles; the members of the Inter-Church Group on Faith and Politics who produced the pamphlet *Breaking down the enmity*;[4] The Mixed Marriages Association in the North and the Association of Interchurch Families in the South; the Quaker canteen for the families of prisoners at the Maze prison; and the organisers of the ecumenical carol service held each year at St Anne's Cathedral in Belfast. We are glad to learn that the Irish Theological Association operates on an ecumenical basis, and that useful ecumenical gatherings have been held at Ballymascanlon, Greenhills, and Glenstal. There is also a range of secular organisations which faithfully carry on their caring work in spite of tension and violence. Here, then, is a rich tapestry of healing and renewal crucial to the promotion and preservation of human rights, and helping to bind the community together.

The same impulse and commitment generated Christian initiatives in the Republic during this period. In Dublin, eminent politicians joined the first public protest outside the headquarters of the Provisional wing of the IRA.

Christian action includes factual or interpretative statements. Both the Irish and British Councils of Churches have pointed in numerous statements to the complex web of historical, political, and economic forces which have made Ireland what it is today. The Churches, with their majesty and power, their universality and profound traditions, command unique resources, and yet they are trapped in a situation which is, at least in part, of their own making.

At the same time, we should mention some of the shortcomings of the British and Irish Churches. The British Council of Churches (BCC), for instance, gave less prominence to 'Bloody Sunday' than to more distant events in Southern Rhodesia (now Zimbabwe) and South Africa. The British Council of Churches, as a matter of policy, is guided by the local ecumenical council, so that it reacts to events in Northern Ireland only at the request of the Irish Council of Churches. Such an arrangement has inhibited comment on Irish questions by the BCC, lest such comment be construed as interference in the affairs of a sister council. Better understanding of the situation in Ireland has been fostered by the recent meeting of the BCC Assembly in Cork (1986). But sensitivity to the wishes of the Irish Churches has tended to make it difficult for the British Churches to take seriously British responsibility in and for Ireland.

A similar situation exists for the Roman Catholic Church, where the different jurisdictions of episcopal conferences have inhibited the hierarchies in Great Britain from commenting on Irish questions without the agreement of the Irish Bishops. A joint liaison committee of the three episcopal conferences in these islands now exists, and it remains to be seen how effective this consultative machinery will be.

In any case, the processes of consultation and co-ordination make it difficult to respond quickly to human rights violations or other important matters. The voices of the Churches of Great Britain have been at best muted when the United Kingdom has been condemned for its actions in Northern Ireland by the European Commission and Court at Strasbourg. This failure by the Churches of Great Britain to recognise the sins of omission and commission by their own government is as much part of the problem as is the sectarianism and bigotry sometimes exhibited by Churches in Ireland.

The Irish Churches have suffered, as has the whole of Irish society, from the emigration of talented people, and the consequent paucity of irenic leadership. It has been estimated that over 80 per cent of Northern Ireland students who study outside Northern Ireland do not return there after graduation. In the South, despite a surge in the economy in the 1960s, the employment situation has improved little since partition: it has been estimated that 31000 people left the Republic of Ireland to find their fortune elsewhere in 1985–6. Social workers estimate that 2000 Irish men or women leave each month to live in Great Britain. Since 1983, about 100000 people have emigrated, mostly to the United Kingdom, the United States of America, and Canada. No one who has travelled the world, and particularly the Southern hemisphere, can fail to be impressed with the courage and creative energy of Irish men and women in the mission field, engaged in immense ventures demanding heroism and calling for commitment of the highest order, and who possess a vigorous personal theology which is intellectually questing. Also apparent is the high achievement by Irish men and women from both sides of the border in the corporate and political fields, especially in the United States of America, the United Kingdom, and the older Commonwealth countries. The history of Ireland today, and certainly the record of the Churches, might have been different if a proportion of these men and women had remained in the land of their birth.

There are important exceptions to the loss of talent from Northern Ireland, for instance in the fields of medical science, art, and poetry; and there remain some exceptional individuals in all walks of life, including the institutional Churches. But no community can sustain a persistent human haemorrhage for long without dire consequences.

All communities in these islands suffered substantial loss of life in two world wars, which in Ireland compounded the drain of human resources caused by high emigration. The Republic of Ireland remained neutral during the Second World War, but nonetheless many Southern Irishmen fought and died in both conflicts. It is estimated that some 54500 people from the two parts of Ireland died as a result of the two wars. This represents for both North and South another critical loss of human potential.

Moreover, Ireland did not experience the world-wide influx of refugees and migrants from central and eastern Europe immediately following the two world wars, nor the flow of Commonwealth citizens to Great Britain and the old Commonwealth countries:

indeed, Ireland contributed throughout to the outflow.

For half a century, Ireland has produced many Christian leaders of outstanding ability, giving witness to intellectual and spiritual leadership; yet many of these have decided to live and work outside Ireland. To that degree, the Christian base is weakened. It is not simply a question of a lack of individual leadership here or there, but a cumulative drain over decades and even generations, which may account for a theological impoverishment and an inability to address the wider issues arising from the use of religion in support of partisan politics. The burden of leadership falls on a few.

The outflow of talent from both communities, and the absence of large-scale immigration, has reinforced social introversion, or what Bishop Philbin (formerly of Down and Connor) described as a 'siege mentality'. This may be one reason why the incipient peace movements described above did not flourish over a long enough period. This does not detract from the strength of character needed to plant the seeds of peace in the first instance. But too often social introversion has hindered progress. The outward flow of emigration cannot easily be reversed: it is virtually self-perpetuating: 'Things fall apart; the centre cannot hold'.

In 1976, a joint working party of Protestant and Catholic leaders, chaired jointly by Bishop Cahal Daly and the Rev. Dr Eric Gallagher, issued an agreed report entitled *Violence in Ireland – a report to the Churches*. It is an extremely valuable document, declaring in its 16 recommendations much that we would wish to declare ourselves on this subject. Its conclusions are reproduced in our Appendix 5. The report was well received, but little was done to implement the recommendations. Inertia was present. Today, 10 years after the report was published, there is some evidence that its recommendations on informing the authorities of illegal activities may have helped to increase the flow of such information. The recommendation in favour of peace education gave rise to the appointment by the Irish Council of Churches of a staff member to this work, linked with the director of the Roman Catholic Commission for Justice and Peace. The clauses dealing with education and social investigation remain unimplemented.

Although a measure of continuity is given to Presbyterianism and Methodism by virtue of the offices of Clerk of the Assembly and the Secretary of Conference respectively, mainstream Methodists and Presbyterians change their presiding officers annually, which complicates inter-Church co-operation, particularly as Catholic leaders enjoy life appointments. Although the Catholic Church can act quickly in emergencies through the Cardinal or the Bishops, it can also be as cumbersome at other times as the Protestant Churches. Individual clergymen, especially Protestants, are always afraid of dividing their congregations. This acts as a real restraint on action and encourages conformity. For instance, under their form of Church government, a Presbyterian minister who encounters strong opposition within his congregation may feel he must move to another charge, if he can get a call, otherwise he will be unemployed and may well have to emigrate. It is only human under these circumstances to be cautious in challenging traditional attitudes.

From time to time, specific initiatives have been taken by the Churches. In the past decade, the heads of the four main Churches have begun to practise some of the basic virtues of ecumenism. Given Irish traditions, that is a brave adventure. In their individual or collective statements, they have effectively outlawed illegal and subversive organisations like the IRA and the Ulster Volunteer Force (UVF). They have condemned violence, upheld human rights, and appealed for peace. In Derry, the Roman Catholic Bishop, Edward Daly, has consistently condemned the violence in his city as 'cowardly and immoral'. Repeating the words of Bishop Philbin, he has said that the IRA is 'of the devil'.[5] He has warned that men and women who kill others for political purposes in Ireland were following 'the gospel of Satan' and were, in effect, 'excommunicating themselves'. The present Catholic Bishop of Down and Connor, Dr Cahal Daly, who has often acknowledged that there are virtues in Protestantism, has consistently rejected violence as a means for attaining political objectives. Typical was a declaration, delivered at Mass in the Falls Road, Belfast, when Bishop Daly said:

> These are days of decision for Christians, days of choice. They call for a new form of 'No', a decisive Christian 'No' ... 'No' to violence and the threat of violence. 'No' to talk of force and to men in para-military or pseudo-military dress and regalia. 'No' to false leaders who would set our two communities at one another's throats.

The Bishop condemned such violence as 'a grievous sin against God', and he advised that it represented an act of 'appalling recklessness and irresponsibility' in the prevailing social situation.[6] This is powerful language in Catholic Ireland.

The Moderator of the General Assembly of the Presbyterian

Church in Ireland, the Rt Rev. Dr John Thompson, in condemning violence whether perpetrated from within the Protestant or Catholic communities, said recently, 'An area which concerns us all is that of law and order. The responsibility of all in positions of power in our society to act and speak within the law is of paramount importance at the present time'.[8] The Church of Ireland Archbishop of Armagh, Dr Robin Eames, speaking in 1986 on the uncertainties created by the Anglo–Irish Agreement, soundly condemned all sectarian murders 'and sectarian rhetoric which has sullied the name of Protestantism'. He pointed to 'a lesson of history [that] you cannot legislate for reconciliation. Reconciliation is a process. It becomes a reality when people want it to be a reality'.[8] In recent years, therefore, the main Church leaders have been clear in their renunciation of violence to secure political objectives. That key paramilitary groups have ignored the advice underlines the increasing gap between Church leaders and the men and women of violence. This remains a challenge for the Churches.

We know the perception of people is that Church leaders prefer not to speak out. We know also that a conciliatory statement one week may be followed by an abrasive one the next. The challenge to the Churches is to maintain a consistent standard in judging policies and acts of the two communities.

Occasionally Church leaders take explicitly 'political' initiatives. For instance, a group of Protestant Church leaders led by the Rev. William Arlow, then associate secretary of the Irish Council of Churches, and including prominent clergy from the British and Irish Councils of Churches, met Provisional IRA and Sinn Fein leaders at a hotel in Feakle, in the Irish Republic, around New Year's Day 1974–5. The Provisionals had proposed an 11 day cease-fire over Christmas and New Year, and Merlyn Rees had said that activity by the security forces would be related to the level of paramilitary violence. The republicans asked that the UK Government should agree 'to withdraw from Ireland within twelve months of the adoption of [a] new all-Ireland constitution' and to amnesty 'all political prisoners in Britain and Ireland'. Church leaders passed on the gist of what the Provisionals were demanding to British ministers, but it was inconceivable that such an ultimatum could be accepted. All that Merlyn Rees could do was to say that a genuine and sustained cease-fire 'would create a new situation'.[9] The cease-fire fizzled out during 1975.

Opinions differ about the significance of the Feakle meeting. It involved some of the most senior men from the Protestant Churches. It was an act of great courage, almost of desperation, for leaders of major Churches, revolted by the continuing shedding of innocent blood, to meet republican paramilitaries. It was widely regarded as a naive intervention, and it showed that the Protestant Churches could not bring the violence to an end simply by irenic appeals. While widely misunderstood at the time, and despite being unsuccessful in ending the violence, it nonetheless represented an unusual and brave example of Christian leadership.

CHALLENGES

Regardless of the waxing and waning of violence in Ireland, fundamental challenges face Christians and the Churches throughout the archipelago. All these challenges are tangled with forces more or less demonic, which make for the tragedy of Ireland.

In the North, the Protestants face the task of developing a more tolerant attitude to Catholics. Whatever reservations they may have about the doctrines of the Church of Rome, Protestants should be encouraged to treat individual Catholics with humanity, recognising that unless human and civil rights of all are respected, the minority cannot be expected to play a responsible role in the affairs of Northern Ireland. The consequences of emigration, unemployment, and poverty demand energy and creativity. The rejection of political violence must be unconditional.

The Catholics in both parts of Ireland could make a point of understanding the fears of the Protestant community in the North, their belief that the ties with Great Britain are under threat, their sense that the Anglo–Irish Agreement was concluded behind their back, as it were, their worries that the Protestant community is being systematically exterminated in the border areas.

In the Irish Republic, a Roman Catholic electorate which determines the Constitution, laws, and social standards of society could develop a more pluralistic attitude. The problem was highlighted during the course of our work when the people of the Republic voted on constitutional amendments in a way that suggested to Northern Protestants that the Republic did not respect the consciences of those citizens who were not Catholics. Protestantism has for 400 years been an authentic and important thread in the tapestry of

Irish history. The Northern Protestant has a powerful case when he asks: 'Why should I join a united Ireland when, in my lifetime, I have seen the people of my tradition in the Republic of Ireland drop from over 10 per cent of the population to less than 4 per cent today?' Whilst this fall in the Protestant population includes the departure of the armed forces of the British Crown and civil servants and their families, such a Northern reaction cannot be dismissed as mere bigotry. Given the Protestants' fixity of purpose and strength of conviction, it is not likely to weaken because conditions get worse.

The Churches in Great Britain could be more effective if they were to realise that they are part of the problem, and share in the responsibility for the present unhappy state of affairs. British Churches are not at present well geared to deal with the situation in Northern Ireland. Departments of community affairs or social responsibility are preoccupied with problems in Great Britain itself; departments of international affairs are precluded from dealing with Northern Ireland since it is not foreign territory. All Churches are hesitant to act without the wholehearted backing of their counterparts in Ireland. The three Catholic hierarchies have established a liaison committee to deal with issues affecting Northern Ireland, and the Society of Friends has a committee on Northern Ireland representing members in Great Britain and both parts of Ireland. Other than these, the Churches in Great Britain are not well equipped to respond quickly to developments.

But this is not simply an organisational question. There is a widespread mood in Great Britain, inside and outside the Churches, that the Northern Ireland problem is boring, incomprehensible, and insoluble, that the people of Northern Ireland have only themselves to blame for the current mess. We have written in Chapter 4 that the two communities in Northern Ireland are trapped in a situation which they have inherited from the past. Great Britain is similarly trapped: the Government cannot impose a solution, but neither can it now disengage with honour.

We would encourage the Churches throughout Ireland and Great Britain to strengthen their teaching ministries, countering ignorance, and showing how Christian faith and obedience can help to create new conditions throughout Ireland. We would like to see many more links between the Churches of Great Britain and Ireland, reinforcing those links which have already been forged, some of them at parish level. Much Roman Catholicism in Great Britain is of Irish origin, just as much Protestantism in Ireland is of Scottish or English origin.

There are many areas of social concern where the people of these islands face common problems.

Religious discord in Ireland and racial tensions in Great Britain offer similar challenges to committed Christians. The recent Church of England report on inner city deprivation, *Faith in the City*, offers an agenda for co-operation and mutual support by the Churches. The spread of drug abuse and alcoholism, the threat of AIDS, the growth of petty criminality and urban violence, the freedom of the media, these are all areas for co-operation. We could envisage inter-Church pastoral groups ministering to Irish immigrants in Great Britain; there is scope for the joint training of clergy. All the Churches can play a part, for human and civil rights are not likely to be respected if social and religious institutions are fragmented.

The Churches of ethnic minorities in Great Britain may have a special role in helping the larger Churches to understand what it means to belong to a minority, to be the victim of discrimination, to be misunderstood or despised.

Christians have a common mission in an increasingly secular world. Each of us needs help in escaping from the attitudes of the past.

We cannot close this chapter without paying tribute to those Christian men and women throughout Ireland who work for peace and understanding, for tolerance and a new way forward, and whose strength and creativity are a direct expression of their Christian faith and experience. But for them, Northern Ireland would be in a far worse condition today than it is. No matter how much legislation is enacted for civil and human rights, a community incessantly at war may destroy itself, so that there are neither victors nor vanquished. Until Christians are reconciled to each other and shift social action from violence and revenge to constructive and positive new ventures in politics and social affairs, little is likely to change. The 'new humanity' of which Paul wrote can flourish in Ireland again, for it was here, 1600 years ago, that those who lived in beehive-like dwellings kept the Faith on the Western edge of Europe.

Notes and References

1. *Church and Nation in a Secular Age* (London: Darton, 1983) p. 3.
2. Brian Faulkner, *Memoirs of a Statesman* (ed. by John Houston) (London: Weidenfeld and Nicolson, 1978) pp. 47–9, 58–9; Terence O'Neill, *Autobiography* (London: Hart-Davies, 1972) pp. 103, 106; James Callaghan, *A House divided: The dilemma of Northern Ireland* (London: Collins, 1973), p. 47.
3. Eric Gallagher and Stanley Worrall, *Christians in Ulster, 1968–1980* (Oxford: Oxford University Press, 1982) p. 180.
4. Draft for discussion published in 1984 and available from 8 Upper Crescent, Belfast 7; or 35 Lower Leeson Street, Dublin 2; or 211 Church Park, Portadown (price 50p plus postage).
5. 21 June 1974.
6. 12 November 1986.
7. 13 March 1987.
8. 21 October 1986.
9. For two accounts of the Feakle meeting and the cease-fire, one sympathetic and written by a participant, and one detached and from a ministerial point of view, see Gallagher and Worrall *Christians in Ulster*, pp. 1–2, 96–102, 106; and Merlyn Rees, *Northern Ireland: a personal perspective* (London: Methuen, 1985) pp. 150–81.

8 Political Violence and the Rule of Law

TERRORISM AND COUNTER-TERRORISM

The situation of violence and counter-violence in Northern Ireland since 1968 has few parallels in Western Europe. Resort to the bullet rather than the ballot threatens the lives of innocent people, but it does more than that: it erodes the rule of law and impairs the whole fabric of human society. Each incident of sectarian violence tempts the paramilitaries of the other side to undertake acts of retribution. The security forces are always vulnerable to attack, and any indiscriminate or excessive use of force by them is likely to lead to a fresh outbreak of terrorism. There have been times when the security forces have felt threatened by extremist elements from both ends of the spectrum.

When organised subversion exceeds a certain critical point, the government in a democracy is likely to seek parliamentary approval for emergency legislation which is virtually certain to infringe civil rights and freedoms. Moreover, the security forces are composed of fallible human beings in uniform. We have been especially appalled during our work to hear of people being killed or wounded 'indirectly', 'unintentionally', or 'by mistake', whether such killings were committed by republican or loyalist paramilitaries or by the security forces.

During a recent discussion on terrorism at the United Nations, it became clear that a main aim of terrorists is not to defeat government forces in armed struggle, but to demonstrate that established authority cannot assure the security of ordinary people. A secondary aim is to provoke the security forces to over-react. The common thread of terrorism is the use of violence to instil fear and thus extract concessions. It does not require great numbers to do that. Although terrorists may use the concept and language of human rights, their real aim is to achieve a political goal by intimidation rather than persuasion.

It was inevitable that a large part of our report should be concerned with Northern Ireland, but we have no wish to give the impression that civil and human rights are never endangered elsewhere in these

164

islands. Nor do we consider that threats to liberty deserve attention only when there has been a resort to violence. The claims of black minorities in the inner cities are compelling, even if they do not take to the gun. But Northern Ireland is the region where our two states face a common danger and have a common responsibility.

Because human beings have a tendency to pursue their own interests at the expense of other people, sometimes destructively, it is necessary to establish a government system so as to create the conditions in which human personality can develop. Government is grounded in a mixture of consent and coercion. Nevertheless, the same tendencies in human nature that make it necessary for the state to employ coercion are also present in the agents of the state and others who exercise power, so that those who wield power, including the agencies of government, must themselves be subject to law. In any society, and particularly in a divided society, the police can come to represent the outlook and interests of one group, or at least can seem to do so. In Great Britain, this has happened in relations between the police and minority communities in inner city areas, as well as with strikers on picket lines. In Northern Ireland, the police are mainly Protestant, though every effort is now made to recruit on a non-communal basis. What is needed is a system by which police behaviour is monitored impartially and an aggrieved citizen can be confident that complaints will be dealt with honestly and effectively.

In various parts of this Report, mention has been made of the effect of terrorism on the life of Northern Ireland. The statistics of terrorism may give some idea of what is involved but cannot reveal the full effect on the lives of those who have suffered or how the question of terrorism pervades the whole of society. Because terrorism directly challenges the whole community, government has the duty to adopt adequate measures to combat it. Some of these measures inevitably infringe or curtail a number of established civil rights. It is crucial, however, that when considering the type of emergency laws which exist and how the powers they confer are exercised, there be no confusion about the extent and nature of the terrorist threat. The forms of intimidation practised by terrorists in Northern Ireland amount to a total denial of fundamental human and civil rights. Murder, bombing, abduction, secret courts, and punishment shootings are all part of the tactics employed. Those who deny the most basic rights of others have little credibility when they criticise the security forces – a point underlined by Article 17 of the European Convention on Human Rights when it states that nothing in the Convention implies a right 'to engage in any activity . . . aimed at the destruction of any of the rights and freedoms' set forth in the Convention. We have said that government is based on a mixture of consent and coercion. If the consent of the people is withheld, as happened in Iran under the Shah and in the Philippines under Marcos, and as is the case today with the apartheid *régime* in South Africa, the government has lost its legitimacy, whatever its monopoly of uniforms and whips and guns. The authority of government is not derived from its monopoly of force, but from the consent of the people in whose name it acts.

Critics of constitutional democracy sometimes point to the violence implicit in 'the system' as a justification for resort to counter-violence for political goals – what is sometimes called 'institutional violence' or 'systemic violence'. As John Rawls has observed, 'To employ the coercive apparatus of the state in order to maintain manifestly unjust institutions is itself a form of illegitimate force that men in due course have a right to resist'.[1] For subversive elements in Northern Ireland, the main aim of political protest is to expose the brutality of the system. They welcome rather than deplore an excessive response by the security forces, because it reveals what they believe is the true situation for all to see. Terrorism in its military role tends to commit acts of indiscriminate violence; in its political role, it seeks to discredit the security forces and to undermine public confidence in all forms of established authority. The difficulty for the believer in civil liberties is that the effort to discredit security forces may be conducted in the language of human rights.

Christians down the centuries have believed that the powers that be are ordained of God, and that we are all subject to the higher powers. But those theological statements of Paul are to be understood in the context of the New Testament as a whole, and made at a time when Christians to all intents and purposes took no part in the public affairs of a pagan empire. That was to change with the conversion of Constantine and the writings of Augustine of Hippo, who began the task of identifying the circumstances in which Christians are justified in using armed force in defence of Christian values and institutions. At first, the Christian tradition about the just use of force was applied only to wars between rulers, but from the time of Thomas Aquinas in the thirteenth century, there has also been a doctrine about the use of force in rebellion against unjust authority.

The doctrines of the just war and the just rebellion consist of restrictions rather than permissions. Rebellion is justified only if the established *régime* is intolerably evil and after every effort has been made to achieve change by peaceful means. In our view, there is not a vestige of a basis for the use of violence for political ends in Northern Ireland today. There are, however, a number of pitfalls in assessing whether peaceful ways of achieving change have been exhausted. The nationalist community can appeal to history, the unionist community to present realities, as evidence that political aspirations have been frustrated or disregarded. The legal proscription of organisations advocating political violence makes it difficult to assess the paramilitary claims that they enjoy the support of their respective communities: we would simply note that where paramilitary organisations have political counterparts, as in the case of the IRA and Sinn Fein, and where these political counterparts have submitted themselves to the vote of the people, the results do not justify the claim that they have a mandate from a majority of their own community to resort to armed struggle. Never since the onset of the present troubles has Sinn Fein achieved a majority of nationalist votes in the North, and its electoral support in the South is now derisory.

Northern Ireland faces particular problems because of differences of aspiration about the status of the region, to some extent coloured by memories of past injustices. It is in this situation that ministers, officials, and leaders of opinion seek to promote respect for the institutions of law and government. This will not be achieved by gimmickry; the only realistic means of developing confidence in public institutions in Northern Ireland is for these institutions to be seen to be above factional interest.

From time to time there are unionist demands for 'unleashing' the security forces in Northern Ireland, for the unionist community considers that the Government has not taken seriously enough its positive obligation to maintain order. We want to see the security forces as effective as is humanely possible, but always subject to the law and to such checks and balances as are necessary to ensure that the interests of the whole of society rather than one segment are protected.

The underlying principles of maintaining law and order are that the security forces shall use as much force as is strictly necessary (the principle of proportion) and only against those believed to be breaking or threatening to break the law (the principle of discrimination). These principles are not simply matters of prudence: they are grounded in a long tradition of Christian reflection on the use of force; they are the touchstone of weapons and tactics in ever new and changing contexts.

Those who take up arms against the state and claim to be engaged in a war cannot, at the same time, claim to be treated by the security forces as civilians. The British Government maintains that what is happening in Northern Ireland is not war but criminal terrorism, and so the security forces must be careful to observe the rules for preventing crime and apprehending criminals with the minimal force that is required. This can confront the security forces with difficult operational decisions, especially when a legitimate action against persons carrying arms has the unintended and indirect effect of harming the innocent, or when paramilitaries conceal themselves in the peaceable population. If mistakes occur, as they will, it is better to admit them than to attempt to cover them up: in the long run, a policy of official candour will increase public respect for the security forces rather than the reverse – and it is in the long run that attempts to conceal mistakes are so often exposed.

We turn now to some particular aspect of the maintenance of law and order in Northern Ireland. We cannot be comprehensive, nor are we in a position to give authoritative judgements on all matters of concern, for we lack expertise on the operational problems facing the security forces and the prison service, and on some issues we do not have access to confidential information on which official policy is based. We focus, therefore, on certain topics which have a direct human rights dimension.

STATES OF EMERGENCY

The international code on human rights recognises that emergencies may occur in which it may be necessary to abridge the rights of citizens in some respects. One Article of the European Convention on Human Rights says that in time of 'war or other public emergency threatening the life of the nation' a derogation may be entered to permit measures 'strictly required by the exigencies of the situation' (Article 15). There are, however, certain Articles in the Convention from which there can be no derogation, such as those prohibiting torture and slavery. The UN Covenant on Civil and Political Rights has a similar provision, defining the emergency and the permitted measures in the same terms, and with a longer list of Articles from which derogation is not permitted. But the UN Covenant goes further than the European Convention in one respect, in that the existence of the emergency has to be 'officially proclaimed' (Article 4).

Emergency provisions are a common feature of national constitutions or laws. Sometimes they involve the declaration of a state of siege or a state of emergency. Various emergency laws also exist in the United Kingdom. The Acts authorise the making of regulations to protect the essentials of life in emergencies, but such regulations can be made only in the event of a declaration of an emergency.[2] These statutes are intended to cope with disruption caused by national catastrophes, or by widespread strikes, rather than that arising from terrorism. In the Irish Republic, provision similar to the British legislation is made by an Act which also requires the declaration of a state of emergency.[3] In addition, the Constitution permits derogation from the Constitution by legislation 'for the purpose of securing the public safety and the preservation of the State in time of war or armed rebellion'. This can include an armed conflict to which the Irish Republic is not a party if parliament so resolves.[4] Such resolutions were passed in 1939 with regard to the Second World War, to be revoked in 1976 and replaced by a resolution relating to the troubles in Northern Ireland. This resolution permitted the passing of a law containing limited powers of detention without charge or trial,[5] similar to the seven-day detention power in the United Kingdom.[6] The Irish statute is not currently in force but can be reactivated by Order.

Currently no declared state of emergency exists anywhere in the United Kingdom. The British Government had at one time entered derogations with the United Nations and the Council of Europe with regard to the provisions in Section 12 of the Emergency Provisions Act, which permitted detention without charge or trial for unlimited periods, but these derogations have now been withdrawn. However, the Government keeps the Emergency Provisions Act on the Statute book, so that powers to detain without trial are held in reserve. Though the powers are not currently in force, they could be reactivated by Order in Council, which could take effect without prior parliamentary approval. The Government's case for this is that, should conditions in Northern Ireland deteriorate rapidly, the Northern Ireland Secretary would be able to reintroduce detention without trial without the need for new legislation.[7]

We have grave reservations about this situation. Emergencies are exceptional states, and emergency powers are exceptional powers. They should be available to a democratic government only when a real emergency actually exists. Moreover, the decision to bring these powers into operation should be subject to more effective parliamentary control. Even then, their operation should be limited to the actual duration of the emergency, and the measures authorised should be only 'to the extent strictly required by the exigencies of the situation'. We consider it wrong in principle that any government should keep such powers in a cupboard to which it has the only key. Regrettably, this is the position in a number of countries governed by oppressive *régimes* and has been rightly condemned from many quarters. We do not think it ought to continue to be the position in the United Kingdom, and we therefore urge that the relevant section of the Emergency Powers Act be repealed. We note that this recommendation was also made by the Baker report,[8] but is not contained in the Bill currently before parliament implementing some of Sir George Baker's recommendations.

PROSCRIBED ORGANISATIONS

Membership of a proscribed organisation is an offence in Northern Ireland under the Emergency Provisions Act and in Great Britain under the Prevention of Terrorism Act. However, the lists of proscribed organisations are different as there are six organisations which are illegal in Northern Ireland but not in Great Britain. The Secretary of State for Northern Ireland, for the purposes of the Emergency Provisions Act, may by Order add to the list any organisation that appears to him to be concerned in promoting or encouraging terrorism. He can also remove an organisation from the list. The Home Secretary may make similar Orders for the purposes of the Prevention of Terrorism Act. In either case, the Orders do not take effect unless approved by resolutions of both Houses of Parliament.

These powers to proscribe organisations caused us difficulty. A number of us regard as fundamentally objectionable the proscription of any organisation as such. They take the view that while terrorist *acts*, including the making of common arrangements in the form of a conspiracy to commit violence, are rightly criminal, membership of an organisation is evidence of nothing more than an undesirable disposition, and a mere evil disposition has never been a crime in any part of the United Kingdom. This view was put to the late Sir George Baker in the following terms: 'What ought to be illegal . . . is not their beliefs or objectives . . . but rather the means they use to implement those beliefs and objectives'.[9] Those who take this view would prefer the legal proscription of all organisations to be lifted, while ensuring so far as possible that any members of those organisations who actually carry out, or conspire to carry out, criminal acts are brought to justice under the ordinary law of the land.

The case for the continued proscription of terrorist organisations is that it is an expression of the outrage of ordinary citizens at terrorism and the acts of the proscribed organisations. Without measures like proscription, it is argued, otherwise law-abiding citizens might be provoked into taking the law into their own hands and engaging in reprisals. Reprisal outrages do already occur: without proscription, their incidence might well be higher. There is also the practical consequence that proscription may help to stem the flow of funds to the proscribed organisations. To de-proscribe an organisation might be taken to imply that the organisation had changed, or that the view which society takes of it had changed.

We are concerned that the list of proscribed organisations is not the same in all jurisdictions in the United Kingdom. It would be absurd if those who plan or support terrorism in one jurisdiction were able to operate with greater freedom in another. If someone in Great Britain were to join an organisation proscribed in Northern Ireland but not in Great Britain, such as the Ulster Volunteer Force, he would commit no crime; but if such a person were then to travel to Belfast for some innocent purpose, such as supporting his football team, he would be guilty of a serious crime the moment he set foot in Northern Ireland. If proscription is to remain, we recommend uniformity throughout the United Kingdom, and also uniformity between the United Kingdom and the Republic, if that were possible.

EXCLUSION ORDERS

Under the Prevention of Terrorism Act, Ministers may issue Orders excluding a named person from entering the United Kingdom if there is reason to believe that the person is coming to commit, prepare for, or instigate acts of terrorism. Similar Orders may be issued to prevent persons moving from Northern Ireland to Great Britain or vice-versa.

There is an administrative procedure for review of Orders, but no right of appeal.[10]

The exclusion of persons from Northern Ireland or from Great Britain raises grave issues. Preventing citizens of a country from moving freely within that country involves an infringement of their human rights. The Universal Declaration of Human Rights affirms the right of everyone to freedom of movement within the borders of the state (Article 13), and this freedom is included in the UN Covenant on civil and political rights, to which the United Kingdom is a party.

The Standing Advisory Commission on Human Rights (SACHR) has consistently objected in principle to the use of these Orders within the United Kingdom, on the ground that they deprive a person of a basic human right without a judicial hearing.[11] This view found considerable support in the annual review of the Act for 1985 submitted by Sir Cyril Phillips. He recommended that no further Orders be made and suggested that the power to exclude should not be renewed. Lord Colville, in the review for 1986, took the same view. He recognised that the ending of the power to exclude from one part of the United Kingdom to another would result in more intrusive port procedures, but this he considered to be more acceptable than a system of internal exile.[12] We entirely share these views.

THE SECURITY FORCES

Government security policy in the past decade has been to rely as much as possible on the ordinary criminal process, as modified by emergency legislation. With this has gone an attempt to put the main burden of maintaining order on the Royal Ulster Constabulary and, where possible, to use the Ulster Defence Regiment and the army as a back-up force. This policy has two drawbacks. First, increased police powers and emergency procedures have come to be regarded as part of the normal administration of justice. Secondly, the continuation of emergency procedures year after year has alienated some sections of the community.

An example of the danger of alienating ordinary citizens concerns the power to stop and question for the purpose of ascertaining a person's identity and his or her possible knowledge of recent terrorist incidents.[13] It has been alleged that the army, rather than operating within the legislation, is illegally taking a census, particularly when it counts the occupants of houses late at night. The army, on the other hand, denies that the power has been used unlawfully.

In part, the problem reflects the fact that action taken to deal with terrorism often becomes irksome and an intrusion into private lives, and this quickly leads to resentment. But the problem arises in part from the different perceptions of those involved, and this could be minimised by a more careful and considerate exercise of power and a greater willingness by ordinary citizens to co-operate with those responsible for maintaining law and order.

The Police Authority in Northern Ireland is appointed by the Secretary of State, constituted so as to reflect as wide a cross-section of the community as possible. If, in the future, there should be a devolution of functions in Northern Ireland, we hope that the Police Authority would be reconstituted so as to contain a substantial cross-community element appointed by an elected Northern Ireland assembly.

A crucial issue in Northern Ireland, and in many parts of Great Britain as well, is how confidence in the policy may be maintained. No doubt some authoritarian personalities are attracted to the police, and the police are exposed to exceptional temptations to behave roughly, take short cuts, or engage in crooked practices.

Catholics number about 40 per cent of the population of Northern Ireland but only about 9 per cent of the Royal Ulster Constabulary. We understand that some 12 per cent of recruits in 1984 were Catholics. If this trend should continue, it will be many years before the proportion of Catholics in the RUC corresponds to their proportion of the population as a whole. We hope that conditions will soon exist in which members of the minority community will be willing to join the police service in increasing numbers.

Police forces throughout the democratic world receive complaints from members of the public, and Northern Ireland is no exception. In 1985, 2254 cases of complaint against police officers were recorded. During the course of the year, 3237 complaints from 1985 or previous years were dealt with by the RUC, of which 618 were anonymous or could not be properly investigated, 1349 were withdrawn, 1219 were not substantiated, and 51 were substantiated and were dealt with by internal disciplinary procedures or by the Courts, depending on the nature of the offence.

Some dissatisfied complainants took their cases to the Police Complaints Board, which was established in 1977 to examine complaints of misconduct by members of the Royal Ulster Constabulary. In 1985, the Board dealt with 1866 cases of complaint of which 1306 were anonymous, repetitive, incapable of completion, or subsequently withdrawn. The remaining 560 cases contained 1261 items of complaint, mainly alleging assault, incivility, oppressive conduct, or harassment. Of these, 11 cases resulted in prosecutions by the Director of Public Prosecutions for assault and theft; three cases of discreditable conduct were dealt with internally by the Deputy Chief Constable; in 6 cases the Board recommended disciplinary charges of abuse of authority or disobedience to orders; and in one case the Board itself directed disciplinary charges of abuse of authority. Informal disciplinary action in the form of advice or a warning was taken in 36 cases.[14]

That the Complaints Board is not a front for the RUC can be illustrated by a difference of opinion between the Board and the Deputy Chief Constable over when it is 'reasonable' to stop and search persons suspected of carrying drugs.

> The mere fact that a person is known to have a previous conviction for unlawful possession of an article or that a person is carrying a particular kind of property or is dressed in a certain way or has a certain hairstyle is not, of itself, a reasonable ground for suspicion.[16]

We would add that the statistical element of the 1985 report of the Police Complaints Board was the least intelligible of those reports we saw from statutory bodies in our areas of concern.

A revised procedure for complaints against the police was under review as we finalised our Report. A new commission is to be created with additional powers to supervise police investigations into serious complaints, and with procedures for dealing informally with less serious complaints. The Standing Advisory Commission on Human Rights considers that the new procedure will be 'both elaborate and complex' and that 'it will be very difficult for ordinary members of the public to understand it properly'.[16] The same might be said of existing procedures!

RIOTS

Both the UN Code of Conduct for law enforcement officials (Article 3) and the Council of Europe's Declaration on the Police (para. 12) seek to place limits on the force used in police responses to public disorder. Social changes and the alienation of persons from authority give rise today to potential or actual situations of disorder. Unwise counter-measures by the police can have the effect of escalating the disorder. In Northern Ireland, the use of CS gas at the beginning of the troubles, and more recently of plastic bullets, has raised serious questions about police procedures.

Apart from Northern Ireland, plastic bullets are available to the police and have been used during the past 10 years in Belgium, Switzerland, and Spain; they are available but have not been used in Great Britain, Cyprus, Luxembourg, and Portugal. Other non-lethal means of riot control include mounted police, harassing gas such as CS, and water cannon. CS or similar chemical agents have been used over the past 10 years in Northern Ireland, as well as in Cyprus, Denmark, the Federal Republic of Germany, the Netherlands, and Switzerland. Water cannon, presently under consideration in Great Britain, have been used within the past 10 years in Belgium, Cyprus, the Federal Republic of Germany, the Netherlands, and Switzerland. We understand that neither CS gas nor water cannon is available to the police in the Republic of Ireland. As a final resort, fire-arms are carried as part of regular police equipment in a number of West European countries. Other technical aids such as barriers, shields, truncheons, and irritants added to water are commonly available.

Difficult operational decisions have often to be made about the use of such devices. It is the duty of the security forces to prevent or quell disorder, yet they must achieve this by using limited force and in such a way as to avoid an escalation or spreading of disorder. Common law allows the use of reasonable force but gives no further guidance, for the courts have said that it is largely a matter of fact whether the force used in a particular situation was reasonable.

Guidance to the police in Northern Ireland on the use of fire-arms is given in the Chief Constable's Force Orders and to the army by the Yellow Card. We believe that urgent consideration should be given to the publication of the guidance given to the security forces on the use of lethal fire-arms, perhaps in the context of the Code of Practice for the exercise of emergency powers by the security forces, so that ordinary citizens may be fully aware of the situation. We know that there are one or two cogent arguments against the course we recommend, but much current suspicion against the security forces in Northern Ireland is based on garbled information. This is one case where openness is of crucial importance, even if there are some risks.

Two international treaties to which the United Kingdom is a party affirm the right to freedom of assembly, subject to such restrictions as may be necessary in a democratic society to maintain order and to protect the rights and freedoms of others.[17] This balances the scales in favour of permitting demonstrations and places an onus on those who would restrict them. In considering restrictions, we would distinguish between genuine demonstrations and coat-trailing exercises which are intended to provoke. In practice, it is not always easy to distinguish between the two. Moreover, there may be occasions where a number of otherwise legitimate demonstrations clash, or where a demonstration which would be unobjectionable at one site may cause a problem at another.

Public parades have been a feature of life in Northern Ireland for many generations. Hundreds of parades, large and small, by such organisations as the Orange Order, the Apprentice Boys of Derry, and the Ancient Order of Hibernians, take place from spring until early autumn each year. Most of these take place without incident, but a number cause local tension and have sometimes been the occasion of riots and conflict with the police.

Tension usually rises because a right is claimed to parade along routes which are regarded as 'traditional'. Parades sometimes pass through areas now mainly inhabited by people from the other community, and such parades are regarded as provocative assertions of territorial domination. Unionists, in particular, have sometimes asserted an inalienable right to parade where their forefathers did, even in areas where the majority of the inhabitants is now Catholic. If a choice has to be made, we would attach more importance in the circumstances of today to the maintenance of intercommunal harmony than to the assertion of a right to parade along a traditional route.

In his annual report for 1985, the Chief Constable proposed that an independent public tribunal be established to decide on the holding and routeing of parades. There are two aspects to this problem, decisions on routeing and decisions to ban. Under the Public Order Act 1986 decisions on *routeing* in Great Britain are taken by the police, with the possibility of an application to the courts for a judicial review. Decisions on *bans* are taken by district councils (in London by the Home Secretary) on the recommendation of the police, with the possibility of judicial review. In Northern Ireland, rerouteing decisions are taken by the police, but decisions on bans are taken by the Secretary for State, either on information (but not necessarily a recommendation) supplied by the police or obtained otherwise; judicial review of such decisions is effectively excluded.

In the charged atmosphere that exists in Northern Ireland, it is desirable that political considerations should intrude as little as possible into these decisions. While a wide measure of discretion is unavoidable, there should be an effective means of appealing against a decision. For these reasons, we would favour taking decisions on bans out of the hands of the Secretary of State and giving it to the police (as is the case with routeing), with an appeal on the facts to a court.

When people are killed in terrorist or counter-terrorist operations, the family and friends are entitled to grieve in private, whether at home, during the service, or at the graveside, and others have the responsibility of respecting the wishes of family and friends. We are aware of the republican tradition of marking such events with paramilitary displays, and we have also heard of paramilitary attacks under the cover of funerals. We consider that the wishes of the family for privacy should always be respected. The Catholic Church insists on dealing only with the next-of-kin and not with paramilitary organisations and requires an undertaking that there will be no flags, emblems, political banners, or paramilitary displays in the church or its immediate vicinity. If these guidelines are followed, the security forces will not need to intrude or impose themselves on funerals or burials.

THE COURTS

There has been continuing concern in Northern Ireland about the use of courts which have no juries for those charged with terrorist offences. It should be noted that trial by jury is not a right protected by the international code of human rights. Many West European countries do not have juries, and even in Great Britain the vast majority of criminal cases, albeit of a 'relatively minor nature, are tried by magistrates without a jury.

Non-jury trials for those charged with serious crimes were introduced in Northern Ireland in 1973, following the report in 1972 of a Commission under the chairmanship of Lord Diplock, hence the popular term 'Diplock Courts'. The Act was amended in 1975 and consolidated in 1978; a fresh amending Bill is currently before parliament. These procedures were justified by the fear of intimidation of witnesses, and after some apparently perverse jury verdicts. Their operation was reviewed in 1975 by a Committee under the chairmanship of Lord Gardiner, and again in 1984 by Sir George Baker. While a number of amendments to the procedures were made in 1975 and are proposed in the current Bill, their basic features remain the same. The right to trial by jury is removed with regard to a number of offences such as murder, offences in connection with fire-arms and explosives, listed in a schedule to the Act (hence the term 'scheduled' offences). Trial for these offences is by a High Court or Crown Court judge sitting alone, who must deliver a full written judgment, from which there is an automatic right of appeal in all cases to a higher court. There is a power for the Attorney General to 'deschedule' certain cases, and the Secretary of State may add to or subtract from the list.

We accept the need for a special procedure, but it does not follow that the procedure now in force is the only possible one.[18] One alternative would correspond to the Special Criminal Court in the Republic of Ireland, a three-judge collegiate court. At its outset, it was subject to considerable criticism, but now seems to be generally accepted. It has been argued that an important obstacle to the introduction of a three-judge court in Northern Ireland is the shortage of judges and the virtual impossibility of recruiting enough additional judges, given the age structure of the Northern Ireland Bar and the reluctance of some barristers to accept appointment.[19] One alternative to a three-judge court is the possibility of a court consisting of a judge, who would alone decide issues of law, and two lay assessors who, together with the judge, would decide issues of fact. This model was used by the United Kingdom in the past for some colonial emergencies.

Most of us are uneasy at leaving decisions of such importance to one person, particularly as they often turn on an assessment of the character and credibility of the witnesses and the accused. Such assessments are always subjective, and it is impossible to be sure that the interaction between the judge and the others in the courtroom does not on occasion affect this assessment. It is true that this factor is minimised by an unlimited right of appeal, but consideration of the written transcript by the appeal court may not eliminate the effect of such factors. Most of us consider that two or three heads are better than one, but two members of the Working Party take the view that the sole and undivided responsibility of a single experienced lawyer with judicial qualities has been satisfactory, and that the onus is on those who are uneasy about the present system to show that the change would be an improvement. This latter consideration is of some weight, as there is no evidence of case-hardening of judges, and there has been no recent equivalent in Northern Ireland of the cases in England where it has been convincingly argued that juries have wrongly convicted in terrorist cases. It is sometimes said that a change from single-judge courts would, at least, produce greater public confidence in the administration of justice, but two of us regard that as a cosmetic argument and suspect that many of the present critics would then seek another reason for attacking the judicial system.

In recent times, there have been a number of major terrorist trials in Northern Ireland in which the Crown case was largely based on the evidence, often uncorroborated, of a witness who was an accomplice in the crimes charged. These witnesses have been called 'converted terrorists' by the authorities, but are more frequently referred to as 'supergrasses' because of the large number of defendants charged on their evidence.

There is nothing new in accomplices turning Queen's evidence against their former partners in crime. This has happened particularly in connection with organised crime because, in some high-level drug prosecutions, the only incriminating evidence has come from others lower down the criminal hierarchy. The police tactics in these cases is to encourage lesser figures to testify against their fellows, or to become paid informers who can be sent back into the criminal underworld to gather evidence of future crimes.

The legal position in the common law world and beyond is that accomplices are competent to give evidence: but since the last century, the common law has recognised that reliance on the word of a participant in crime against his accomplices carries distinct risks. Accomplices will inevitably be people who have committed crimes, probably involving dishonesty. They will have an incentive for giving evidence in return for immunity for their crimes, or for bail and a lenient sentence, or for money and protection. There is the risk that turning Queen's evidence may be self-serving exercises by criminals anxious to play down their own involvement or wishing to use the occasion to settle old scores.

Terrorism and organised crime have led to the encouragement of supergrasses as a matter of policy in several European countries. Italy is a particular example where there has recently been what is probably the largest ever supergrass case, with some 240 Mafia suspects on trial. But in Italy specific legislation was enacted to provide a legal *régime* to govern the use of supergrasses, and the immunities and rewards are regulated by that legislation. The Government in the Federal Republic of Germany failed to get parliamentary approval for similar legislation. But proceeding this way ensured that there was a public debate and a means of ensuring public support before the event. In the United Kingdom, virtually everything has been left to the discretion of the prosecuting authorities, whose decisions are shrouded in secrecy. The result has been recrimination and acrimony, and a further erosion of support for the judicial process.

Parliament at Westminster has played a relatively insignificant role in controlling the use of the legal powers involved, though the courts seem now to treat supergrass evidence with care, in some cases declining to convict and in most others quashing convictions on appeal.

One particular aspect of these trials that has caused us concern is that they have frequently involved a large number of defendants, in one case no fewer than 45. The number of defendants is primarily a matter for the prosecuting authorities, though we understand that there have been virtually no applications for separate trials. This practice was criticised by Sir George Baker, who recommended that in future there should be no more than 20 defendants in any one trial.[20] We agree with this, and we also hope that extreme care will be exercised in future before launching new cases of this nature.

'Justice delayed is justice denied': a problem connected with the supergrass trials is that of delay. In many cases the delay before trial is unacceptable, even if it is caused, as is sometimes the case, by the defendant wanting a particular lawyer and having to wait until he becomes available. Delay in the judicial process is not confined to Northern Ireland: the average period between committal and trial is less in Northern Ireland than in Great Britain.[21] But what concerns us has been the *exceptional* delay in *some* trials, sometimes as long as two years. We think there should be fixed limits for the period from arrest to committal and from committal to trial, as there are in Scotland. It is unsatisfactory that in Northern Ireland, with its particular problems concerning the criminal justice system, there should be such long delays, and we support the recent proposal of the Standing Advisory Commission on Human Rights for a full report on this subject by the Government.[22]

We have considered the fact that for certain serious offences in

Northern Ireland, the onus of proof is on the accused not the prosecution. This was a matter to which Sir George Baker gave considerable attention, and he found 'a surprisingly large number' of similar provisions in Acts and Regulations. Baker quoted the almost unanimous view of lawyers that this provision should be used 'carefully, cautiously and sparingly',[23] a view which we share.

We have heard of a number of complaints that a more extensive and generous provision of legal aid is needed in Northern Ireland. The present arrangement is that the Legal Aid Scheme is administered by the Incorporated Law Society of Northern Ireland, which reports annually to the Lord Chancellor. The latter appoints a Legal Aid Advisory Committee which comments on the annual report of the Law Society and advises him about the working of the Legal Aid Scheme. We have urged in Chapter 2 that adequate legal aid be provided for aggrieved citizens who wish to use the complaints procedures under international human rights treaties.

We support the recommendation of the Standing Advisory Commission on Human Rights that the United Kingdom should ratify the UN Convention against torture without reservation or interpretative declaration which would detract from the force of the Convention,[24] and we urge the Republic of Ireland to do the same.

PRISONERS

Both the United Nations and the Council of Europe have Standard Minimum Rules for the Treatment of Prisoners, and the United Nations has recently also adopted Standard Minimum Rules for the Administration of Juvenile Justice. We would urge the Governments of both states to ensure that these are fully respected throughout their penal systems and, where they are not, to carry out any necessary reforms as soon as possible.

In the United Kingdom, prison conditions are supervised by HM Chief Inspector of Prisons and local Boards of Visitors. The Chief Inspector publishes reports on each institution inspected, as well as annual reports: these make depressing reading. According to the Inspector, the conditions in United Kingdom prisons, especially local ones, are often nothing less than scandalous. We are disturbed by the slow pace at which these criticisms are being met.

The Boards of Visitors have two main functions. One is to inspect prisoners, receive complaints from them, and draw the Governor's attention to these and to any shortcomings which they observe themselves. The other is to hear the most serious disciplinary charges against prisoners and award punishments for these, including loss of remission (which effectively amounts to the imposition of additional terms of imprisonment).

It is difficult to see how these two functions can be compatible. In an extreme case, a prisoner might complain to a member of the Board of Visitors about his treatment at the hands of the prison staff and later find himself charged before the Board to which that member belongs with the disciplinary offence of making a 'false and malicious allegation against an officer'. As long ago as 1975, a Committee chaired by Lord Jellicoe, and jointly established by JUSTICE (the UK section of the International Commission of Jurists), the National Association for the Care and Settlement of Offenders, and the Howard League for Penal Reform, published a report called *Boards of Visitors of Penal Institutions* which recommended that these functions should be separated and assigned to different institutions. That recommendation had still not been acted on in 1983, when it was endorsed by another JUSTICE Committee, under the chairmanship of Sir Brian MacKenna, in a report called *Justice in Prison*, which also proposed a wide range of other reforms in the prison system, founded on the requirements of the human rights treaties by which the United Kingdom is bound.

These recommendations, and similar ones made by other bodies such as the Prison Reform Trust, still await implementation. We do not doubt the goodwill of the Prison Department of the Home Office, which is only too conscious of the stresses within the prison system. But the pace of reform seems to us excruciatingly slow, and we would urge the Government of the United Kingdom to do all in its power now to accelerate it.

Persons found guilty of murder or other serious offences but who were under the age of 18 when they committed the crime are detained at the Secretary of State's pleasure (SOSP); this was originally meant for the benefit of young offenders when capital punishment was mandatory for murder. According to the Children and Young Persons (Northern Ireland) Act 1968,

> Sentence of death shall not be pronounced ... if it appears to the Court that at the time when the offence was committed, he was under the age of eighteen ... but in lieu thereof the Court shall sentence him to be detained during the pleasure of [the Secretary of State].

The same system of indeterminate sentences operates in Great Britain and the Republic of Ireland. In Scotland, it is known as detention without limit of time.

Whatever may have been the original intention, the giving of indeterminate sentences in Northern Ireland does little to wean the young offenders from the terrorist organisations. Internal reviews of cases take place in the Northern Ireland Office after three and then six years from the date of committal to prison; after eight years there is a review by the Life Sentence Review Board. If the Board considers that a provisional date should be set for release on licence, they will seek the approval of Ministers and the judiciary who must, by law, be consulted in cases of murder. The final decision rests with the Secretary of State. In exceptional circumstances, a case may go to the Review Board after less than eight years.[25]

There were 62 SOSP prisoners in Northern Ireland when we began work in 1984, but the number has been reduced to 40 because of releases, as follows:

Released in 1985	7
Released in 1986	10
Released in 1987	5
Provisional release dates set for 1987 and 1988	6
Others	34
	62

Of the 34 outstanding cases, four are at an advanced stage of judicial and ministerial consultation.

Article 10(3) of the UN Covenant on Civil and Political Rights requires that juvenile offenders in the penitentiary system 'shall be segregated from adults and be accorded treatment appropriate to their age and legal status'. On the face of it, the practice of imposing an SOSP sentence on a juvenile murderer, rather than the mandatory life sentence which an adult would receive, conforms with this requirement. But a life sentence is technically determinate (even though in practice, in most cases, it operates as an indeterminate sentence), while an SOSP sentence is intended from the beginning to be indeterminate. Indeed, a situation can arise in which a juvenile who is found guilty of murder is automatically sentenced to detention for an indeterminate period and then finds himself in a different position from an accomplice who perhaps was only a year or two older. How long the sentence will be and where it should be served is entirely a matter at the discretion of the Secretary of State. In the event of release, the offender is released on licence in whatever form and under whatever conditions are prescribed by the Secretary of State.

Sir George Baker noted in his report in 1983–4 that 27 SOSPs had been in custody for over eight years, and three for over 10 years. 'Their youth has gone. Some are afraid to leave the compounds for cellular accommodation in the H blocks.' To be imprisoned without a release date is particularly demoralising for young people, especially as adult prisoners qualify for 50 per cent remission in Northern Ireland. Baker concluded, 'I am not sentimental, but there is a case for compassion and the giving of a hope of release'.[26] We agree.

Ministers, judges and, officials, however humane, must be cautious about releasing people who have committed terrorist offences in the past, and might do so again if released. We would make the following five proposals.

1. In a recent case (2 March 1987), the European Court of Human Rights considered the case of a man, Robert Weeks, who had been released from prison on licence and then had his licence revoked by the Home Secretary. The Court's judgment was that this was a violation of the European Human Rights Convention as the applicant had not been able to challenge the Minister's decision in appropriate court proceedings.

It follows from the decision of the European Court of Human Rights in the *Weeks* case that anyone subject to an SOSP sentence will henceforth be entitled to periodic reviews of that sentence by an independent tribunal having the power to order his release, and operating the usual safeguards of what the common law calls 'natural justice', including in particular the prisoner's right to full disclosure of everything that is alleged against him or that might influence the tribunal in its decision.

2. When Sir George Baker reported at the beginning of 1984, there were 30 SOSP prisoners who had been in custody more than eight years. Since then, 28 prisoners who had been in custody have been released, given provisional dates for release, or are in the pipeline. Presumably this covers all, or virtually all, of Baker's 30. By now, however, more than 20 additional prisoners sentenced in 1977–9 will have been in custody more than eight years, and five more will have exceeded eight years in 1988. We suggest that a target date be set, perhaps the end of 1988, for a Ministerial or judicial review of *all*

SOSP prisoners who will then have been in custody for more than eight years.

3. Although we have been assured by civil servants and prison staff that a prisoner always knows when the reviews are taking place, we have also been told by members of the Boards of Visitors that this is not always the case. It should be remembered that for a considerable period of time paramilitary commanders within the prison compounds refused to allow prisoners to take part in the review process. The Northern Ireland Association for the Care and Resettlement of Offenders comments:

> the whole process is conducted behind closed doors. There are no firm guidelines available to the prisoner or his family as to how and when various reports are made or as to how the case is presented before the Life Sentence Review [Board].[27]

In order to avoid uncertainty, we suggest that prisoners should be given information *in writing* before each review, and asked to sign a form acknowledging that they have understood what the procedure will be.

4. We consider that prisoners being reviewed should have the advice of clergy, a lawyer, a doctor, or a family member.

5. As soon as possible, and certainly if responsibility for prisons should ever be devolved, we would like the review boards to include a non-official element, like the Parole Board in Great Britain.

FINDING THE RIGHT BALANCE

A recurrent theme in the story of special legislation is the underlying conflict between two concepts: whether to seek to stamp out paramilitary activity through coercion or to dissolve it through conciliation. In our view, the issue is not a matter of choosing one concept or the other: it is one of finding a balance between the two. The essence of special legislation is to shift the balance in the direction of coercive values by giving the authorities additional powers designed to safeguard lives and property. Such protection is, and must remain, a primary objective. As Lord Gardiner stated in his report, 'where freedoms conflict, the state has a duty to protect those in need of protection'.[28]

Where, then, should the balance be drawn? One approach is a pragmatic one which involves a consideration of the existing law and the extent to which it should be modified in order to secure certain objectives: thus the Emergency Provisions Act takes the form of a number of specific departures from the ordinary law. Another possible approach is to consider the legislation as a whole from the viewpoint of principle and in the context of human rights treaties to which the United Kingdom is a party.

We would like to see an early review of emergency legislation in the light of the United Kingdom's international obligations. It is understandable that some of this legislation grants to the executive broad discretionary powers which are subject to few controls and with only limited rights of appeal. In almost every case, we would prefer a proper legal *régime*. Within such a *régime*, we would favour the establishment of a parliamentary committee, on the lines of a select committee, with responsibility for scrutinising and reviewing anti-terrorist legislation. We see a regulatory procedure of this nature as vital in ensuring the acceptable operation and public accountability of emergency legislation.

In our study we have noted, and often quoted from, the many reports on human and civil rights in Northern Ireland, and on security measures. But we have also been struck by the relative paucity of parliamentary debate on emergency legislation. Perhaps parliament has allowed some of its responsibility to be exercised by committees of inquiry. We do not intend any reflection on those who have worked as members of these review bodies to say that they have sometimes been used as ways of avoiding or shelving awkward problems. We think the primary and often the best place for discussion of these issues, and the detailed supervision of the operation of emergency laws, is parliament, and especially the House of Commons. We recall that the creation of a parliamentary committee in a new 'Northern Ireland legislative assembly was discussed in the Northern Ireland Constitutional Convention. We do not think the suggestion should be allowed to die.

Notes and References

1. *A Theory of Justice* (Oxford: Clarendon Press, 1972) p. 391.
2. Great Britain 1920 and 1964; Northern Ireland 1926.
3. Protection of the Community (Special Powers) Act 1926
4. Article 28(3).
5. Northern Ireland (Emergency Provisions) Act 1978.
6. Prevention of Terrorism (Temporary Provisions) Act 1984.

7. *Eleventh Annual Report of the Standing Advisory Commission on Human Rights, 1984–5*, (London: HMSO, 1985). para. 71(a).

8. *Review of the Operation of the Northern Ireland (Emergency Provisions) Act 1978* (London: HMSO, 1984) (Cmnd 9222, Baker) para. 236.

9. As note 8, para. 412.

10. *Twelfth Annual Report of the Standing Advisory Commission on Human Rights, 1985–6* (London: HMSO, 1986) p. 13; Nicholas Scott, MP, in reply to Parliamentary Question from Kevin McNamara, issued as press release by Northern Ireland Office, 24 February 1987. *Tenth Annual Report of the Standing Advisory Commission on Human Rights, 1983–4*, para. 40; *Eleventh Annual Report . . . , 1984–5*, paras 61–3; *Twelth Annual Reports . . . , 1985–6*, Chapter 7 (all London, HMSO).

12. *The Prevention of Terrorism (Temporary Provisions) Act 1984: review of the year 1985* by Sir Cyril Philips, para. 21; *Report on the Operation in 1986 of the Prevention of Terrorism (Temporary Provisions) Act 1984* by Viscount Colville, paras 2.3.6–7.

13. Northern Ireland (Emergency Provisions) Act 1978, Section 18.

14. *Police Complaints Board: Annual Report 1985* (London: HMSO, 1986) para. 40 and pp. 14, 16–7, Tables I, II, IV, V; letter from Brian McClelland, 3 March 1987.

15. *Police Complaints Board: Annual Report 1985* (London: HMSO, 1986) para. 16.

16. *Eleventh Annual Report of the Standing Advisory Commission on Human Rights, 1984–5*, pp. 30–1, 55–74; *Twelfth Annual Report of the Standing Advisory Commission for Human Rights, 1985–6*, pp. 169–72 (Chapter 10 and Appendix H).

17. UN Covenant on Civil and Political Rights, Article 21; European Convention on Human Rights, Article 11; Convention Against Racial Discrimination, Article 5(d) (ix).

18. Cmnd 9222, pp. 63–75, paper prepared by John Jackson in Annex A to Appendix D.

19. *The Prevention of Terrorism . . . Act 1984*, paras 115–18.

20. *The Prevention of Terrorism . . . Act 1984*, para. 172.

21. As note 8, para. 7 of Appendix E and Table 8 in Annex A of Appendix E (pp. 80, 94).

22. As note 8, p. 12.

23. As note 8, paras 210, 213.

24. *Eleventh Annual Report of the Standing Advisory Commission on Human Rights, 1984–5*, paras 20–40 and Appendix A (pp. 41–54).

25. As note 8, para. 95.

26. *Life Sentence Prisoners in Northern Ireland: an explanatory memorandum* (Belfast: Northern Ireland Office, 1985) para. 15.

27. *Detention at the Secretary of State's Pleasure* 22 Adelaide Street, (Belfast: NIACRO, 1984) p. 9.

28. *Report of the Committee to consider, in the context of civil liberties and human rights, measures to deal with terrorism in Northern Ireland* (London: HMSO, 1975) (Cmnd 5847, Gardiner) para. 15.

9 Towards Peaceful Coexistence

In the American Declaration of Independence, Thomas Jefferson derived 'inherent and inalienable rights' from the fact that 'men' are created 'equal and independent'. That was to use the language and concepts of the eighteenth century. 172 years later, when the UN General Assembly came to prepare the first article of the Universal Declaration of Human Rights, three issues had to be resolved. The first draft of the Declaration, using the language and ideas of Jefferson, had begun, 'All men are brothers'. Not surprisingly, the UN Commission on the Status of Women objected to the use of sexist language, so the text was amended.

The second issue was whether or not the Declaration should refer to a Divine Creator. The revised draft at that stage now read 'All human beings are born free and equal in dignity and rights. They are endowed by nature with reason and conscience and should act towards one another in a spirit of brotherhood'. Brazil wanted the second sentence to affirm that human beings are created in the image of God. This proposal proved to be extremely contentious, and the Brazilian amendment was withdrawn in exchange for the omission of the words 'by nature'. At a later stage, the Netherlands proposed to insert a reference to the divine origin and immortal destiny of human beings, but this proposal was also withdrawn when it became clear that it would be defeated if put to the vote. The result was that the UN Declaration of Human Rights makes no mention of God, or even of nature.[1]

The third issue in 1948 arose when South Africa wanted to change 'dignity and rights' in the first sentence to 'fundamental rights and freedoms', on the ground that while everyone might be entitled to certain rights which were therefore fundamental, not everyone was entitled to *all* rights. The South African amendment was defeated, and South Africa abstained when the Declaration as a whole was subsequently put to the vote.

It was in keeping with the spirit of the times that the UN Declaration should begin with rights. It was, however, impossible to ignore responsibilities and the rights of others, so the penultimate article of the Declaration reads, 'Everyone has duties to the community ... In the exercise of his rights and freedoms, everyone shall [accord] due recognition and respect for the rights and freedoms of others'.

Sir George Baker, in his report on emergency legislation in Northern Ireland, wrote that he had felt increasingly the need for a society for the furtherance of human *duties* to counter-balance those who struggle so valiantly, and so rightly, for human rights.[2] We have sought in this Report to give equal weight to rights and responsibilities, for they belong together. We have noted, all the same, that minorities tend to stress rights while majorities stress responsibilities.

In Northern Ireland there is the paradox that the two communities consider themselves both a majority *and* a minority, depending on which entity is being considered – the six counties of Northern Ireland, the island of Ireland, the United Kingdom, or the whole archipelago. Because of this paradox, we have not been taking sides when trying to give equal weight to rights and responsibilities.

In considering these rights and responsibilities, we note that our two states are near neighbours on the Western periphery of Europe. In spite of a troubled history of conflict and injustice, we are now bound together by many ties of sentiment and common interest. We have inherited similar legal traditions and democratic institutions; our economies tend to prosper or languish in tandem; we listen to the same sorts of music, read the same sorts of literature, enjoy the same sorts of art; many of us have voting rights in each other's countries; and both states belong to the Council of Europe, the European Community, and the United Nations.

At the same time, our peoples have their own distinctive folk-memories of the past, with different heroes and villains, different perspectives on the same historical events, and consequently with different aspirations for the future. And we do some important things differently: the Irish Republic chooses its parliament by proportional representation, for example, the United Kingdom by the first-past-the-post system; the United Kingdom seeks national security by membership of a military alliance, the Irish Republic by its commitment to neutrality.

We look forward to increasing co-operation between the peoples of our two states on a neighbourly and humanitarian basis. To take one example, the lifeboat service for these islands has been a single institution since 1825. We understand that there has been no pressure to separate the service into two parts,[3] and there seem to us to be overwhelming pragmatic and humanitarian reasons for keeping that situation as it is.

We believe that such inter-state co-operation could be progressively extended. We have looked, for example, at the possibility of amalgamating the systems for admitting undergraduates to universities and other institutions for higher education in the two states, in the light of the report which Professor Gareth Williams prepared for the National Economic and Social Council in Dublin and the Northern Ireland Economic Development Office.[4] It seems clear that a full merger of admission systems is not at present possible, but we endorse many of the less ambitious recommendations of Professor Williams. In particular, we hope that as the Irish Republic develops the Distance Education Centre (created in 1982), full use will be made of the experience and course materials of the Open University in the United Kingdom. Much of the material made for the Open University at Milton Keynes takes insufficient account of the needs of students in Northern Ireland (and, indeed, in Scotland and Wales), so material would no doubt need adapting for it to be useful in the Irish Republic.[5] We understand that discussions on two-state co-operation on higher education have been going on for several years but are now languishing, and we agree with Professor Williams that it is time to give these discussions 'a new impetus'.[6] We would also encourage increasing co-operation between other bodies with similar or identical functions, such as the Arts Council of Great Britain, the Arts Council of Northern Ireland, and the Arts Council in Dublin.

In the island of Ireland, there is already a great deal of cross-border co-operation at every level. Professor John Whyte, a member of this Working Party, found that in 1973 there were 151 all-Ireland non-governmental organisations and 66 all-archipelago bodies. All the main Churches are organised on an all-Ireland basis, for example, and several of the dioceses and districts straddle the border. Several sports are organised on an all-Ireland basis, including cricket, golf, rugby, and tennis. The Irish Congress of Trade Unions operates throughout Ireland, as do a great many academic and professional associations. There are other matters, such as the two official boards for tourism and the two sports councils, where an all-Ireland approach might in time be possible without offending national susceptibilities. This was hinted at in the report on Anglo–Irish Joint Studies, submitted to the two heads of government in November 1983 (para. 3.15).

During the course of our work, we came across several cases of apparent misrepresentation in Northern Ireland newspapers. This is the sort of issue which comes within the ambit of the United Kingdom Press Council. Of more than 1100 complaints dealt with by the Council in 1985, only six came from Northern Ireland: one was disallowed, two were withdrawn, and three were upheld.

Brian Garrett, a member of this Working Party, suggested in 1974 that, in view of disquiet among the general public about the influence of the media, an all-Ireland press council should be set up on a voluntary basis, to deal with matters such as intrusion into privacy or breach of confidentiality, where there is normally no legal remedy available to aggrieved parties. If there should be constitutional obstacles to an all-Ireland body, he wrote, 'let some instrument be devised so that the UK Press Council established a local Northern Ireland section capable of working in harmony with a separate Press Council established in the Republic'.[8] We believe these ideas should be explored further.

THE CHURCHES

Because of the way in which this Project was established, it is natural that we should have asked ourselves what Christians and the Churches might now do to promote inter-communal understanding, justice, and peace. The Roman Catholic church in these islands is organised in three hierarchies: England and Wales, Scotland, and Ireland. Most of the other Churches in the United Kingdom and the Republic of Ireland co-operate in two ecumenical councils, the British Council of Churches in Great Britain and the Irish Council of Churches in the two parts of Ireland.

We have encountered nothing but friendliness in our relations with Churches in the two states, and we would like to thank the many Church members, both clerical and lay, who have gone out of their way to answer our questions or help us in other ways. On one occasion, a Roman Catholic archbishop happened to come into one of our meetings by mistake, and he was readily persuaded to stay until the end of the session and play a full part in the discussion of Church schools. The two ecumenical councils and one of the Roman Catholic hierarchies made financial contributions to our work, as did 11 Churches, three religious communities, five parish councils, the Free Church Federal Council in London, and the Catholic Institute for International Relations.

Co-operation between Catholics and Protestants in Ireland is more limited than it is in Great Britain. The Irish Council of Churches and its constituent members work with their Catholic counterparts in a Joint Working Group on Social Problems, and there is also a Churches Central Committee for Community Work. We publish as our Appendix 5 the conclusions of an inter-Church working party in 1976 as an illustration that joint conclusions are possible even in a sensitive field. We warmly commend those in the various Churches who have been pioneers of bridge-building.

We found some readiness on the part of Church representatives to criticise Churches of another tradition. Irish Catholics were quick to criticise the Churches in Great Britain for not speaking out after outrages by the security forces in Northern Ireland. Irish Protestants and, indeed, many others, among them Roman Catholics, denounced the Catholic Church for playing what they regarded as an obscurantist role in the referenda in the Republic on abortion and divorce. British Protestants criticised Irish Catholics for not opposing political violence with enough clarity, and Irish Protestants for being unadventurous in relations with the Catholics. And so on.

We suspect that some criticism was based on ignorance or misunderstanding of the facts – though there are plenty of disgraceful pages in the histories of all Churches in these islands. We understand why Irish Protestants should have been dismayed that the results of the referenda seemed to show that the people in the South are not yet willing to make their society truly pluralistic, in which it would be as easy for non-Catholics as for Catholics to follow their own informed consciences. We would add, however, that we were impressed at the trouble taken by the Government of the Republic to canvass the views of Protestant leaders several months before the amendment on divorce was submitted to the vote.

Some of us are disappointed that Church leaders from the two traditions in Ireland have not always been even-handed in their denunciation of political violence. As there have been over 1500 incidents since 1968 in Northern Ireland leading to fatalities, it is no doubt difficult to think of fresh ways of denouncing each new outrage, especially if the speaker should have underlying sympathy for the goals (if not the methods) of the persons or organisation being denounced. We recall that Pope John Paul II used unequivocal language at Drogheda in 1979:

Violence is a lie . . . Violence destroys what it claims to defend . . .
On my knees I beg you to turn away from the paths of violence.

But the Pope went on to condemn 'conditions which give excuse or pretext to men of violence'. He appealed for respect for the 'inalienable rights' of every human being.[9]

There has been enough internecine criticism by Christians in or about Ireland, and we do not wish to add to it. Genuine ecumenical co-operation that is not merely cosmetic requires that we be as ready to admit our own shortcomings as to criticise the failings of those of other traditions. Those of us from Great Britain and the Irish Republic have asked ourselves what we might do to help Christians in Northern Ireland so that they may be agents of intercommunal harmony. Our first task is to understand better what it means to be a minority, to enter with sympathy into the disappointment and despair of our own minorities, to work with them and for them as they struggle for their own human and civil rights.

We also need to redouble our efforts at ecumenical co-operation. Some of this has to be done in formal ways by the headquarters of the different Churches, but we are impressed at the opportunities at the diocesan and parish levels. We have in mind, for example, the effective partnership of Roman Catholic, Anglican, and Free Church leaders in the Liverpool area. There is much that Christians can do together without violating their own traditions. We need to use our imaginations to discover new ways of overcoming the divisions we have inherited from the past.

We welcome all signs that Christians in Great Britain are taking seriously their responsibilities towards their fellow citizens in Northern Ireland. This may require structural changes, so that the Churches in Great Britain can promptly and responsibly relate to religious or secular events in Northern Ireland, and back up words with deeds when appropriate. But it is also a question of attitude. Christians in Great Britain need to cultivate an approach of humility and concern, treating members of both communities in Northern Ireland as people who are trapped in a tragic situation, but entitled to the same respect as all other citizens of the United Kingdom.

All the Churches can contribute to inter-Church dialogue and co-operation without endangering their own distinctive beliefs and practices. Many towns and cities in the two states are twinned with foreign municipalities. We would like to see links of this sort between institutions in Great Britain and similar bodies in Ireland, between Churches, trade unions, schools, youth groups, and so on. We would like to see exchanges of clergy, doctors and nurses, teachers, community workers, trade union members, and the like.

GRIEVANCES REMOVED

Two issues of symbolic importance to both communities, to which we devoted attention in the first two years of our work, have recently been resolved: the use of the Irish language in street names, and flags and emblems.

An Act of the Stormont Parliament in 1949 prohibited the use of any language other than English in the naming of streets.[10] It is clear from the debates in the Northern Ireland Parliament at the time that this prohibition was introduced in order to prevent Irish from being used. Many might regard this as a minor irritant, especially since it was not strictly enforced. The law permits street and house names, traffic signs, and public notices to be displayed in Gaelic as well as in English in Scotland, in Welsh in Wales,[11] in Manx in the Isle of Man, in Norman-French in the Channel Islands, and in Chinese in Soho. We see no compelling reason why Irish should not be used in Northern Ireland where this is the wish of local residents and so long as it is done unprovocatively. A *communiqué* following a meeting of the Anglo–Irish Ministerial Conference indicated that this particular provision may be repealed in the near future.

Another Stormont Act gave the police power to prohibit the display of any flag or emblem, other than the Union flag, whose display might lead to a breach of the peace.[12] The Act was clearly directed at the Irish tricolour, which a number of nationalist organisations made a point of displaying at functions and parades. Unionists regarded the Irish tricolour as signifying opposition to the very existence of Northern Ireland. Excluding the Union flag from the prohibition was based on the argument that to display the national flag of the United Kingdom could never lead to a breach of the peace. While the Act did not actually prohibit the display of emblems other than the Union flag, it was widely regarded by the nationalist community as having that effect.

The Act had been falling into desuetude. We were intending to recommend the repeal of the Flags and Emblems Act, believing that the Union flag needs no special protection as its display in normal circumstances would not lead to a breach of the law.* We learned as our Report was being finalised that this is included in a new Order for Northern Ireland.

---

*One member of the Working Party would have disagreed with such a recommendation. He maintains that Northern Ireland is now the only part of the archipelago where it might be a crime to display the national flag: 'This is neither right nor fair'.

Notes and References

1. John P. Humphrey, *Human Rights and the United Nations: a great adventure* (New York: Transnational, 1984) p. 60.
2. *Review of the Operation of the Northern Ireland (Emergency Provisions) Act 1978* (London: HMSO, 1984) (Cmnd 9222, Baker) para. 32(2).
3. Letter from James L. Kavanagh, national organiser of the RNLI for the Republic of Ireland, 5 March 1987.
4. *Higher Education in Ireland: Co-operation and complementarity (Dublin: National Economic and Social Council; Belfast: Economic Development Office, 1985).*
5. *Proceedings of the joint conference on higher education* (Dublin, 6 November 1985), pp. 4, 35–6, 50, 65–6, 73, 80–1.
6. *Higher Education in Ireland* pp. 5 and 47.
7. See John Whyte, 'The Permeability of the United Kingdom – Irish Border: a preliminary reconnaissance', *Administration*, 31 (3) (1983) pp. 300–15.
8. Brian Garrett, 'Free expression and the case for an Irish Press Council', *Irish Times*, 20 December 1974.
9. *Ireland: In the footsteps of St. Patrick* (Boston: Daughters of St Paul, 1979) pp. 39–40.
10. Public Health and Local Government (Miscellaneous Provisions) Act (Northern Ireland) 1949.
11. Welsh Language Act 1967.
12. Flags and Emblems (Display) Act (Northern Ireland) 1954.

10 Your Rights are my Responsibility

In this final chapter, we shall try to bring together the arguments which have led us from our premises to our conclusions.

Charged by leading Christians to consider human rights and responsibilities, we have naturally approached this task from a Christian perspective. In Chapter 1, we found that the modern concept of human rights, however much it may be open to rhetorical exaggeration for political or ideological purposes, is not only well grounded in political philosophy but has a secure theological base in Christian tradition – as indeed it has in those of other religions. It may be significant that we reached this unanimous conclusion despite the differences between the Churches and backgrounds from which we ourselves came.

We conclude, therefore, that respect for the human rights and fundamental freedoms of all human beings is a high obligation for all Christians, as indeed it is for all people of goodwill. This obligation entails, for every individual and for all groups in which individuals join together, the conscientious discharge of responsibilities without which none of these rights can be preserved or enjoyed. This dependence of the rights of some on the responsibilities of others can be most succinctly summarised in the title we have chosen for this concluding chapter: your rights are my responsibility.

In Chapter 2, we have explained the legal revolution which has taken place in the past few decades through the establishment of an international and secular code of human rights *law*. The effect of this is that the modern nation state is no longer free to treat its citizens in any way it pleases but is now bound to obey the norms which international law prescribes in this field. Accordingly, the primary responsibility to ensure and respect human rights and fundamental freedoms falls upon the state and its public authorities, and our first recommendations are therefore addressed to the governments of the two states with which we are here concerned: the United Kingdom and the Republic of Ireland.

We also address recommendations to individuals and organisations (including the Churches) in the two states. This is necessary because our mandate specifically asked us to review non-governmental responsibilities.

THE RESPONSIBILITIES OF GOVERNMENTS

In every country, including the two from which we come, the state is the single most powerful entity and therefore in the best position, through legislation or administrative action, either to ensure or to deny human rights and fundamental freedoms to its inhabitants. Our first concern is therefore that our two states should do everything in their power to ensure the best possible protection for all the human rights and fundamental freedoms of all their inhabitants in each of their respective territories. Because they are close neighbours, have many common interests, and share common traditions developed over many centuries, our next concern is that the extent and the means for this protection should, so far as possible, be the same in each of them.

In fact, we have found that, in both the states, the degree of protection for human rights and freedoms available to their inhabitants is not yet as high as it could be. (In the case of the United Kingdom, the most cogent evidence for this proposition is to be found in the mounting series of cases which Her Majesty's Government has lost before the European Court of Human Rights at Strasbourg.) Also, the extent of the protection differs in several respects between the two states. Having considered these issues as thoroughly as we can, we have unanimously concluded that the single most important recommendation we can make in this field is that each of the two states should incorporate in its domestic laws all the human rights and freedoms which it is already bound by international law to respect and ensure, and so to provide its inhabitants with direct remedies in their national courts for any alleged violations of them rather than leave them to resort, if they can and if they know how, to the competent international organs. This can best be done by incorporating the European Convention on Human Rights into the national legal systems of both the United Kingdom and the Republic of Ireland, so removing our two states from the diminishing minority of European nations which do not already have such provision.

We have carefully reviewed the various theoretical and practical objections which have been raised against this proposal, and we are satisfied that these can readily be overcome and are in any case far outweighed by the benefits which it can offer. In this connection, we should add that we are well aware of the differences between a state which, like the Republic of Ireland, has a written constitution and one which, like the United Kingdom, has not.

In order to eliminate the disparities in the protection of human rights and fundamental freedoms *between* our two states, we also recommend to each of their governments that they should ratify various treaties which the other one has already ratified, but which it has not. The most important of these are the twin International Covenants on Human Rights which have been ratified by the United Kingdom but not so far by the Republic of Ireland. In this connection, we also recommend the ratification by both states of certain of the Additional Protocols to the European Convention, and their subsequent incorporation into domestic law.

Once all this is done, there will be domestic remedies in both states for all violations of human rights. But if these remedies are to be accessible to their citizens, lawyers must learn to use them, and litigants who cannot afford them must have access to legal aid. We think it would also be highly desirable to establish human rights commissions in England, Wales, Scotland, and the Irish Republic, analogous to the one already operating in Northern Ireland.

Human rights are, by their nature, of universal application. But their importance becomes especially acute where there are minorities, ethnic, religious, linguistic, or other. The existence of such minorities, their concern for the preservation of their integrity and cultural identity, and their particular aspirations, often raise difficult problems. The main contribution which the international code of human rights law makes to the solution of such problems is the concept of non-discrimination, for the code contains an over-riding requirement that, *in respect of their human rights and fundamental freedoms*, all human beings must be treated equally, regardless of what particular group they belong to. In addition, the code guarantees to members of minorities the right to enjoy their own culture, to profess and practise their own religion, and to use their own language. But beyond this, the code has little to say about them: in particular, it does not set out any general principle or any particular political model which can be expected to fit every case or to resolve all the problems which the existence of minorities can create.

NORTHERN IRELAND: A SPECIAL CASE?

From these general considerations, we have turned to the particular problems of Northern Ireland. This is the principal place where the interests of our two states intersect, where human rights problems are present in their most acute form, and where our Churches evoke exceptional loyalty. We know only too well that there are many other areas in each of the two states where there are groups with legitimate grievances, but for the reasons just cited we make no apology for devoting far more attention to Northern Ireland.

The recommendations which we make are put forward from our perspective of human rights and responsibilities in an all-archipelago interdenominational Christian setting. We claim no particular originality for them, nor do we imagine for a moment that, even if all of them were to be implemented, they would provide a 'solution' to problems which have their roots in centuries-old divisions and are manifested in sincere and deeply-held convictions. But we believe that their adoption could perceptibly improve matters in the short term, and could establish the beginnings of a new approach and a subtle but important shift in attitudes, which could yield much greater benefits in the longer term.

Many factors which affect Northern Ireland are common to the rest of these islands – and indeed to much of Western Europe – such as the steady decline of certain industries, unemployment, tensions between central and local government, changing social patterns and mores, and rival historic claims by different groups to particular territories. We therefore thought it right to look at several other places in Western Europe with a past history of conflict between rival groups of inhabitants, for which workable solutions have been found in recent times. We are of course well aware that each of these situations is unique, and that none of the successful solutions could be bodily transplanted to another place. However, we believe that there are at least two general lessons that can be learned from these examples, and it is to these that we now turn.

CONSTITUTIONAL STATUS

We observe that, in all the successful solutions to conflicts involving minorities, one common cluster of features is an unqualified acceptance by all the states concerned of each others' sovereignty and of secure and recognised boundaries between them, and an unqualified renunciation of territorial claims upon each other. For this reason, we recommend that the Republic of Ireland should complete the task which it has already begun at Sunningdale and in the Anglo–Irish Agreement and review the wording of Articles 2 and 3 of its Constitution in such a way as to preclude any further interpretation of them as an immediate claim to the territory of Northern Ireland.

Beyond that, there is a further problem. Though the Irish Constitution contains an excellent bill of rights, it also still reflects the social teaching of the Catholic Church as it was in the 1930s, now some two generations ago, and long before the radical reforms wrought by the Second Vatican Council. While Ireland is becoming a more pluralistic society, its legal institutions still lag some way behind these developments. For example, legislation to outlaw racial discrimination is only just being introduced, and there is still no possibility of civil divorce, even for those whose religion does not forbid it. We know that we are not alone in thinking that a major constitutional and legislative review is becoming decidedly overdue.

Similarly, we regard it as important that, so far as possible, Northern Ireland should not be treated differently from the rest of the United Kingdom in respect of the laws and administrative procedures which obtain there, at all events so far as concerns human rights and fundamental freedoms. For example, we find it anomalous and undesirable that religious discrimination should be against the law in Northern Ireland but not in Great Britain, and that racial discrimination should be illegal in Great Britain but not in Northern Ireland. We therefore recommend that all such legislation should be extended to cover the whole of the United Kingdom. Likewise, we find it odd that emergency legislation should remain on the statute book even though in the official view there is now no emergency there, and that there are organisations which are proscribed in Northern Ireland which are not proscribed in Great Britain. In all these matters, we recommend that the two governments should seek to harmonise their laws both throughout and between their countries.

THE RESPONSIBILITIES OF INDIVIDUALS, AND OF THEIR ASSOCIATIONS

But even when governments have done all they can to respect human rights in their laws and administrative practices, that will be of little avail unless individual members of society and the associations which they form consistently collaborate in upholding this respect.

This brings us to the second lesson which we have learned from the other cases we have looked at in Western Europe: no solution to such conflicts is possible unless there is a fundamental willingness among all those concerned to resolve their differences peacefully and to respect each others' cultures and legitimate aspirations. In Northern Ireland, there is a profound conflict between two such aspirations: that for a united Ireland, on the one hand, and that for continued union with Great Britain on the other. We see nothing inherently illegitimate or morally blameworthy in either of these, *provided they are pursued by lawful and peaceful means*. While there are undoubtedly other countries in the world governed by *régimes* so oppressive that such aspirations cannot be peacefully pursued, we are unanimous in our view that the United Kingdom does not, by even the remotest stretch of the imagination, fall into that category. Accordingly, we are convinced that there is no case whatever for resort to any form of violence or any other unlawful conduct in pursuit of the aspirations of either of the communities in Northern Ireland. Indeed, we cannot see how the existing problems there can even begin to be resolved unless and until *all* the inhabitants of Northern Ireland agree to respect the laws and institutions of the state in which they happen to live, the unionist community agrees to respect the rights and aspirations of the nationalist community (including its aspiration for a united Ireland by peaceful means), and the nationalist minority agrees to respect the democratic rights of the unionist majority, including its desire for continued union with the rest of the United Kingdom.

This requirement of respect for each others' differences entails a number of consequences. One is that neither of the groups concerned should be denied any opportunities open to the other to take part in the political processes which shape the affairs of the state in which they live. Ever since partition, the nationalist community in Northern Ireland has complained of being excluded from the making of political decisions, and even in recent times an attempt at 'power-sharing' failed. Today, the unionist community complains that, unlike the SDLP, its political representatives were not consulted by the United Kingdom Government during the negotiations which culminated in the Anglo–Irish Agreement. Nor does there seem to be any realistic possibility for anyone resident in Northern Ireland, of either community, to play an active part in the affairs of either the Conservative Party or the Labour Party, from one of which (or both, in time of war) all Governments of the United Kingdom have been formed since partition. So long as such grievances exist, they constitute major obstacles to the achievement of peaceful co-existence, and we therefore recommend that they should be removed as quickly as possible.

Another important problem area may be found in the field of education. The international code of human rights law affirms the right of parents to ensure that the education of their children conforms with their own religious and philosophical convictions. Included in that right is the right to withdraw children from acts of worship or from religious teaching which is at variance with their own beliefs. But these rights have to be balanced by the responsibility of all schools to serve the interests of the community as a whole, and the responsibility of the state to ensure that all schools, whether state-controlled or independent, will promote mutual understanding, tolerance, and friendship, rather than divisiveness.

In the complex situation in Northern Ireland, the right balance may not be easy to achieve, but there are now significant parallels in other parts of the United Kingdom. The presence of substantial religious and ethnic minorities in some cities has created a demand for ethnic or religious schools. At the same time, in the interests of the community as a whole, there has been a movement towards fully integrated schooling at all levels, and some schools which draw their pupils from different communities have experimented imaginatively with forms of ecumenical and inter-faith worship. In Northern Ireland, there has been a similar development in the establishment of half a dozen or so integrated interdenominational schools, usually founded on parental initiatives. We believe that these have significant potential for the healing of community divisions and that they deserve the fullest support of the Churches and the secular authorities. In particular, the Churches should not delay in setting up chaplaincies at these schools, to provide pastoral care for staff and pupils.

THE RESPONSIBILITIES OF THE CHURCHES

We make no apology for having devoted much space in our report to the role of the Churches. They have nurtured some heroic acts of witness and service and have sustained patient attempts at mediation and bridge-building. But at the same time, they cannot avoid at least some responsibility for the persistence of sectarianism and at times even bigotry. Though Christians in Great Britain may sometimes feel tempted to recall to Christians in Northern Ireland those priorities of reconciliation, community, and mutual love which are the heart of Christian ministry and proclamation, we must also recall that the Churches in Great Britain (and indeed in the Republic of Ireland) must bear their own share of responsibility for some of the present evils, and that they have unique opportunities to make positive contributions towards their removal.

For various reasons, to do partly with the organisation of denominational and ecumenical bodies, and partly with a persistent apathy among Church members, the Churches in Great Britain have for a long time failed to speak out with enough courage or to act with enough compassion and understanding towards their fellow Christians in Northern Ireland. Similarly, the Roman Catholic Church in Ireland, though it has recently been more explicit in its condemnation of violence and has become more considerate to other religious communities, still needs to become more sensitive to the needs of the whole of society and to strengthen its ministry of reconciliation. We believe that greater co-operation and mutual understanding between the Churches throughout these islands is a key which could unlock many spiritual resources that undoubtedly exist in Northern Ireland, as they exist elsewhere, for the resolution of conflict and the ending of anger and fear; and a number of our more detailed recommendations are intended for that end.

RESPONSIBILITY FOR SECURITY

We recognise that the UK Government bears the ultimate and ineluctable responsibility for the maintenance of law and order in Northern Ireland, and that the current situation there presents exceptional problems to the security forces, the judiciary, and the penal system. It would be outside our competence to make recommendations on operational matters, but it is an important part of our task to draw attention to areas where particular policies may run the risk of failing to respect human rights and fundamental freedoms. The following matters have caused us particular concern:

1. there is still a power, now only very rarely exercised, to make exclusion orders which prevent British citizens from travelling freely between different parts of the United Kingdom
2. the official guidance given to the security forces in Northern

Ireland on the use of lethal weapons is not made public, a fact which needlessly increases fear and suspicion

3. decisions to ban marches are taken by the Secretary of State, and are not subject (as they would be in the rest of the United Kingdom) to judicial review

4. although the *average* period between the committal and trial of an accused person is less in Northern Ireland than in Great Britain, there have in some cases been delays of up to two years

5. young persons convicted of serious offences are detained at the Secretary of State's pleasure and given what is in effect an indeterminate sentence, which can sometimes be even longer than that given to an adult convicted of a similar offence

6. for many serious offences, there is no right to trial by jury; while we appreciate the special risks of intimidation of witnesses and jurors, this must nonetheless remain a source of concern.

Many of these issues have been considered in a number of official reports, most recently in 1984 by the late Sir George Baker. In addition to them, there are still other matters outstanding. Neither the United Kingdom nor the Republic of Ireland, for example, has yet ratified the UN Convention against Torture, and HM Inspector of Prisons still has cause to draw annual attention to the appalling conditions in many British prisons, which fall far short of the requirements of both the UN's and the Council of Europe's Standard Minimum Rules for the Treatment of Persons in Detention.

But here again, responsibility must be shared between government and people. While the primary responsibility falls upon government, both to maintain law and order and to ensure that its own forces fully respect the human and civil rights of all its citizens, and that they do not abuse their powers for illegitimate ends, those citizens in their turn have a responsibility to co-operate fully with the security forces and to give them all possible help in the discharge of their difficult and dangerous duties.

A BRIDGE FOR THE FUTURE?

One of the central Christian virtues is hope, and that is the note on which we would wish to end. In the course of our study, we have been greatly impressed by the contrast between the cold and humourless bigotry of a few misguided fanatics, and the warm and cheerful tolerance and the courage in adversity demonstrated by the great majority of the members of both the communities in Northern Ireland. In an important study prepared for the United Nations,[1] Francesco Capotorti described the ' 'subjective criterion' for the definition of a minority which, he said,

> has been defined as a will on the part of the members of the groups in question to preserve their own characteristics.

In that sense, both the communities of Northern Ireland are minorities. But Capotorti goes on to say:

> When their rights are guaranteed and fully respected, minority groups can serve as a link between States which have among their population persons belonging to the same ethnic and linguistic group, and thus help strengthen co-operation and promote peaceful and friendly relations between the countries concerned.

There, it seems to us, lies the hope for the future. For if harmony were at last to be achieved in Northern Ireland, that presently unhappy land could be transformed from a battleground into a bridge and serve as a future object lesson for other warring communities, of which the world tragically still has far too many.

We conclude the Report with a summary of our main recommendations which, if adopted, would improve the quality of life for all of us in these islands.

The Governments of the United Kingdom and the Republic of Ireland

1. Incorporate the European Human Rights Convention and Protocol no. 1 into domestic law (pp. 37–41, 42, 88, 106, 112, 116, 144, 197–8).
2. Ratify and similarly incorporate Protocol no. 7 to the European Human Rights Convention (pp. 42, 88, 198).
3. Ratify the Optional Protocol to the UN Covenant on Civil and Political Rights (in the case of the Republic, after ratifying the Covenant itself) (pp. 35, 41–2).
4. Ratify the UN Convention against torture (pp. 181, 204).
5. Establish human rights commissions in England, Wales, Scotland, and the Irish Republic, similar to the Standing Advisory Commission in Northern Ireland (pp.138, 198).
6. Explore the possibility of uniformity in proscribing terrorist organisations (pp. 171, 200).

7. Observe the UN's and the Council of Europe's Standard Minimum Rules for the treatment of offenders (pp. 181, 204).
8. Ensure that adequate legal aid is available for human rights complainants (pp. 43, 181, 198).
9. Review the Gareth Williams proposals for collaboration on higher education with a view to speedy implementation of those outstanding proposals that are now practicable (p. 190).
10. Increase functional co-operation between the two states (pp. 189–90).

The Government of the United Kingdom

11. Ratify and incorporate into domestic law Protocol no. 4 to the European Convention on Human Rights (pp. 42, 88, 198).
12. Ensure same basic civil rights throughout the United Kingdom (pp. 97–8, 100–2, 106, 119, 134–5, 200).
13. Repeal 'state of emergency' legislation (pp. 169–70, 186, 200).
14. Pending repeal of emergency legislation, arrange for better parliamentary supervision (pp. 170, 186).
15. Some members of Working Party opposed to *any* proscription of undesirable organisations, majority consider that proscription of terrorist organisations should be uniform throughout the United Kingdom (pp. 170–1, 200).
16. Terminate exclusion orders (pp. 172, 203).
17. When there is devolution of functions in Northern Ireland, some members of the Police Authority to be appointed on cross-community basis by Northern Ireland Assembly (p. 173).
18. Publish guidance to the security forces on the use of force (pp. 175, 203–4).
19. Decisions on banning and routeing of parades in Northern Ireland to be by Chief Constable, with appeal to the courts (pp. 177, 204).
20. Majority of Working Party favour three-judge courts or single judge with two assessors (pp. 178–9, 204).
21. Avoid supergrass trials with many defendants (pp. 179–80).
22. Study possibility of establishing time limits from arrest to trial (pp. 180, 204).
23. Accelerate review of role of Boards of Visitors (p. 182).
24. New safeguards for prisoners detained at the Secretary of State's Pleasure (pp. 184–5, 204).

The Government of the Republic of Ireland

25. Review Articles 2 and 3 of the constitution regarding territorial claim (pp. 110–1, 199–200).
26. Ratify the two UN Covenants on human rights (pp. 34, 41, 112, 116, 198).
27. Ratify UN Convention aginst racial discrimination (pp. 41, 112, 114–15, 135).
28. Incorporate Protocol no. 4 of the European Convention into domestic law (pp. 42, 88, 198).
29. Undertake constitutional and legal review so as to ensure full respect for minority rights, including rights of non-Christians and non-believers in any religious faith (pp. 110, 115, 144, 200).

Christians and Churches in the Two States

30. Establish more bilateral links between Churches in Great Britain and the two parts of Ireland (pp. 161, 193).
31. Include an ecumenical element in training of clergy (pp. 132, 162).
32. Strengthen teaching ministry (p. 161).
33. Explore possibility of inter-Church ministry to Irish immigrants in Great Britain (p. 162).

Christians and Churches in Great Britain

34. Learn from ethnic minorities in Great Britain what it feels like to be a minority (pp. 162, 193).
35. Recognise that the people of Northern Ireland are fellow-citizens of the United Kingdom deserving of respect and equal rights (pp. 193, 203).
36. Review structures so that Churches can respond effectively to Northern Ireland issues (pp. 155, 161, 193, 203).

Protestants in Northern Ireland

37. Respect the human and civil rights of the Catholic minority, notwithstanding the fact that most of them aspire to Irish unity (p. 160).

Roman Catholics in the Irish Republic

38. Ensure full respect for rights of minorities (p. 160).

Roman Catholics Throughout Ireland

39. Understand the aspirations and fears of Northern Protestants (pp. 160, 203).

Churches and Secular Authorities in Northern Ireland

40. Support integrated education, Catholic and Protestant Churches to appoint chaplains (pp. 127–8, 202).

Church Members and Non-Governmental Organisations in the Irish Republic

41. Work for ratification of UN Covenants on human rights (p. 41).

Churches, Trade Unions, Professional Associations, Schools, Youth Groups, etc. in Great Britain and the Two Parts of Ireland

42. Arrange for 'twinning' and exchanges in both directions (pp. 161, 193).

Lawyers in the Two States

43. Familiarise themselves with complaints procedures to European Human Rights Commission and UN Human Rights Committee (pp. 43, 198).

Press of the Two States

44. Consider the possibility of a Press Council for the two parts of Ireland, or close collaboration between the Northern Ireland element of UK Press Council and a similar body to be established in the Irish Republic (p. 191).

A Member of Parliament in the UK

45. If blasphemy remains a crime, seek opportunity to introduce a Private Member's Bill extending blasphemy to cover offensive references to non-Christian faiths (p. 51).

Conservative and Labour Parties in Great Britain

46. Review policies about membership in Northern Ireland (pp. 67–8, 201–2).

Political Parties in Great Britain and the Irish Republic

47. Discuss and then support incorporation of the European Convention on Human Rights into domestic law (p. 39).

United Kingdom Government and Local Authorities

48. Permit 'local option' regarding day of rest in areas where non-Christians predominate (pp. 45, 51).

Reference

1. Francesco Capotorti, *Study on the rights of person's belonging to ethnic, religious, and linguistic minorities* (New York: United Nations, 1979) (doc. E/CN 4/Sub.2/384/Rev.1).

Appendix 1

Pros and cons of incorporating the European Convention on Human Rights into domestic law: extracts from a Report of the Standing Advisory Commission on Human Rights (Northern Ireland) (1977)[1]

6.04 On the one hand it may be argued that:

(1) It is complacent to assume that there is no need for new legal safeguards in Northern Ireland or indeed elsewhere in the United Kingdom. The existing legislative and common law safeguards against abuse of power are less comprehensive and effective than in many advanced democratic countries. For example:

    (a) there are inadequate constitutional guarantees against the abuse of power by the government or Parliament;

    (b) there is no modern and coherent system of administrative law enabling the citizen to obtain prompt, speedy and adequate legal redress for the misuse of administrative powers by public authorities;

    (c) there are important gaps in our legal system where basic rights and freedoms (e.g. in relation to freedom of expression, conscience, and association, respect for privacy and family life, or the right to a fair and public hearing in the determination of civil rights or criminal charges) are not adequately guaranteed;

    (d) the need for greater protection is especially important in relation to the increased powers and responsibilities of regional and local government and private institutions whose activities affect the basic rights and freedoms of the citizen; and

    (e) the absence of a Bill of Rights enforceable by the courts against the misuse of public powers may have contributed to the present situation in Northern Ireland.

(2) A Bill of Rights would remove certain fundamental values out of the reach of temporary political majorities, governments, and officials and into the realm of legal principles applied by the courts. This would not be undemocratic because the exercise of political power in a democracy should not be beyond criticism or restraint.

(3) A Bill of Rights would be especially important in the context of the devolution of the present powers of Central Government in maintaining the national framework of law and order, and guaranteeing the basic rights of citizens throughout United Kingdom.

(4) A Bill of Rights would encourage a more actively and socially responsive judicial role in protecting basic rights and freedoms; it would alter the method of judicial law-making, so as to enable the courts to recognise the fundamental importance of certain values and the relationship between them.

(5) The European Convention contains a minimum Bill of Rights for Council of Europe countries and is also being used as a source of

guidance about common standards within the European Community in relation to human rights questions arising under the EEC Treaty. The enactment of a Bill of Rights in this country would enable the United Kingdom to be manifestly in conformity with its international obligations and would also enable the citizen to obtain redress from United Kingdom courts without needing, except in the last resort, to have recourse to the European Commission in Strasbourg.

(6) A Bill of Rights would not necessarily hamper strong, effective and democratic government because it could recognise that interference with certain rights would be justifiable if they were necessary in a democratic society, for example, in the interests of national security, public safety or the economic well-being of the country, for the prevention of disorder or crime, for the protection of health or morals, or for the protection of the rights and freedoms of others.

(7) The generality of a Bill of Rights makes it possible for the interpretation of such a document to evolve in accordance with changing social values and needs. This process of giving fresh meaning to basic human rights – and the obligations which flow from them – from generation to generation is valuable for its own sake, as a means of educating public opinion, and as a rallying point in the State for all who care deeply for the ideals of freedom.

(8) A Bill of Rights would not be a substitute for more specific statutory safeguards against specific abuses (e.g. anti-discrimination legislation or the Parliamentary Commissioner for Administration): It would supplement and strengthen those safeguards where they were incomplete.

(9) Although it would be difficult and perhaps divisive to envisage introducing a wholly new and comprehensive Bill of Rights except as part of a widely supported major constitutional settlement, this does not rule out more limited guarantees (e.g. on the lines of the European Convention); nor would such limited guarantees involve fettering the ultimate sovereignty of Parliament.

On the other hand it may be argued that:

(1) Because of the general nature of Bills of Rights and the increased powers of judicial law-making which they require, the scope and effect of such documents is uncertain and unpredictable.

(2) A Bill of Rights would create expectations which could not be satisfied in practice. It would be regarded as a panacea for all grievances whereas its real value (if any) would be only a limited one. It would be least effective when it was most needed: i.e. to protect fundamental rights and freedoms against powerful currents of intolerance, passion, usurpation and tyranny.

(3) A Bill of Rights might be interpreted by the courts in a manner which would hamper strong, effective or progressive government, and the role of the courts would result in important public issues being discussed and resolved in legal or constitutional terms rather than in moral or political terms. It would risk compromising the necessary independence and impartiality of the judiciary by requiring the judges to work in a more political arena.

(4) Most Bills of Rights stem from a constitutional settlement following revolution, rebellion, liberation or the peaceful attainment of independence. It would be difficult and perhaps divisive to seek to obtain a sufficient degree of political consensus about the nature and scope of a Bill of Rights in present circumstances.

(5) Human Rights are at least as well protected in the United Kingdom as in countries which have Bills of Rights since they are adequately safeguarded by traditional methods, i.e., legislative measures to deal with specific problems, combined with the unwritten but effective constitutional conventions; the sense of responsibility and fair dealing in legislators and administrators; the influence of a free press and the force of public opinion; the independence of the judiciary in upholding the rule of law; and free and secret elections.

(6) The United Kingdom differs from many advanced democratic countries in lacking (a) a written constitution, (b) a system of public law, and (c) a codified legal system. A Bill of Rights involves features of all three of these distinctive characteristics of other legal systems. It would therefore represent a fundamental departure from the existing legal tradition.

(7) A Bill of Rights which did not (i) contain a modern definition of the rights and freedoms relevant to the particular circumstances obtaining whether in the United Kingdom in general or in Northern Ireland in particular, (ii) have priority over other laws, (iii) create legally enforceable rights and (iv) apply to violations of human rights by private individuals and organisations as well as by public authorities would not satisfy some prominent supporters of such a measure. On the other hand a Bill of Rights which did have these characteristics would be unlikely to obtain widespread public support.

(8) A Bill of Rights would create wasteful duplication in relation to existing statutory safeguards for human rights and would generate unnecessary litigation.

(9) In Northern Ireland existing safeguards (e.g. Part III of the Northern Ireland Constitution Act 1973) have not in practice tended to be relied upon by those alleging that their human rights have been infringed. There is no evidence that this situation would be altered by the introduction of a Bill of Rights.

6.05 None of the arguments which we have summarised on each side of the question is 'right' or 'wrong'. Some of the arguments on each side are controversial, but there are important points in all of them. However, the unanimous conclusion which we have reached . . . is that the legal protection of human rights in Northern Ireland should be increased and that one of the ways in which this should be done is by the enactment of an enforceable Bill of Rights. We believe that the most appropriate way of doing this would be to incorporate the European Convention into the domestic legal system of the United Kingdom.

6.06 We would summarise our main reason [for considering it desirable to introduce some form of enforceable Bill of Rights] by referring to:

(a) the value of ensuring express compliance with the international obligations imposed by the European Convention which are designed to secure to everyone within the United Kingdom the rights and freedoms guaranteed by the Convention and to provide effective remedies for violations of those rights and freedoms by public authorities;

(b) the value of giving explicit and positive recognition in our constitutional and legal system to respect for basic human rights and freedoms;

(c) the need for effective legal safeguards against the misuse of power by public authorities;

(d) the necessity in a genuinely democratic society to ensure that governments respect the rights and freedoms of minorities;

(e) the importance of legislating expressly for comprehensive and effective guarantees of human rights which are applicable to the United Kingdom as a whole so that the basic rights of the individual do not depend upon the particular part of the United Kingdom in which the individual was born or lives;

(f) the importance of having general principles or criteria to assist legislators and administrators, as well as judges, in matters concerning human rights;

(g) the need to encourage legislators, administrators and judges to be more systematically and consciously concerned with fundamental values when they perform their public functions (as part of the necessary process of adaptation to the legislative, administrative and judicial techniques of the other member countries of the European Community and of the Council of Europe);

(h) the advantages of a more actively and socially responsive judicial role in settling constitutional disputes and in protecting basic rights and freedoms;

(i) the need to remove the uncertainties about the present status and effect of the European Convention in the law of the United Kingdom;

(j) the benefits of a Bill of Rights as a source of public education about the values of a democratic society.

Some of these reasons, although of general application, have a particular relevance to the situation in Northern Ireland today . . .

6.07 The present state of opinion . . . demonstrates wide agreements, both in Northern Ireland and among political groups and independent experts in Great Britain, in favour of modelling a Bill of Rights upon the European Convention rather than attempting to introduce a Bill of Rights which stands free from the Convention. We share this view. We doubt whether a sufficient degree of consensus could be obtained (whether in Northern Ireland alone or in the United Kingdom as a whole) as to the scope and effect of a free-standing Bill of Rights, especially if, as some have argued, such a change were to be made in advance of a new constitutional settlement involving entrenched rights and legal restraints on Parliamentary sovereignty, judicially enforced.

Reference

1. *The Protection of Human Rights by Law in Northern Ireland* (London: HMSO, 1977) (Cmnd 7009) paras 6.04–6.07.

Appendix 2

**How an individual may bring proceedings in Strasbourg against the
United Kingdom or the Republic of Ireland**

Like all legal proceedings, complaints to the European human rights
institutions in Strasbourg involve many technicalities and are therefore best
conducted by lawyers familiar with the procedures. However, lay people can,
if they wish, institute such proceedings on their own. What follows here is a
rough guide to the general requirements; a booklet containing more detail,
and called *Step-by-Step Booklet on Lodging an Application with the
European Commission of Human Rights*, is obtainable from the Council of
Europe.[1]

COMPETENCE

The Commission can deal only with complaints about alleged violations of
one or more of the rights and freedoms specifically protected by the
European Convention on Human Rights, or by one of two Protocols (the
First and Fourth) to that Convention. The First Protocol deals with the right
to property, the right to education, and the right to free elections; the Fourth
Protocol deals with imprisonment for debt and freedom of movement. The
Republic of Ireland has ratified both these Protocols; the United Kingdom
has so far ratified only the First, and the Commision cannot entertain
complaints against the United Kingdom in respect of the rights which the
Fourth protects. The Republic has made some reservations about free legal
aid, education, and extradition, and the United Kingdom has made a
reservation about education; these may affect complaints in respect of the
relevant rights.

Before instituting a complaint, it is *essential* to read the Convention or the
relevant Protocol with great care and to understand clearly what rights and
freedoms it covers, and what it does not. The language of these instruments is
fairly general, but has now been interpreted in many cases both by the
Commission and the Court. It is, therefore, highly advisable to read and
understand not only the instruments themselves but the relevant decisions
and reports of the Commission and the judgements of the Court, which have
interpreted them. It should be emphasised that this is a task which may
require considerable legal skills.

Complaints may be made only by individuals or non-governmental
organisations who have suffered a personal detriment as the result of a
violation of one of the protected rights or freedoms, where the responsibility
for the violation rests with a public authority of the state against which the
complaint is made, and not with a private person or organisation.

Before complaining to the Commission, it is necessary for the complainant to have tried all available means to obtain redress in the state against which he or she complains and, in particular, to have taken all available legal proceedings for such redress. After that, the complaint must be lodged within a period of six months.

PROCEDURE

In order to lodge a complaint, all that is needed is a letter sent to the Secretary, European Commission of Human Rights, Council of Europe.[1] The letter should contain a brief outline of the complaint, an indication of the rights and freedoms thought to have been violated, a list of the local remedies which the complainant has tried to obtain, and a list of all official decisions (with copies of them) about the case.

The Secretary to the Commission will reply to this letter and will probably ask for more information, as well as possibly giving advice about the further procedure. At some stage, he will send the complainant a form to be completed, and the complaint will then be formally registered.

After that, the Secretary will keep the complainant informed of the progress of the application. At this stage, all the proceedings are in writing, and nothing is made public.

ADMISSIBILITY

At the next stage, the Commission decides whether the application is 'admissible' – that is to say, that all local remedies have been tried, that the application was made within the six-month period, and that it is not 'manifestly ill-founded'. If the Commission decides that the application is not admissible, that is the end of the matter: there is no appeal.

FURTHER STAGES

If the Commission decides that the application is admissible, free legal aid becomes available to the applicant if he or she cannot afford a lawyer's fees. From that point on, the commission examines the facts of the case and the arguments of the applicant and the state complained against, and also places itself at the disposal of the parties in order to reach a friendly settlement. For all these purposes, the Commission may invite the parties to a hearing in Strasbourg, hear witnesses, and carry out investigations in other places.

If no friendly settlement is reached, the Commission draws up a report, giving its opinion as to whether there was a violation. This report is sent to the government of the state complained against, and also to the Committee of Ministers of the Council of Europe.

At this point, there are two possibilities: the case can be decided either by the Committee of Ministers or by the European Court of Human Rights. It can be referred to the Court either by the state concerned or by the Commission; if it is not referred to the Court, then the formal decision is made by the Committee of Ministers.

THE COURT

If the case is referred to the Court, that is the start of a new procedure. Formally, the applicant plays no part in this: the parties are the Commission, which has referred the case, and the state complained against. In practice, however, the Court generally allows the applicant to appear and to take an active part in the proceedings. Sometimes it will allow outsiders with a general interest in the subject matter (for example, non-governmental organisations) to submit written memorials to the Court.

The Court holds formal hearings and eventually delivers a formal judgement, which is binding on the state concerned. If the Court finds that there was a violation, it may also order compensation to be paid to the applicant.

These proceedings can take a considerable time to reach their conclusion. Before the Commission they may, in some cases, take as long as five years; before the Court they may take another two.

Reference

1.　BP431, R6, 67006 Strasbourg Cedex (France).

Appendix 3

UN declaration on the elimination of intolerance and discrimination based on religion or belief, 25 November 1981

Article 1

1. Everyone shall have the right to freedom of thought, conscience and religion. This right shall include freedom to have a religion or whatever belief of his choice, and freedom, either individually or in community with others and in public or private, to manifest his religion or belief in worship, observance, practice and teaching.

2. No one shall be subject to coercion which would impair his freedom to have a religion or belief of his choice.

3. Freedom to manifest one's religion or belief may be subject only to such limitations as are prescribed by law and are necessary to protect public safety, order, health or morals or the fundamental rights and freedoms of others.

Article 2

1. No one shall be subject to discrimination by any State, institution, group of persons or person on the grounds of religion or belief.

2. For the purposes of the present Declaration, the expression 'intolerance and discrimination based on religion or belief' means any distinction, exclusion, restriction or preference based on religion or belief and having as its purpose or as its effect nullification or impairment of the recognition, enjoyment or exercise of human rights and fundamental freedoms on an equal basis.

Article 3

Discrimination between human beings on the grounds of religion or belief constitutes an affront to human dignity and a disavowal of the principles of the Charter of the United Nations, and shall be condemned as a violation of the human rights and fundamental freedoms proclaimed in the Universal Declaration of Human Rights and enunciated in detail in the International Covenants on Human Rights, and as an obstacle to friendly and peaceful relations between nations.

Article 4

1. All States shall take effective measures to prevent and eliminate discrimination on the grounds of religion or belief in the recognition, exercise and enjoyment of human rights and fundamental freedoms in all fields of civil, economic, political, social and cultural life.

2. All States shall make all efforts to enact or rescind legislation where necessary to prohibit any such discrimination, and to take all appropriate measures to combat intolerance on the grounds of religion or belief in this matter.

Article 5

1. The parents or, as the case may be, the legal guardians of the child have the right to organise life within the family in accordance with their religion or belief and bearing in mind the moral education in which they believe the child should be brought up.

2. Every child shall enjoy the right to have access to education in the matter of religion or belief in accordance with the wishes of his parents or, as the case may be, legal guardians, and shall not be compelled to receive teaching on religion or belief against the wishes of his parents or legal guardians, the best interests of the child being the guiding principle.

3. The child shall be protected from any form of discrimination on the grounds of religion or belief. He shall be brought up in a spirit of understanding, tolerance, friendship among peoples, peace and universal brotherhood, respect for freedom of religion or belief of others, and in full consciousness that his energy and talents should be devoted to the service of his fellow men.

4. In the case of a child who is not under the care either of his parents or of legal guardians, due account shall be taken of their expressed wishes or of any other proof of their wishes in the matter of religion or belief, the best interests of the child being the guiding principle.

5. Practices of a religion or belief in which a child is brought up must not be injurious to his physical or mental health or to his full development, taking into account article 1, paragraph 3, of the present Declaration.

Article 6

In accordance with article 1 of the present Declaration, and subject to the provisions of article 1, paragraph 3, the right to freedom of thought, conscience, religion or belief shall include, *inter alia*, the following freedoms:

(a) To worship or assemble in connection with a religion or belief, and to establish and maintain places for these purposes;

(b) To establish and maintain appropriate charitable or humanitarian institutions;

(c) To make, acquire and use to an adequate extent the necessary articles and materials related to the rites or customs of a religion of belief;

(d) To write, issue and disseminate relevant publications in these areas;

(e) To teach a religion or belief in places suitable for these purposes;

(f) To solicit and receive voluntary financial and other contributions from individuals and institutions;

(g) To train, appoint, elect or designate by succession appropriate leaders called for by the requirements and standards of any religion or belief;

(h) To observe days of rest and to celebrate holidays and ceremonies in accordance with the precepts of one's religion or belief;

(i) To establish and maintain communications with individuals and communities in matters of religion or belief at the national and international levels.

Article 7

The rights and freedoms set forth in the present Declaration shall be accorded in national legislations in such a manner that everyone shall be able to avail himself of such rights and freedoms in practice.

Article 8

Nothing in the present Declaration shall be construed as restricting or derogating from any right defined in the Universal Declaration of Human Rights and the International Covenants on Human Rights.

Appendix 4 [*]

AGREEMENT BETWEEN [THE GOVERNMENT OF THE UNITED KINGDOM OF GREAT BRITAIN AND NORTHERN IRELAND AND THE GOVERNMENT OF THE REPUBLIC OF IRELAND] [THE GOVERNMENT OF IRELAND AND THE GOVERNMENT OF THE UNITED KINGDOM]

[The Government of the United Kingdom of Great Britain and Northern Ireland and the Government of the Republic of Ireland] [The Government of Ireland and the Government of the United Kingdom];

Wishing further to develop the unique relationship between their peoples and the close co-operation between their countries as friendly neighbours and as partners in the European Community;

Recognising the major interest of both their countries and, above all, of the people of Northern Ireland in diminishing the divisions there and achieving lasting peace and stablity;

Recognising the need for continuing efforts to reconcile and to acknowledge the rights of the two major traditions that exist in Ireland, represented on the one hand by those who wish for no change in the present status of Northern Ireland and on the other hand by those who aspire to a sovereign united Ireland achieved by peaceful means and through agreement;

Reaffirming their total rejection of any attempt to promote political objectives by violence or the threat of violence and their determination to work together to ensure that those who adopt or support such methods do not succeed;

Recognising that a condition of genuine reconciliation and dialogue between unionists and nationalists is mutual recognition and acceptance of each other's rights;

Recognising and respecting the identities of the two communities in Northern Ireland, and the right of each to pursue its aspirations by peaceful and constitutional means;

Reaffirming their commitment to a society in Northern Ireland in which all may live in peace, free from discrimination and intolerance, and with the opportunity for both communities to participate fully in the structures and processes of government;

Have accordingly agreed as follows:

A

STATUS OF NORTHERN IRELAND

Article 1

The two Governments

(a) affirm that any change in the status of Northern Ireland would only come about with the consent of a majority of the people of Northern Ireland;

*The United Kingdom and Republic of Ireland versions are not identical. We have disregarded differences of capitalisation, punctuation, accents, the use of italics, and footnoting: where there are other variations, we give the UK version first in square brackets, then the Republic of Ireland version, also in square brackets.

(b) recognise that the present wish of a majority of the people of Northern Ireland is for no change in the status of Northern Ireland;

(c) declare that, if in the future a majority of the people of Northern Ireland clearly wish for and formally consent to the establishment of a united Ireland, they will introduce and support in the respective Parliaments legislation to give effect to that wish.

B

THE INTERGOVERNMENTAL CONFERENCE

Article 2

(a) There is hereby established, within the framework of the Anglo–Irish Intergovernmental Council set up after the meeting between the two heads of Government on 6 November 1981, an Intergovernmental Conference (hereinafter referred to as 'the Conference'), concerned with Northern Ireland and with relations between the two parts of the island of Ireland, to deal, as set out in this Agreement, on a regular basis with:

  (i)   political matters;
  (ii) security and related matters;
  (iii) legal matters, including the administration of justice;
  (iv) the promotion of cross-border co-operation.

(b) The United Kingdom Government accept that the Irish Government will put forward views and proposals on matters relating to Northern Ireland within the field of activity of the Conference in so far as those matters are not the responsibility of a devolved administration in Northern Ireland. In the interest of promoting peace and stability, determined efforts shall be made through the Conference to resolve any differences. The Conference will be mainly concerned with Northern Ireland; but some of the matters under consideration will involve co-operative action in both parts of the island of Ireland, and possibly also in Great Britain. Some of the proposals considered in respect of Northern Ireland may also be found to have application by the Irish Government. There is no derogation from the sovereignty of either [the United Kingdom Government or the Irish Government] [the Irish Government or the United Kingdom Government], and each retains responsibility for the decisions and administration of government within its own jurisdiction.

Article 3

The Conference shall meet at Ministerial or official level, as required. The business of the Conference will thus receive attention at the highest level. Regular and frequent Ministerial meetings shall be held; and in particular special meetings shall be convened at the request of either side. Officials may meet in subordinate groups. Membership of the Conference and of sub-groups shall be small and flexible. When the Conference meets at Ministerial level [the Secretary of State for Northern Ireland and an Irish Minister designated as the Permanent Irish Ministerial Representative] [an Irish Minister designated as the Permanent Irish Minsterial Representative and the Secretary of State for Northern Ireland] shall be joint Chairmen. Within the framework of the Conference other [British and Irish] [Irish and British] Ministers may hold or attend meetings as appropriate: when legal matters are under consideration the Attorneys General may attend. Ministers may be accompanied by their officials and their professional advisers: for example, when questions of security policy or security co-operation are being discussed, they may be accompanied by [the Chief Constable of the Royal Ulster Constabulary and the Commissioner of the Garda Síochána] [the Commissioner of the Garda Síochána and the Chief Constable of the Royal Ulster Constabulary]; or when questions of economic or social policy or co-operation are being discussed, they may be accompanied by officials of the relevant Department. A Secretariat shall be established by the two Governments to service the Conference on a continuing basis in the discharge of its functions as set out in this Agreement.

Article 4
(a) In relation to matters coming within its field of activity, the Conference shall be a framework within which [the United Kingdom Government and the Irish Government] [the Irish Government and the United Kingdom Government] work together
  (i) for the accommodation of the rights and identities of the two traditions which exist in Northern Ireland; and
  (ii) for peace, stability and prosperity throughout the island of Ireland by promoting reconciliation, respect for human rights, co-operation against terrorism and the development of economic, social and cultural co-operation.
(b) It is the declared policy of the United Kingdom Government that responsibility in respect of certain matters within the powers of the Secretary of State for Northern Ireland should be devolved within Northern Ireland on a basis which would secure widespread acceptance throughout the community. The Irish Government support that policy.
(c) Both Governments recognise that devolution can be achieved only with the co-operation of constitutional representatives within Northern Ireland of both traditions there. The Conference shall be a framework within which the Irish Government may put forward views and proposals on the modalities of bringing about devolution in Northern Ireland, in so far as they relate to the interests of the minority community.

C
POLITICAL MATTERS

Article 5
(a) The conference shall concern itself with measures to recognise and accommodate the rights and identities of the two traditions in Northern Ireland, to protect human rights and to prevent discrimination. Matters to be considered in this area include measures to foster the cultural heritage of both traditions, changes in electoral arrangements, the use of flags and emblems, the avoidance of economic and social discrimination and the advantages and disadvantages of a Bill of Rights in some form in Northern Ireland.

(b) The discussion of these matters shall be mainly concerned with Northern Ireland, but the possible application of any measures pursuant to this Article by the Irish Government in their jurisdiction shall not be excluded.

(c) If it should prove impossible to achieve and sustain devolution on a basis which secures widespread acceptance in Northern Ireland, the Conference shall be a framework within which the Irish Government may, where the interests of the minority community are significantly or especially affected, put forward views on proposals for major legislation and on major policy issues, which are within the purview of the Northern Ireland Departments and which remain the responsibility of the Secretary of State for Northern Ireland.

Article 6

The Conference shall be a framework within which the Irish Government may put forward views and proposals on the role and composition of bodies appointed by the Secretary of State for Northern Ireland or by departments subject to his direction and control including:

the Standing Advisory Commission on Human Rights;
the Fair Employment Agency;
the Equal Opportunities Commission;
the Police Authority for Northern Ireland;
the Police Complaints Board.

D
SECURITY AND RELATED MATTERS

Article 7

(a) The Conference shall consider:
   (i)   security policy;
   (ii) relations between the security forces and the community;
   (iii) prisons policy.

(b) The Conference shall consider the security situation at its regular meetings and thus provide an opportunity to address policy issues, serious incidents and forthcoming events.

(c) The two Governments agree that there is a need for a programme of special measures in Northern Ireland to improve relations between the security forces and the community, with the object in particular of making the security forces more readily accepted by the nationalist community. Such a programme shall be developed, for the Conference's consideration, and may include the establishment of local consultative machinery, training in community relations, crime prevention schemes involving the community, improvements in arrangements for handling complaints, and action to increase the proportion of members of the minority in the Royal Ulster Constabulary. Elements of the programme may be considered by the Irish Government suitable for applications within their jurisdiction.

(d) The Conference may consider policy issues relating to prisons. Individual cases may be raised as appropriate, so that information can be provided or enquiries instituted.

E
LEGAL MATTERS, INCLUDING THE ADMINISTRATION OF JUSTICE

Article 8

The Conference shall deal with issues of concern to both countries relating to the enforcement of the criminal law. In particular it shall consider whether there are areas of the criminal law applying in the North and in the South respectively which might with benefit be harmonised. The two Governments agree on the importance of public confidence in the administration of justice. The Conference shall seek, with the help of advice from experts as appropriate, measures which would give substantial expression to this aim, considering *inter alia* the possibility of mixed courts in both jurisdictions for the trial of certain offences. The Conference shall also be concerned with policy aspects of extradition and extra-territorial jurisdiction as between North and South.

F
CROSS-BORDER CO-OPERATION ON SECURITY, ECONOMIC, SOCIAL AND CULTURAL MATTERS

Article 9

(a) With a view to enhancing cross-border co-operation on security matters, the Conference shall set in hand a programme of work to be undertaken by [the Chief Constable of the Royal Ulster Constabulary and the Commissioner of the Garda Síochána] [the Commissioner of the Garda Síochána and the Chief Constable of the Royal Ulster Constabulary] and, where appropriate, groups of officials in such areas as threat assessments, exchange of information, liaison structures, technical co-operation, training of personnel, and operational resources.

(b) The Conference shall have no operational responsibilities; responsibility for police operations shall remain with the heads of the respective police forces, [the Chief Constable of the Royal Ulster Constabulary maintaining his links with the Secretary of State for Northern Ireland and the Commissioner of the Garda Síochána his links with the Minister for Justice] [the Commissioner of the Garda Síochána maintaining his links with the Minister for Justice and the Chief Constable of the Royal Ulster Constabulary his links with the Secretary of State for Northern Ireland].

Article 10

(a) The two Governments shall co-operate to promote the economic and social development of those areas of both parts of Ireland which have suffered most severely from the consequences of the instability of recent years, and shall consider the possibility of securing international support for this work.

(b) If it should prove impossible to achieve and sustain devolution on a basis which secures widespread acceptance in Northern Ireland, the Conference shall be a framework for the promotion of co-operation between the two parts of Ireland concerning cross-border aspects of economic, social and cultural matters in relation to which the Secretary of State for Northern Ireland continues to exercise authority.

(c) If responsibility is devolved in respect of certain matters in the economic, social or cultural areas currently within the responsibility of the Secretary of State for Northern Ireland, machinery will need to be established by the responsible authorities in the North and South for practical co-operation in respect of cross-border aspects of these issues.

G

ARRANGEMENTS FOR REVIEW

Article 11

At the end of three years from signature of this Agreement, or earlier if requested by either Government, the working of the Conference shall be reviewed by the two Governments to see whether any changes in the scope and nature of its activities are desirable.

H

INTERPARLIAMENTARY RELATIONS

Article 12

It will be for Parliamentary decision [in Westminster and in Dublin] [in Dublin and in Westminster] whether to establish an Anglo–Irish Parliamentary body of the kind adumbrated in the Anglo–Irish Studies Report of November 1981. The two Governments agree that they would give support as appropriate to such a body, if it were to be established.

I

FINAL CLAUSES

Article 13

This Agreement shall enter into force on the date on which the two Governments exchange notifications of their acceptance of this Agreement.

In witness thereof the undersigned, being duly authorised thereto by their respective Governments, have signed this Agreement.

Done in two originals at Hillsborough on the 15th day of November 1985.

[For the Government of the United Kingdom of Great Britain and Northern Ireland:

MARGARET THATCHER

For the Government of the Republic of Ireland:

GARRET FITZGERALD]

[For the Government of Ireland

Gearóid Mac Gearailt

For the Government of the United Kingdom

Margaret Thatcher]

Appendix 5

Conclusions of the Inter-Church report, *Violence in Ireland*[1]

1. In spite of the complicated historical and social issues involved and without prejudice to any legitimate political aim, we find unanimously that there is no justification in the present situation in Ireland for the existence of any para-military organisations.
2. It follows that we see no justification for the campaigns of bombing and killing being carried on in Northern Ireland, in the Republic of Ireland and in Britain.
3. We uphold the right of any group to express its views in peaceful demonstration and in seeking electoral support.
4. We recommend that the Churches actively support peace and reconciliation movements.
5. While we recognise that the authorities can make mistakes or be guilty of abuses, we recommend that the Churches jointly remind their members that they have a *prima facie* moral obligation to support the currently constituted authorities in Ireland against all paramilitary powers and that to do so is not in any way to prejudge longer-term political and constitutional developments. In particular, where an individual has information about violent activities of paramilitary organisations he or she may be assuming a personal moral responsibility if, after taking account of all the personal, family and other dangers involved, he does not put such information before the authorities. Furthermore the Churches should be prepared to offer strictly confidential advice through their clergy to their members when faced with these terrible questions.
6. We recommend that the Churches support the principle of a Bill of Rights to protect minorities. We are in favour of extending the functions of the Commissioner of Complaints in Northern Ireland.
7. We suggest the setting up of a Christian Centre of Social Investigation which would conduct research into problems underlying social and communal unrest and would monitor continuously progress made in removing the basic grievances of discrimination and injustice within civil society that are related to the occurrence of violence. Other problems to be investigated underlie our further recommendations and they are problems which must not be shelved if such a centre cannot be established.
8. We recommend action by the Churches to ensure that their worship is not exploited by paramilitary organisations at funerals and commemorations.
9. We recommend all possible support for the family as a social unit, both through Christian pastoral care and through practical measures set out in the Report.
10. We recommend urgent experiment and enterprise in the Youth Service

designed to make an appeal to those sections of youth hitherto not attracted to its activities. We urge further effort to establish and maintain interdenominational activities for youth.

11. We hold that the Churches should set an example to society in the place they give to women thus encouraging them to take their rightful, confident place in society.

12. We call for a sustained and far reaching programme of education within the Churches themselves by which their members may be made more aware of the political and social implications of Christianity for Irish society as well as of the democratic methods available for promoting justice and peace.

13. We urge upon the attention of the Joint Committee appointed to monitor mixed marriages the special circumstances existing in Northern Ireland.

14. We recommend the establishment of a Joint Committee to consider closer contact and co-operation between Roman Catholic and other schools.

15. We regard the growth of community awareness in many areas as potentially one of the more positive developments of recent years and we urge local congregations to make every effort to play a part in these developments.

16. We suggest that all political leaders should be encouraged to see their task as that of reaching a just agreement with their opponents rather than of achieving victory over them; and that to this end they should be open to any reasonable settlement proposed.

Note

1. Report of a working party appointed by the Irish Council of Churches and the Roman Catholic Joint Group on Social Questions (1976) pp. 90–3.

Suggestions for Further Reading

Philosophy and Christian Ethics

Breaking down the enmity: faith and politics in Northern Ireland. 1984 (available from 8 Upper Crescent, Belfast 1, or 211 Churchill Park, Portadown, or 25 Lower Leeson Street, Dublin 2).

Cohn, Haim H. *Human Rights in Jewish Law* (New York: KTAV, for the Institute of Jewish Affairs, London, 1984).

Fairweather, Ian C. M. and James I. H. McDonald *The Quest for Christian ethics* (Edinburgh: Hansel, 1984).

Falconer, Alan D. 'The Churches and Human Rights', in *One in Christ*, 13 (4) (1977) pp. 321–49.

Falconer, Alan D. (ed.) *Understanding human rights* (Dublin: Irish School of Ecumenics, 1980).

Gallagher, Eric, and Stanley Worrall *Christians in Ulster, 1968–1980* (Oxford: Oxford University Press, 1982).

Habgood, *Church and Nation in a Secular Age* (London: Darton, 1983).

Henley, John 'Theology and Basis of Human Rights', *Scottish Journal of Theology*, 38 (3) (1986) pp. 361–78.

Hersch, Jeanne (ed.) *Birthright of Man* (Paris: UNESCO, 1969).

Khan, Muhammas Zafrulla *Islam and Human Rights* (London: The Mosque, 1967).

Lutheran World Federation *Theological Perspectives on Human Rights* (Geneva: Lutheran World Federation, 1977).

McDonagh, Enda (ed.) *Irish Challenges and Theology* (Dublin: Dominican Publications, 1986).

Mackie, Steven G. *Ireland's conflict diminishes me* (Geneva: World Council of Churches, 1975).

Mayo, Bernard *The philosophy of right and wrong* (London: Routledge, 1986).

Miller, Allen O. *A Christian Declaration on Human Rights* (Grand Rapids, Mich.: Eerdmans, 1977).

Minorities in Ireland (Belfast: Irish Council of Churches, Advisory Forum on Human Rights, n.d., but probably 1985).

Mitchell, Basil *Law, Morality, and Religion in a Secular Society* (London: Oxford University Press, 1967).

Rosenbaum, Alan S. (ed.) *The philosophy of human rights: international perspectives* (London: Aldwych, 1981).

Stackhouse, Max *Creeds, Society and Human Rights* (Grand Rapids, Mich.: Eerdmans, 1984).

Swidler, Arlene and Leonard (eds) *Human Rights in Religious Traditions* (New York: Pilgrim Press, 1982).

The Church and Human Rights (Vatican City: Pontifical Commission, 1975).

Violence in Ireland: a report to the Churches (Belfast: Christian Journals; Dublin: Veritas, 1976).

Walsh, Michael, and Brian Davies (eds) *Proclaiming Justice and Peace* (London: Collins–CAFOD, 1984).

Whyte, John H. *Church and State in Modern Ireland*, 2nd edn (Dublin: Gill and Macmillan, 1980).

Law, Government, and Politics

Adams, Gerry *The Politics of Irish Freedom* (Dingle, Republic of Ireland: Brandon, 1986).

Arnold, Bruce *What kind of country: modern Irish politics, 1968–1983* (London: Cape, 1984).

Barritt, Denis, and Arthur Booth *Orange and Green* (Northern Friends Peace Board, 1972).

Boyle, Kevin, and Tom Hadden *Ireland: a positive proposal* (Harmondsworth: Penguin, 1985).

Boyle, Kevin, Tom Hadden, and Paddy Hillyard *Law and State* (London: Martin Robertson, 1975).

Boyle, Kevin, *et al. Ten years on in Northern Ireland* (London: Cobden Trust, 1980).

Brownlie, Ian (ed.) *Basic documents on human rights* (Oxford: Clarendon Press, 1971).

Buckland, Patrick *A history of Northern Ireland* (Dublin: Gill and Macmillan, 1981).

Callaghan, James *A House divided: the dilemma of Northern Ireland* (London: Collins, 1973).

Campbell, Colin (ed.) *Do we need a bill of rights?* (London: Temple Smith, 1980).

Capotorti, Francesco *Study on the rights of persons belonging to ethnic, religious and linguistic minorities* (New York: United Nations, 1979) (UN doc. E/CN 4/Sub.2/384/Rev.1).

Cristescu, Aureliu *The right to self-determination: historical and current development on the basis of United Nations instruments* (New York, United Nations, 1981) (UN doc. E/CN 4/Sub.2/404/Rev.1).

Daes, Erica-Irene A. *The Individual's duties to the community and the limitations on human rights and freedoms under Article 29 of the Universal Declaration of Human Rights: a contribution to the freedom of the individual under law* (New York: United Nations, 1983) (UN doc. E/CN 4/Sub.2/432/Rev.2).

Espiell, Hector Gros *The right to self-determination: implementation of United Nations resolutions* (New York: United Nations, 1980) (UN doc. E/CN 4/Sub.2/405/Rev.1).

Fawcett, James *The international protection of minorities* (London: Minority Rights Group, 1979) (Report 41).

Faulkner, Brian *Memoirs of a statesman* (ed. by John Houston) (London: Weidenfeld and Nicolson, 1978).

FitzGerald, Garret *Towards a new Ireland* (Croydon: Charles Knight, 1972).

FitzGerald, Garret *Irish Identities* (London: BBC, 1982).

Gifford, Tony *Supergrasses: the use of accomplice evidence in Northern Ireland* (London: Cobden Trust, 1984).

Greet, S. C. and A. White *Abolishing the Diplock Courts* (London: Cobden Trust, 1985).

Haagerup, N. J. *The situation in Northern Ireland* (European Parliament, 1984) (doc.1–1526/83).

Hadden, Tom, and Paddy Hillyard *Justice in Northern Ireland* (Cobden Trust: 1973).

Harmless weapons (Chichester: Barry Rose, for the Council for Science and Society, 1978).

Hewitt, Patricia *The abuse of power: civil liberties in the United Kingdom* (Oxford: Robertson, 1982).

Jackson, Harold, and Anne McHardy *The Two Irelands*, 3rd edn (London: Minority Rights Group, 1984) (Report 2).

Kenny, Anthony *The road to Hillsborough* (Oxford: Pergamon, 1987).

Kilbrandon, Lord (Chairman) *Northern Ireland: report of an independent Inquiry* (1984, available from 9 St James's Square, London, SW1Y 4LE).

Lyons, F. S. L. *Ireland since the famine* (London: Collins, 1973).

Moody, T. W. *The Ulster Question, 1603–1973*, 3rd edn (Cork: Mercier Press, 1978).

Murphy, Dervla *A place apart* (Harmondsworth: Penguin, 1979).

Murphy, Dervla *Changing the problem* (Gigginstown, Republic of Ireland: Lilliput, 1984).

New Ireland Forum. Proceedings, studies, and report (Dublin: Stationery Office, 1984).

Northern Ireland Assembly: first report from the Devolution Committee (Belfast: HMSO, 1984).

O'Brien, Conor Cruise *States of Ireland* (London: Hutchinson, 1972).

O'Malley, Padraig *The uncivil wars* (Belfast: Blackstaff, 1983).

O'Neill, Terence *Autobiography* (London: Hart-Davies, 1972).

Oliver, John *Ulster today and tomorrow* (London: PEP, n.d., Broadsheet 574).

Palley, Claire *Constitutional law and minorities* (London: Minority Rights Group, 1978) (Report 36).

Prior, Jim *Balance of Power* (London: Hamish Hamilton, 1986).

Protection of Human Rights in Northern Ireland (London: Amnesty International, 1985).

Rea, Desmond (ed.) *Political cooperation in divided societies* (Dublin: Gill and Macmillan, 1982).

Rees, Merlyn *Northern Ireland: a personal perspective* (London: Methuen, 1985).

Rights of Nationalities and Protection of Minorities (Munich: Internationales Institut für Nationalitätenrecht und Regionalismus, 1984).

Seighart, Paul *The Lawful Rights of Mankind* (Oxford: Oxford University Press, 1985).

Tajfel, Henri *The social psychological of minorities* (London: Minority Rights Group, 1978) (Report 38).

Walsh, Dermot *Use and abuse of Emergency Legislation in Northern Ireland* (London: Cobden Trust, 1984).

Watt, David (ed.) *The constitution of Northern Ireland: problems and prospects* (London: Heinemann, 1981).

Zander, Michael *A Bill of Rights*, 3rd edn (London: Sweet and Maxwell, 1985).

INCOME AND EXPENDITURE TO 30 SEPTEMBER 1985 (2), (6), 30 SEPTEMBER 1986 (3), (7), AND 20 MAY 1987 (4), (8)

(1)	Income			(5)	Expenditure		
	(2) 1984–5	(3) 1985–6	(4) 1986–7		(6) 1984–5	(7) 1985–6	(8) 1986–7
	£	£	£		£	£	£
Balance brought forward	–	3367	2041	Travel	3276	5065	4969
Editorial and publication reserve	–	3500	7500	Accommodation and meals	1518	1702	1537
		6867	9541	Office expenses	547	586	1624
					5341	7353	8130
Church agencies	1433	3000	2362	Editorial and publication expenses	–	–	7500
Charitable trusts	8991	6092	5850	Reserve	3500	7500	7500
Individuals	1701	392	–	Balance	3367	2041	2541
Bank interest	83	543	418				
	£12208	£16894	£18171		£12208	£16894	£18171

Financial Contributions Towards the Project

Fifty-four individuals, Churches, parishes, religious communities and charitable trusts made financial contributions to the project, varying in amount between £5 and £5000. In 1985, an old age pensioner sent his Christmas bonus. Some contributors do not wish to be named. To them, and to the following, we express our thanks: L. M. Allen, Abbot of Ampleforth, Abbot and Community of Glenstall Abbey (County Limerick), Baptist Union of Great Britain and Ireland, Baptist Union of Scotland, Bishop of Bangor, in memory of Lucy Bourne, British Council of churches, Denis Buxton Trust, Barrow and Geraldine S. Cadbury Trust, Central Board of Finance of the Church of England, Alison M. Douglas, Edith M. Ellis 1985 Trust, European Human Rights Foundation, Free Church Federal Council, GSC Trust, A. B. and M. L. Gillett Charitable Foundation, Golders Green Quakers, Thomas W. Greaves Charitable Settlement, Sir Halley Stewart Trust, Catherine and Paul Hickinbotham, Lord Hylton, Ireland Fund, Ireland Yearly Meeting of the Society of Friends, Irish Council of Churches, Livingstone Trust, London Yearly Meeting of the Society of Friends, A. H. Marsden, Methodist Church, National Catholic Fund, New Sheffield Trust, Quaker Peace and Service, Radley Charitable Trust, Sir James Reckitt Charity, Joseph Rowntree Charitable Trust, Bishop of Salisbury, Church of Scotland, Kathleen Slack, Stonegate Trust, C. B. and H. H. Taylor 1984 Charitable Settlement, United Reformed Church, Westcroft Trust, and Kenneth Whitaker.

Index